Under The Stars

Foundations of Steiner Early Childhood Education
Collected Essays

Renate Long-Breipohl

Under the Stars © 2012 Renate Long-Breipohl
Renate Long-Breipohl is hereby identified as the author of this work in accordance with Section 77 of the Copyright, Designs and Patent Act, 1988. She asserts and gives notice of her moral right under this Act.

Published by Hawthorn Press, Hawthorn House,
1 Lansdown Lane, Stroud, Gloucestershire, GL5 1BJ, UK
Tel: (01453) 757040 Fax: (01453) 751138
Email: info@hawthornpress.com

Website: **www.hawthornpress.com**

All rights reserved. No part of this book may be reproduced, stored in a retrieval system or transmitted in any form by any means (electronic or mechanical, through reprography, digital transmission, recording or otherwise) without the prior written permission of the publisher.

Cover design and typesetting by Bookcraft, Stroud, Gloucestershire
Cover photo by Robin Scagell/Galaxy Pictures

Reprinted 2013 by Berforts Information Press Oxford

Printed on environmentally friendly chlorine-free paper manufactured from renewable forest stock.

Every effort has been made to trace the ownership of all copyrighted material. If any omission has been made, please bring this to the publisher's attention so that proper acknowledgement may be given in future editions.

British Library Cataloguing in Publication Data applied for.

ISBN 978-1-907359-16-3

This book is dedicated to the children and colleagues whom I have met in my life and my work in Australia and in many countries around the world.

Contents

Foreword vii
Introduction xi

Chapter 1
Recognizing and Nurturing the Life Forces of the Young Child 1

Chapter 2
Thinking and the Consciousness of the Young Child 23

Chapter 3
The Development and Education of the Will 46

Chapter 4
Relationships in Early Childhood: Attachment, Separation and Individualization 68

Chapter 5
Children in the Modern World 87

Chapter 6
'Moving with Soul': Supporting Movement Development in the Early Years 102

Chapter 7
Self-directed Play in Early Childhood: A Chance for the Child, a Challenge for the Educator 122

Chapter 8
Art Experiences in Early Childhood Education 139

Chapter 9
In Search for Reality: Self-development and Child Observation 162

Chapter 10
'Under the Stars' 174

Bibliography 197
Index 200

Foreword

Steiner Waldorf Early Childhood has been waiting for this treasure for many years. Renate Long-Breipohl is well known amongst Waldorf circles as an enthusiastic and enlightening lecturer, and has written articles for many journals throughout the world. Her clarity of thought, new insights and deep study of the topics covered in this profound and practical anthology of well researched articles, will be a gift for anyone concerned with early childhood. From her understanding of child development, to research on play, she has deepened our knowledge, providing food for thought for students, teachers, researchers and educators within and outside the Steiner Waldorf movement.

The first chapter of this anthology focuses on recognizing and nurturing the life forces of the young child. It describes connecting and repeating growth activities in developing, in particular, the neural pathways, the nerve sense system and the organs, as well as human connections, first through the ability to imitate and then in social connecting, culminating in the transformation of the etheric forces at around seven. The role of the adult in creating a nurturing environment in order to protect these life forces so that the children can develop a healthy physical body is described in detail.

In the second chapter Renate explores the quality of thinking and the conscious development of the young child. She relates it to the development of walking and speaking, and gives wonderful examples in descriptive pictures from her observations of children. She connects Rudolf Steiner's ideas with modern neuro-scientific research (such as Sally Goddard Blythe's), and the importance of the thinking of the adult in developing a moral sense in the child.

The chapter on understanding the development and education of the will forces of the young child investigates the stages of their development from birth to 21. Enabling the child to master his own will, and the creation of a mood of love, warmth and joy around the child, are parts of the adult's role, and not least, the adult's own self education in being a model worthy of imitation. As Renate says at the end of this chapter, the reflective practice of the educator helps develop a spiritual connection to the young child, through which education can become fully effective. Moral education, a moral attitude, the moral world and the human virtues of Gratitude, Truthfulness and Beauty are also addressed in this chapter.

The fourth chapter on relationships covers attachment, separation and individualization. Forming relationships, bonding and imitation work on a deep level with the emerging individuality of the child. Renate gives some wonderful examples based on experiences in Steiner early childhood settings. Her observations clearly define the differences between the anxious, dependent, defiant and independent child.

We all have questions relating to what is now called Indigo or Star children. These, and other 'special children of the 21st century', are referred to in the chapter on 'Children in the Modern World'. The prevalence of children with additional needs today, including ADHD, Autistic Spectrum disorders, symptoms, possible causes, behaviours and attributes are described in such a way as to raise questions in the reader. We are given the gift of Steiner education through the insights of Rudolf Steiner, to enable us to work with these questions.

'Moving with Soul' is a wonderful way of describing how children move, and how we as adults can support their movement development. In this chapter, Renate describes the development of movement from pre-birth to three, and upwards. Again, modern research underpins what Renate is saying about our relationship to the spatial dimensions of our earthly existence; from making judgments and discrimination to the development of thinking. Our adult influence as a role model, our archetypal gestures, working with a breathing rhythm and our self-development are shown through loving examples and deepening of soul, which Renate brings with such joy.

'Self-directed Play: A Chance for the Child, a Challenge for the Educator' doesn't even need introducing we all know this is essential for the development of a healthy child, a healthy adult, and a healthy social life! Renate has recently published a research study (*Supporting*

Self-directed Play in Early Childhood; WECAN) on this subject. In this chapter Renate looks at the different types of play, giving wonderful examples, referencing different educationalists. She describes how we as educators can understand, support, facilitate, deepen and strengthen opportunities for play.

I found the chapter on art experiences in early childhood fascinating, particularly looking at the adult's role in introducing an aesthetic element into our work. Renate refers to the questions raised by Susan Howard, an American educator and teacher trainer, on how the teacher, the educator, is personally engaged in artistic activity for our own self-development and in the classroom. Are the environment, toys and materials imbued with an aesthetic sense of beauty? Are the artistic activities (storytelling, painting, modelling, music, etc.) which we introduce suitable and do we understand which gift each brings? Mentioning the 'art of clothing' certainly opened my eyes to what impressions we make unconsciously.

The next chapter explores self-development and child observation. Here Renate looks at our responsibilities as adults who need to recognize the individual child in the world today. She shows us how to enter into the world of the child with love and joy to develop detailed observations and to stop making assumptions about any given situation. Using the three principal human virtues to develop these faculties, together with the schooling of thinking in our inner life, helps us to (hopefully) make the right judgment.

The last chapters help us to understand the incarnation process as a guide to our own self-development. Renate points us towards the contemplation of the cosmos, and the mysteries of the Zodiac. She gives a beautiful description in the beginning of Part 2, the Adult's Work, where she says, 'Through her activity the educator also builds up a field of warmth in which the child can nest himself and in which he can experience closeness to another human soul'. The images and activities, and the virtues of each Zodiac sign, help us to become human beings worthy of this incarnating soul.

I wish I had the insights given in this remarkable book when beginning my training in Steiner Waldorf Early childhood education. I wish I had them in order to deepen my work as a kindergarten teacher with young children. I am grateful to Renate for providing them now to support my work with students and practitioners in the classroom, and to enrich my life's work on this subject.

Janni Nicol, 2012
Steiner Waldorf Early Childhood Representative, Author, Consultant and Trainer

Introduction

The first Waldorf kindergarten opened its doors at Easter 1926 on the grounds of the Waldorf school in Stuttgart, Germany, one year after Rudolf Steiner's death. Elizabeth Grunelius was the founding kindergarten teacher. She had prepared herself for this task ever since 1920, when Steiner had asked her to join the college of teachers of the first Waldorf school as the craft teacher and with the special task of setting up a Waldorf kindergarten. Steiner was very aware of the need for such a kindergarten, in which an education in harmony with the principles of the newly founded Waldorf school could be offered to children younger than the school entry age, which at that time in Germany was the seventh year. However, financial constraints and the immensity of the task of building and developing the school delayed the commencement of the kindergarten for several years. Steiner himself did not live to see the opening of the kindergarten, but he was able to advise Grunelius on the principles underlying early childhood education and on their implementation.[1]

Already in 1906 Steiner had given a series of public talks on the education of the child, which were published the following year in a booklet entitled *The Education of the Child in the Light of Spiritual Science.* Here he develops how education can arise out of an understanding of the essential nature of the child. He describes the young child as experiencing himself[2] as being one with the environment. As a consequence of this consciousness of oneness, learning by imitation and example is all-important for education in the early years. 'There are two magic words which indicate how the child enters into relation with his environment. They are: Imitation, and example … What goes on in his physical environment, this the child imitates, and in the process of imitation his physical organs are cast into the forms which then become permanent.'[3]

Steiner also describes how the soul-spiritual being of the child is working within the processes of physical growth and development. He therefore stresses the need for creating the right conditions for the healthy growth and development of the child. Already in this early publication he points to environmental influences and educational practices that are counterproductive to the health of the child and the development of natural faculties such as memory, imagination and play.

Elizabeth Grunelius worked in the Stuttgart Waldorf Kindergarten for 12 years and was then invited to the USA to set up a kindergarten in Kimberton. Later she helped to set up a second kindergarten at Adelphi College, USA, and another in Chatou, France. It was not until 1950 that she published a book on Steiner early childhood education: *Early Childhood Education and the Waldorf School Plan*. This was republished in England, then translated into German in 1955, and French in 1957.

Her book has been a guideline for Steiner Waldorf early childhood education ever since, although especially in the 1950s and 1960s when literature on Waldorf kindergartens was scarce. From the perspective of someone writing about Steiner education today this is amazing. We have to assume that during the first 25 years of the Waldorf kindergarten much of the founder's insights and knowledge were passed on to aspiring Waldorf kindergarteners by word of mouth and through a kind of apprenticeship learning.

Only in 1951 did the first international Waldorf kindergarten conference take place, in Hannover. Now an annual event, the conference was supported by Elizabeth Grunelius well into the 1980s and organized by her colleague and former student Klara Hattermann. Hattermann was instrumental in setting up the first training seminar for Waldorf kindergarteners in Stuttgart/Germany and, together with Dr Helmut von Kügelgen, she was closely involved in the founding of the International Association of Waldorf Kindergartens (IAWK) in 1969. Part of the Association's mission is to support training for Waldorf early childhood educators and hold conferences so that those working in Steiner Waldorf early childhood education are well prepared for their task and conscious of the foundations of this education. From 1970 onwards there has been a continuous stream of conferences and training seminars, and courses for Steiner early childhood educators have spread to many parts of the world.

Looking back to the 1970s, and even the 1980s, it is striking how few publications were available to students of early childhood education, especially with respect to its foundations in Steiner's spiritual science.[4] One reason for this might be that in the early days individuals wishing to work in Steiner education would have studied Steiner's work extensively before becoming educators. In particular, they would have studied the important lectures Steiner gave to teachers after the first Steiner school opened in 1919, in which he extended and deepened much of what he had already discussed in 1907. Thus the early teachers did not need an introduction to the fundamentals of spiritual science underpinning Steiner education: they needed to know how this knowledge could be transformed into educational programmes and then implemented.

At Elizabeth Grunelius' suggestion, extracts from Steiner's work with specific bearing on early childhood education were compiled and published in 1971 with the title *Vom Wesen des kleinen Kindes*. Printed in English in 1975 as *Understanding Young Children*, this compilation has become a major resource for studying Steiner's insights into the spiritual foundations of child development and early education. In addition, IAWK published a series of books relating to practical aspects of kindergarten education, such as appropriate toys and toy making, celebrating the seasons and festivals in the kindergarten, painting and drawing, puppetry, movement, and craft for and with children.[5]

Today study materials for educators and parents are readily available in many languages – although not nearly enough in those parts of the world where Steiner early childhood education is still very new, such as in parts of Asia and Africa.

With respect to publications on Steiner early childhood education by other authors than Steiner, it is worth noting that these often came about in the context of concerns about aspects of modern life through which childhood risked losing the qualities necessary for the healthy development of young children. As early as 1950 we can read in the publisher's preface to Elizabeth Grunelius' book: 'It is a characteristic of our time that, while the average life span of the human being becomes longer and longer, the span of childhood gets shorter and shorter. It is increasingly thought of preschool years: How can we make the most efficient use of them to acquire information which can be used for later learning. In this way we speed up the child's approaching adulthood.'[6]

In Germany, the first book to give a comprehensive overview of Steiner Waldorf early childhood education appeared in 1973. Edited by Helmut von Kügelgen, the chairperson of the IAWK, *Plan und Praxis des Waldorfkindergartens* (*Plan and Practice of the Waldorf Kindergarten*) included articles on fundamentals such as imitation and play, storytelling, arts and children's health. It was published in response to moves by the Federal government to lower the school entry age from six to five and to introduce a compulsory preschool year that placed emphasis on the academic subjects for five-year-olds. The government's plans were opposed by the Waldorf Kindergarten Association and other organizations, and the planned changes could be stopped.

Plan und Praxis was compiled to protect childhood and to demonstrate appropriate ways of nurturing children at this time of their lives. As a result, the book focuses on the dangers of early academic instruction for children's health and well-being and describes the alternative practices offered by the Waldorf kindergarten, and their benefits. Interestingly, fewer than half of the articles are by Steiner kindergarten teachers – the majority of authors are other Steiner teachers and doctors.[7]

In the late 1990s and early 2000s, important books for Steiner early childhood education were published, dealing with the impact of electronic media on the young child, the impact of introducing computers into the lives of young children, and the disappearance of play. While the early introduction of academic subjects and the push for structured learning programmes for children at an ever-earlier age are ongoing issues, other questions have come to the foreground. These include changes in the development of movement and thinking in young children, changes in children's ability to play, and changes in the way children form relationships. During the last decade many early childhood educators have authored important publications on the principles and practice of Steiner early childhood education.

This book should be seen in the context of the efforts of experienced early childhood teachers to write about the young child, the education necessary for early childhood, and its spiritual foundations. Through my years of teaching in a Steiner kindergarten and through 20 years of experience training Steiner early childhood educators, I have been confronted with the necessity to gain clarity myself, not only about the aims and methods of Steiner early childhood education but also about the spiritual foundations underlying this successful and convincing approach to early education.

The essays presented here have arisen out of my work over the last 10 years and represent the search for a deeper understanding of Steiner's spiritual insights. The essays do not cover the entire area of early childhood education, but they do cover essential aspects of it.

The way in which Steiner early childhood education was presented in the early days seems insufficient for today's readers. In his booklet *Education of the Child in the Light of Spiritual Science*, Steiner pointed out that practice and its outcomes for the children, not ideas and theories, would prove this education to be right. In 1907, 12 years before the first Waldorf school was founded, he remarked:

> If the knowledge of Anthroposophy were applied in practical spheres like education, the idle talk that this knowledge has first to be proved would quickly disappear. Whoever applies it correctly, will find that the knowledge of Anthroposophy proves itself in life by making life strong and healthy ... a proof stronger than all the logical and so-called scientific arguments can afford. Spiritual truths are best recognized in their fruits and not by what is called a proof, be this ever so scientific.[8]

The fruits of Steiner education still convince those parents who choose it for their children. However, for the inquisitive intellect of the majority of human beings today, this is not entirely satisfactory. We want to know where the theory and practice of Steiner education originated, and what methods were used to prove their validity.

Interestingly, Steiner himself was confronted with this question when he gave a series of lectures about the principles of Waldorf education in Oxford in 1922. He had been invited to speak at a public conference on 'Spiritual Values in Education and Social Life', chaired by Dr Millicent Mackenzie, Professor for Education at Cardiff

University.⁹ From his introductory remarks it seems that Steiner was very aware of the fact that he was speaking at one of the birthplaces of natural science and its epistemological foundations, which had so influenced education throughout the 19th and early 20th century:

> Now I am about to speak of a method of education that may, in a sense, be called new ... However, before anyone strives for something new in any area of human culture, one must first learn to respect what is old. Here in Oxford, I feel the power that lives in these old traditions and how it inspires. One who can feel this may also have the right to speak of what is new.[10]

And a little later he explained his own approach thus:

> What I have to say about education and teaching is based on the spiritual scientific knowledge that has been my life's work ... This education and curriculum is based entirely on knowledge of the human being ... It aims to know all the suprasensory aspects of the human being between birth and death – everything that demonstrates the human place in a suprasensory world.[11]

And then with regard to natural science and its relationship to spiritual science:

> Natural science can indeed help us understand the bodily nature and functions of the human being during physical life. It has not, however, succeeded in reaching the essential spirit of the human being, because it experiments with external tools and observes with the outer senses ... The spiritual view that we represent here does not say that these are the limits of human knowledge, or human cognition. Rather, we must bring forth from the depths of human nature the forces of cognition that can observe the complete human being of body, soul, and spirit – just as a physiologist can observe

the structure of the human eye or ear. If, until now, we lack such knowledge because of our natural scientific education, we must begin to build it up. Consequently, I will speak to you about how to develop a kind of knowledge that assures genuine insight into the inner texture of childhood life.[12]

These extracts from 1922 describe the epistemological situation of two fundamentally different approaches to knowledge, which still prevail today.

It is possible to delineate the spiritual foundations of Steiner education in thought form. It is possible to lay open the spiritual insights out of which the educational aims and practices of Steiner education have arisen. As his remarks from the first Oxford lecture show, Steiner's epistemology entails the possibility of extending the cognitional possibilities of the human being beyond those that are currently achieved and scientifically accepted. The frame of reference for thoughts and ideas at the foundation of Steiner education are derived from such extended cognition. Whether such extended cognition produces valid results or not cannot be the subject of public debate, as such a debate would only make sense within a framework that was familiar to all participants. Otherwise one would risk projecting ideas and experiences derived from cognition within a different frame of reference – in this case the modern scientific one – onto a frame of reference of which one has no experience.

However, results from Steiner spiritual research, including those relating to early childhood, can be described in such a way that the benefits of both ways of approaching reality – spiritual and modern scientific research – are brought together and complement each other in the understanding of the child and child development. It is intended that within this collection of essays the reader may find examples of research from both the natural scientific and the spiritual scientific approach. Together they can provide insights into child development and advice for education which otherwise would not have been possible.

The frame of reference underpinning this publication is the existence of two worlds, the spiritual cosmos and the physical earth environment, which come together in each human being.

The transition from one world into the other is the theme of early childhood. Because of this transitional stage of existence, young children are of a different nature than older children or adults.

> Do we have the right to claim that our intellectual mode of knowledge ever allows us to participate in a child's experience of the outer world – this child who is all sense organ? We cannot do this. We can only hope to achieve this through a kind of cognition that goes beyond itself – one that can enter the nature of all that lives and moves. Intuitional cognition is the only knowledge that can do this.[13]

Results of intuitional cognition will be presented insofar as they are relevant for early childhood education. Intuitional cognition should not be understood as a body of knowledge. It is a method of investigation which led Steiner to significant insights, but it is not complete. It should be actively pursued by all educators who aim to extend their own cognitional faculties in the way described by Steiner, and who will then be able to contribute their own experience to the work in progress of understanding young children.

I have attempted to further develop the understanding of childhood based on two major insights of Rudolf Steiner:

- the incarnation process as a bridge between the spiritual and the physical world, and
- the major role played by spiritual forces of the cosmos and the earth environment in child development.

Incarnation

Incarnation, 'coming into the flesh', has two sides. The spiritual child is understood as descending from the state of pre-birth existence into earth existence and then taking on a physical body so that the child appears as a physical being with a spiritual core hidden within. All that Steiner has described with respect to the development of the child rests upon this duality of spiritual origin and physical manifestation. Various adaptation processes must occur for the child to be able to live a life on earth.

Part of the frame of reference and linked to the incarnation process is Steiner's description of the four bodies of the human being – the physical, etheric, astral body and I body – and their gradual 'births' over the first 21 years of life. Looking at the different times and processes of the maturation of these four bodies, or aspects, of the human being is helpful for explaining and dealing with many issues in child development, as will be detailed later.

Forces

When we enter more deeply into the process of incarnation, we come to understand that forces are active in the growth and development of the child. In the deepest sense the development of the child in body and soul is determined by how these forces, spiritual and earthly, work together, sometimes in unison, sometimes in opposition, yet in the early years guided by the incarnating individuality of the child. Steiner specifies how these spiritual and earthly forces work in such areas as movement, the development of speech and thinking, the will and the play of the child. All essays in this book embrace this theme of forces in child development and unfold it into different aspects of the process.

When Steiner speaks about the duality of physical-etheric forces and soul-spiritual forces in child development they are understood to be of a purely spiritual nature. They are not comparable to 'energy' in the sense of physics, which is still a very refined form of matter. Today it is no longer unusual to speak about spiritual forces or spiritual currents and their manifestation in the physical realm, given the growing popularity in the West of Eastern traditional medicines and alternative methods of healing. Much of what can be experienced in healing resists explanation within the frame of reference of natural science. The understanding of such forces varies and sometimes diverges from Steiner's. However, the direction is certainly similar in that these approaches to health and healing allow for forces other than those known to be caused by physical processes alone.

This book is written by an early childhood educator for teacher trainees, educators and parents who are interested in the deeper aspects of Steiner early childhood education. It originated as much from my own experiences with young children as from Steiner's insights. It is about incarnation, the influence of spiritual forces in the child's development and the appropriate steps the educator can take to support this process, be it through forming relationships, supporting the development of movement and thinking in the child, play, child observation or working on one's inner development. In order to progress further in improving and refining early education, and thus contribute to the future evolution of humanity, a deeper understanding of human existence is needed. Studying the incarnation process of the young child is a good way of gaining a picture of the underlying spiritual reality of human existence. If this book can be a contribution to this as well as to a deeper understanding of the young child, it has fulfilled its purpose.

Comments about the purpose and content of each essay

The first of the essays, 'Recognizing and Nurturing the Life Forces of the Child', relates to what is referred to above as the underpinning frame of reference: the notion of spiritual forces at work in the growth and development of the child in the first seven years. It aims to state that these forces need to be nurtured and protected in early childhood and to provide insights into their nature and functions.

In doing so, reference is made to the work of Ernst Marti and Hermann Poppelbaum, two scientists who have built on Steiner's insights into the nature of etheric forces as the foundation for understanding the laws behind growth, development and life cycles of plants.

The laws of etheric activity in the plant realm can shed light on the growth and development of young children. Steiner himself emphasized the importance of the activity of etheric forces during the gestation period in the womb and in early childhood.[14] Therefore, an overview of the qualities and functions of the four kinds of etheric forces is given in this essay. It may serve as an indicator for pedagogical practice in all three stages of early development between birth and the age of seven.

The following issues are raised:
- establishing and maintaining a healthy body;
- patterns of maturation and sequenced phases of development;
- the activity of connecting–repeating, refining–enhancing and polarization as characteristic for the three different phases of early childhood development;
- the danger of damaging health by drawing on life forces for learning at a time when the formation of the bodily organs is not yet completed.

The journey continues with the development of 'Thinking and Consciousness in the Young Child' and the special importance of the third year of life. Previous stages are discussed as well, since thinking does not appear all of a sudden, but evolves since birth within the processes of learning to walk and to speak.

Steiner identifies two different streams in the process of incarnation: the stream of growth and development, and the stream through which the child's spiritual being enters into the body in the acquisition of uprightness, speech and thinking. Acquiring movement, speech and thinking are spiritual-physical processes in that they originate in pre-birth existence and provide the child with the fundamental faculties for living a human life on earth. Regarding the second aspect, scientific research has now confirmed the decisive role of movement and speech in the development and functioning of the brain and the ability to think and learn. The research of Sally Goddard Blythe is just one example of this.

Steiner's considerations on the child as a spiritual being, as eternal individuality descending to earth, are unique among developmental and educational theories. A typical example of prevailing attitudes in this area is a certain curriculum document which makes mention of the spiritual needs of children among other needs, yet does not explain what these needs are or where they come from.[15]

Steiner was adamant that acknowledgement and understanding of the spirituality of the child should flow directly into an educational practice that considers all aspects of the child. Therefore, thinking is not just treated as a tool to succeed in life. It is understood as holding possibilities for further spiritual development of the human being, for transcending the knowledge and the moral capacities achieved up to now.

Thus, with respect to the third year of life and the development of thinking, Steiner was more concerned about the child experiencing moral actions in his environment, which would imprint themselves deeply into all three soul forces of the child, than about the child being introduced to information and the mental processing of this information. It is against this background of thinking as a soul faculty that Steiner's discovery of the transformation of life forces into forces of thinking needs to be understood.

Coming from the perspective of the future possibilities and tasks of the human being, Steiner observed the trends in the education of his time with great concern. One such trend was the importance placed on ever-earlier intellectual training and achievement in modern society. In opposition to this, Steiner, similar to Piaget, represents a developmental theory of learning which recognizes that there are phases of development and a right time for each new step of learning to occur.

With this in mind we may read Steiner's critique of modern early education as a plea for an undisturbed childhood, for allowing children to perceive and experience the world in their own way until they are ready for the transition to the next stage. Developmentally, this would be sometime around the seventh year.[16]

Steiner spoke about this issue of prematurely addressing the child's thinking in many different contexts, in lectures to teachers as well as to the general public. There is not one single work of his that would summarize it all. The essay on thinking and consciousness of the young child presented here is an attempt to bring together the different aspects of Steiner's complex picture of the development of thinking.

'The Development and Education of the Will', including additional remarks on moral education, illustrates how in Steiner's understanding of early education the will of the child takes centre stage. What Steiner suggests here needs to be considered against the background of the same duality of spiritual forces active behind development as already mentioned in the essays on the life forces and the thinking of the young child.

Especially with respect to the will, we cannot get a true picture of the soul forces of the human being unless we include the spiritual biography of the human being as well: the existence before birth and after death. Steiner states that during life on earth the will does not achieve its goal and remains incomplete. The underlying image is of a transformative process which is not confined to life on earth. Only with this insight can we understand Steiner's notions of 'will grown old' and 'new will'. The former is will that has passed through spiritual existence and is active in the formation of the brain; the latter is will that evolves during life between birth and death. Thus will is seen as the dynamic principle in the human being and in evolution, generally and individually.

Will as a driving force in the life of an individual is clearly visible in young children. Being conscious of the duality of will forces in the human being may help us to better understand children's energetic behaviour. It is expression of the yet unformed 'new will'. Of all human beings, children are the ones most strongly oriented towards the future.

In child development textbooks one will look in vain for a chapter on the child's will. At best one can read about 'motivation'. This is understandable because the full extent of the importance of the will can only be seen if one considers the possibility of a spiritual biography of the human being and the influence of spiritual forces on the human being before birth and after death. Then all that was achieved through the intentionality of the will and human deeds is transformed into a predisposition which will determine structures of the physical brain in the process of preparing for a new incarnation.

Will, as it appears in the child from birth onwards, develops in stages. It is the aim of this essay to bring these stages to the attention of early years educators, as each stage needs to be approached differently. A progression is outlined, from the imitative stage of will development to will coloured by self-feeling or self-interest, and then to the emergence of the child's interest in the world, which overcomes the natural egocentricity of the young child.

Steiner makes the point that the will is the only soul force which needs to be educated: it is born incomplete, whereas the child's thinking is full of wisdom and can unfold by itself, provided the child has a supportive and stimulating environment.

Steiner has given educational advice on how best to deal with the will of young children. Mention should be made here of the importance he attributes to working with imitation and example and to establishing habit. At the same time Steiner is pointing to the ineffectiveness of verbal explanations and admonition.

The issue of educating the will is closely connected with that of 'moral education', which is addressed in an appendix. Moral education has become specifically relevant in our time, the age of the 'consciousness soul', in which each individual human being is called to make their own decisions on what ethics and ideals to pursue. Moral education is education of the will insofar as it deals with a disposition towards doing good.

Steiner has named three moral predispositions that need to be nurtured in the child through the three seven-year phases of growing up: gratitude, love and the will to do one's duty. These are attitudes, or predispositions, which have to grow in the child and cannot be instilled by admonition or punishment. Instead, Steiner points to the three seven-year phases of education, which should be filled with goodness (age 0–7), beauty (age 7–14) and truth (age 14–21). When these ideals permeate the environment of the child, it will be easier for him to develop a predisposition towards morality. It will help to establish a kind of soul habit, through which morality becomes a capacity of the will rather than the intellect – which is virtually powerless when it comes to doing good.

It is a common experience that the best intentions and reasons do not suffice to bring about a good deed, and that admonitions appealing to a child's understanding have little effect. It is worthwhile to consider Steiner's suggestions for moral education, which are directed towards what in modern terms may be called 'intrinsic motivation', that is, one's own wish to do better regardless of external factors like reproach or punishment.

The essay on attachment deals with forming 'Relationships in Early Childhood'. This theme is explored from the spiritual aspect of relationships and its congruence with mainstream research on what is now a hot topic in early education: creating the right conditions for the child to form secure attachment relationships with educators. Easing transitions, enabling children to enter into a closer relationship with an educator preferred by the child, arranging staff schedules in order to avoid a constant change of staff – all these are now high on the agenda in childcare for children under the age of five. Today, educators' attention is directed mainly towards issues of primary attachment due to the large number of families in which both parents are in the workforce and have little time for their children. However, the quality of relationships in care situations and the importance of secondary attachment relationships for the social and emotional development of young children are also being considered.

The conditions needed by children to form secure attachments have been well researched and documented since the 1970s. This essay gives a summary of research on secure and insecure attachments and places it in the context of the entire incarnation process, with particular attention to establishing quality relationships at the different stages of development.

In Steiner education the notion of the repetition of evolutionary stages of humanity in the development of the individual contributes to the understanding of child development and informs pedagogical action. This holds true for pedagogical relationships as well.

The four stages in the development of secure attachment, suggested by John Bowlby and commonly accepted, are placed in the context of qualities within the stages of incarnation of humanity described by Steiner. I suggest that the four evolutionary conditions of warmth, light, water and earth provide a framework which allows us to perceive the spiritual dimension of relationships in the development of the young child: original unity (warmth), seeing the other and forming a relationship (light), letting go of the initial closeness (water), and then becoming independent (earth). Seen in this light, attachment and separation gain significance as archetypal processes with respect to relationships, but also with respect to the necessity of becoming independent.

On the basis of this archetypal dimension of relationships between young children and the adults who care for them, the essay addresses the issue of relationships where children have not been able to pass through the four stages of attachment in the appropriate way. Information on the different forms of insecure attachment is presented and then, in the second part of the essay, the consequences of insecure attachment are discussed on the basis of three illustrative case studies. I suggest that not being able to develop normally through the four stages of attachment has repercussions for children of kindergarten age and beyond. Further reflections relate to the ways in which we can assist the process of forming secure secondary attachment relationships between children and educators.

The essay on 'Children in the Modern World' evolved from reflections on the relevance of principles of Steiner early childhood education today. It was triggered by the interest in Steiner education which arose among parents of children with behavioural difficulties following the publication of the book on the 'Indigo Children' in the USA. This book seemed to have an answer to the question as to why parents were experiencing so many difficulties with respect to their children being strong willed, resisting or even consciously defying their wishes and demands. Parents hailed the book *Indigo Children* as an eye-opener and an explanation for difficulties they had experienced. They took to heart the authors' claim that the difficult behaviour of these children did not arise because of parents' mistakes, but were a new phenomenon of our time – the arrival of a new generation of children, different from any we have seen before.

Because the book mentioned Steiner education as being suitable for Indigo Children, many were enrolled into Steiner schools. The expectation of parents was that these children would be educated by teachers who knew about and cared for their spiritual needs.

Other books followed. Most of the characteristics identified in these children – and summarised in the essay – are derived from observations by psychologists and child counsellors who have met and worked with them. They have been confirmed by teachers who have worked with such children in their classrooms.

What conclusions to draw from these observations remains an open question. Interpretations vary. Some see the children as heralding a new, more spiritually inclined generation. Others prefer to concentrate on the behavioural problems and attribute these to damage caused by environmental factors.

The most thorough treatment of related behavioural issues such as ADHD and the possibility of an evolutionary shift is Eugene Schwartz's book *The Millennial Child*, published in 1999. At that time Schwartz was director of the Waldorf teacher training programme at Sunbridge College. He applied Steiner's notion of the continuous evolutionary process in humanity to the changes observed in human consciousness and the soul forces of thinking, feeling and willing during the 20th century and at the turn of the millennium. He attributed the current shift observed in children's behaviour to an increase in strong yet undeveloped will forces in children today. Steiner himself had pointed to changes in children relating to an increase in spiritual faculties needed for the future tasks of humanity.

Within this framework the issue of behavioural problems and changes takes on a deeper dimension and loses any taint of sensationalism. It is a development that includes children of today as a whole.

With respect to pedagogical practice, all authors cited in this essay agree that the quality of educator–child relationships plays a key role in dealing with the behavioural issues of modern children, be they identified as ADHD children, 'new generation' or labelled with the recent diagnostic term of 'defiance disorder'. The principles of an education that embraces the deeper spiritual aspects of relationships with children, as well as how to arrange life within a kindergarten or child care centre accordingly, is the theme of the last part of the essay.

'Moving with Soul' leads into the pedagogical-therapeutic aspect of working with children. The theme of incarnation is taken up again, but now from the angle of entering into the field of the earth and its forces, and the acquisition of the upright posture by the human being.[17] This uprightness brings about a unique relationship of earth and cosmos compared to the animal world.

It is of great importance for the educator to get a feeling for the wonder of uprightness, towards which young children strive with great effort of will in the first year of life. Steiner urges educators to meet this striving with reverence. The way a child becomes upright reveals aspects of the individuality of the child and of the deep, albeit unconscious, spiritual connection of the young child to the cosmos.

From his work with disabled children, Karl König, a medical doctor and embryologist, has gained insights into the incarnation process and the steps children take to form a relationship to the earth environment.[18] In the light of the three steps outlined by König, the results of recent research into the early development of movement are considered, especially research into the role of the early reflexes, their transformation and the issue of retained reflexes in the development of movement in the child.

The considerations of how to support the development of movement in the young child in Steiner education also relate to the three aspects of the incarnation process as outlined by König. They are used as points of reference for discussing different approaches of working with movement in early childhood. The hand gesture games developed by Wilma Ellersiek are discussed in more detail because the rhythmical-musical quality of these games is so much in harmony with what Steiner emphasizes, namely that truly human movement always involves the soul and therefore has an artistic quality rather than being merely physical exercise.

Through her extraordinary perceptiveness Ellersiek was also able to develop movement sequences which depict archetypal gestures in the nature realm, especially in plants and animals. These are of great relevance for movement education in the later years of early childhood because they support the refinement of movement.

It is the intention of the essay on movement to highlight that there is nothing arbitrary about the child's natural development of movements and gestures: the development of movement is spiritually meaningful. Movement programmes should mirror this meaningfulness, which has its origin in the spiritual connectedness of the human being with cosmos and earth.

'Self-directed Play' is a form of 'being in movement', the most important activity of the young child. The inner and outer world meet in play: the individuality of the child forms connections to the world around him, to nature, to human beings and to the world of man-made things. In play the child makes sense of himself and his surroundings, and this play is a phenomenon in children all around the world from baby age onwards. It used to be entirely the domain of the child, with very little adult interference. The history of education tells what has happened to play ever since well-meaning educators took hold of it as a tool for instruction – not just now, but two hundred years ago.

The reason for this essay stems from developments in the last 40–50 years and the growing worldwide concern about the disappearance of play as 'free', that is, self-initiated and self-directed activity of the child. Two major changes can be identified which have contributed to this development: the growing influence of electronic media in the lives of children, and curriculum reforms that have pushed structured learning more and more into the early years and led to play becoming an educational tool or being replaced altogether by programmed learning. In addition, early childhood educators are now obliged to document programmes, learning processes and children's progress in unprecedented detail.

This has had an impact on Steiner early childhood education. In some instances it has led to reductions in the time allowed for self-directed play in Steiner kindergartens, in favour of structured activities that are easier to plan and document.

The talks on self-directed play which I gave to Australian Steiner early childhood educators and parents some years ago were aimed at emphasizing the meaningfulness of 'free' play and reviving enthusiasm for giving it the time and space it needs to flourish. These talks, which initiated an effort by Steiner early childhood educators to strengthen the quality of play, have been the starting point for a 'play research project'[19] and for the thoughts underlying this essay as well.

It has been written to:

- encourage educators to take a fresh look at play and to become enthusiastic advocates of free, self-directed play;
- give a summary of Steiner's profound insights into the nature of self-directed play;
- present thoughts on play in relation to the process of incarnation, that is, play as an outer and inner will movement within the different dimensions of human activity;
- indicate types of self-directed play which can be observed in children and which together show the complexity of play;
- share reflections and experiences on play facilitation.

The essay on 'Art Experiences in Early Childhood Education' is written from the perspective of an early childhood teacher, not an artist. It may seem inappropriate for a kindergarten teacher to write about the role of the arts in early childhood. However, the arts and kindergarten work are closely connected and Steiner recommended that a kindergarten teacher should practise at least one art form regularly.

It is true that one can only write about those arts which one practises oneself, which in my case is music and, to a lesser degree, painting and drawing. I do not have enough experience to write about modelling with children, eurythmy or storytelling. However, modelling did become part of this essay, thanks to Hanne Huber's work with respect to modelling with beeswax,[20] and also to Michael Howard, a sculptor and teacher who has, in my view, presented very interesting and innovative suggestions for modelling in early childhood education.[21]

Modelling and music play a special role in early childhood education. These art forms mirror the two major spiritual forces which determine growth and learning in early childhood: the etheric 'formative' forces and the soul-spiritual 'musical' forces, the former being closely related to the activity of modelling, the latter to rhythm and music.

An excursion into the realm of colour was added and called 'radiance of colour', a title which emphasizes that painting and drawing are about experiencing colour rather than learning techniques and communicating ideas.

It is also the intention of this essay to collate Steiner's many remarks on the role of the arts for children. Special mention needs to be made of Steiner's recommendations for music education in the early years. His comments on the relevance of the intervals, specifically his comments on the 'Mood of the Fifth', have inspired a fundamentally new approach to the musical education of the young child.

Following Steiner's lifetime, and especially after the 1960s, a number of musicians, singers and instrumentalists have worked with Steiner's insights and composed music for young children, songs of everyday life, which bring the 'Mood of the Fifth' into early childhood education. This is an ongoing process, as it is not easy for educators to embrace the kind of refined, objective musical quality in which Steiner wanted young children to be immersed. It places high demands on the teacher, including the training of hearing, quality of voice and musical expression.

Steiner's approach to musical education is unlike any other and contrary to what would satisfy the musical taste of most contemporaries. It requires teachers to forgo their own musical preferences as adults for the sake of laying foundations in the child: foundations which will unfetter the child from tradition in musical taste and enable him to express himself in a musically creative way at a later age.

The essay on observation, 'In Search for Reality', like the final one in this collection, covers aspects of inner development that relate to the professional work of the teacher. That teachers pursue a path of self-development is an essential condition for maintaining the original intention and the ongoing quality of Steiner education. The necessity of teachers pursuing a meditative practice related to their work makes teaching a vocation rather than a profession and sets Steiner education apart from other educational systems. Through this practice the teacher connects to the realm of human values and to the spiritual cosmos. The essay's treatment of child observation needs to be understood against this background.

The reality expressed in the title is the reality accessed in the spiritual practice of the teacher. It is through this reality that the origins and causes of a child's behaviour may be understood. Many educators are dissatisfied with the limitations of the current observational approach, which is based solely on what the human senses are able to perceive. It is with respect to the need for advanced human understanding in education that Steiner speaks about extending one's faculties of perception.

For Steiner the ability to feel is as much a means of perceiving as the ability to think. When feeling is regarded as a tool for observation, we should add immediately that feeling as a cognitional faculty needs to be trained in order to become more objective and less self-centred. The suggestions in this essay for developing the teacher's observational abilities relate to this refinement of feeling in observing.

This is not to say that exact observational data become irrelevant. On the contrary, they are an indispensable part of gaining knowledge about phenomena behind which the spiritual reality has to be sought. The strict procedures in observing prevent the observer who is using his feeling as a cognitive tool from going off on a subjective tangent and projecting his own preconceived ideas and fantasies onto his observations and interpretations.

Current observational methods focus only on what is sense-perceptible in the child. Yet unless teachers have observational faculties that enable them to understand the hidden spiritual aspects of the child as well, it could be said that the educational task is only half done. Steiner's intention was to develop such methods. Some of these methods, and how we can develop them through our inner life, are the subject of this essay.

'Under the Stars' may be the least accessible of all essays in this collection to readers who are more familiar with conventional education than with Steiner education. It was written with Steiner early childhood educators in mind who are interested in the spiritual significance of the Zodiac and its relevance for their educational practice. As with the essay on observation, the suggestions given are part of a vocational path of inner development. There are teachers who follow a spiritual path of self-development independently of their profession. This is different from what is meant here, namely that the vocation of being an early childhood educator as such places specific requirements on a teacher to serve young children well.

The four major requirements are:

- to not only embrace the concept of incarnation intellectually but also to feel into the meaning and the archetypal human gestures of the early time in life;
- to do justice to the young child's connectedness to the spiritual world in our own educational practice;
- to acknowledge and nurture the natural drive of young children to develop towards the future rather than be limited to what is expected of them in the present;
- to respond to the child's need for closeness to the adult and for protection.

When speaking about the self-development of the educator, we must include the honest assessment of our weaknesses and failures. Specifically when considering the four requirements, we become aware of the need for change and further development in our educational practice.

How can we embrace in our inner work as educators the meaning of the signs of the zodiac? What does serving the four fundamental needs of the young child mean in practice? These are the themes of the essay.

Many of Steiner's lectures elaborate on his insights into the relationship between cosmos and earth. Steiner demanded of educators in the current period of evolution that educational insights must be informed by wisdom drawn from the cosmos. This is a huge undertaking. Only an attempt at a beginning can be made in this essay.

In referring to Steiner's interpretation of the signs of the zodiac, themes related to the cosmos and the incarnation process are reflected upon with respect to their significance for early childhood education. Steiner refers to certain virtues which esoteric tradition associates with specific zodiacal signs, and which Steiner tested through his own spiritual research. To practise these so-called 'monthly virtues' as educators means to direct our thoughts and actions towards this reality, rather than trying to decipher the cosmic script for the purposes of gaining deeper insights into our personal lives. By striving to refine our life of feeling in the practice of these virtues, we express gratitude towards the cosmos. Thus, through intensification of the soul life, a connection can be established between the educator, the work of education, and the cosmos.

Endnotes

1. Lynne Oldfield has given a more detailed overview of the beginnings of the Waldorf School movement and the Waldorf Kindergarten movement in her book *Free to Learn*, Hawthorn Press, Stroud, 2001.
2. To avoid the confusing use of both genders, I will alternate from chapter to chapter.
3. Quote from R. Steiner, *The Education of the Child in the Light of Anthroposophy*, Rudolf Steiner Press, London, 1981, p. 24.
4. Steiner's major lecture series on education was only first published in English in the late 1970s and 1980s.
5. Freya Jaffke was responsible for the content of many of these, as well as the important booklet on *Work and Play in Early Childhood*. Some have been translated and published in the UK by Hawthorn Press and others, and later in the USA by the Waldorf/Steiner Early Childhood Association of North America (WECAN), in particular books on the festivals and the spiritual work of the teacher.
6. E. Grunelius, *Early Childhood Education and the Waldorf School Plan*, Waldorf School Monographs, Spring Valley, NY, 1966, p. 1.
7. In the list of recommended reading on the first seven years at the end of the booklet, Grunelius' book is the only one written by a kindergarten teacher. However, in the advertisement of work materials and workbooks for parents on the next page, most of the authors are kindergarten teachers. Interestingly, this picture has completely changed in the recently published revised edition *What is a Waldorf Kindergarten?* which includes a number of new articles written by kindergarten teachers. The book was published by WECAN, Spring Valley, NY, in 2009.
8. R. Steiner, *The Education of the Child*, p. 44f.
9. Reference is made here to the introduction by Chr. Bamford to this series of lectures published under the title *The Spiritual Ground of Education*, Anthroposophic Press, Great Barrington, MA, 2004.

10 Steiner, *The Spiritual Ground of Education*, p. 1.
11 Ibid., p. 2.
12 Ibid., pp. 3–5.
13 Ibid., p. 8.
14 Steiner, *The Human Soul in Relation to World Evolution*, Lecture 6
15 The needs of the 'spiritual child' were mentioned in the previous Australian early learning framework, *The Practice of Relationships*. See: www.community.nsw.gov.au/DOCSWR/_assets/main/documents/childcare_framework.pdf
16 It is interesting that the seventh year as starting point for formal learning has come back into the general educational debate recently, triggered through students' high achievements in countries such as Finland and Sweden, where formal education starts at age seven.
17 R. Steiner, *A Psychology of Body, Soul and Spirit*, p. 130ff.
18 *Being Human*, 1989. Anthroposophic Press, NY.
19 The project, which was conducted in Australia between 2003 and 2006, is documented in a separate and more detailed publication: R. Long-Breipohl, *Supporting Self-directed Play in Steiner/Waldorf Early Childhood Education*, Waldorf Early Childhood Association of North America, Spring Valley, NY, 2010.
20 Hanne Huber, *Gestalten mit Bienenwachs im Vorschulalter*, Verlag Freies Geistesleben, Stuttgart, 2001.
21 M. Howard, *Educating the Will*, AWSNA Publications, Fair Oaks, CA, 2004.

1

Recognizing and Nurturing the Life Forces of the Young Child

During the first seven years of life, care for child health is of great importance because the child's well-being and learning is relying on a well-functioning body.

Steiner points to two areas which need the educator's special consideration and care in the early years: the child's senses as the means of taking in impressions from the environment, and the child's life or etheric forces[1], which maintain life processes and health within the body. These forces are normally exuberant in the young child, yet they need to be protected from depletion caused by environmental influences.

The following considerations will focus on these life forces. They are divided into two parts. The first part takes a closer look at the different life forces and the role they play in the development of the young child. The second examines ways to nurture these forces, both in the kindergarten and in day-to-day living with young children.

Part 1: Towards an understanding of etheric forces and their role in child development

What is the nature of life forces and how do they manifest?

To understand these forces in a way that can inform educational action, it is best to begin by looking at the realm of nature which displays etheric activity in its purest form: the realm of plants.

Like all living organisms the plant's life cycle of sprouting, growing, blooming, fruit/seed formation, withering and dying is governed by different laws than the mineral realm. The mineral realm is well researched by natural science, but the laws of mineral substances do not explain the phenomena of plant life as they unfold in time through the life cycle of growth, reproduction, decline and dying.

Since ancient times the four different states of matter, or 'elements', have been described as the solid or mineral element, the water element, the air element and the fire or warmth element. In the plant, the mineral and water elements are drawn up from the earth, the air and warmth elements from the cosmos.

Steiner describes how each of these elements are complemented by the activity of corresponding etheric forces: the life ether working in the solid element, the chemical ether in the watery element, the light ether in the airy element and the warmth ether in processes of transformation through warmth.

Ernst Marti describes the function of each etheric force in relation to its element as follows:[2]

Ether	Element
WARMTH ETHER Creating the conditions for life processes to take place Penetrating all etheric processes Ripening Bringing beings to maturity	FIRE Burning away of substance Dying Transformation
LIGHT ETHER Linear, centripetal (from periphery towards centre) A formative force, exerting a force of suction in forming, structuring space, creating boundaries, separating outside from inside	AIR Rarefied substance Dispersed Unformed
CHEMICAL ETHER (also called 'tone ether') Differentiation Bringing order into substance Lawfulness: rhythms, patterns, connections (similar to the intervals in music: two different tones together create one sound)	WATER Dissolved substance Merging, integrating Flow and continuity Water is passive, dense, heavy and tends to spread until a state of balance and calm is reached
LIFE ETHER Centrifugal force (from centre towards periphery) Growing Plasticizing Absorbing, assimilating, restoring, healing Integrating the forces in a living body	EARTH Substance in its solid state Rigid, cold, impermeable

The working of the ethers in the elements can be illustrated through the example of a flowering plant:

Etheric forces in the lower part of the plant take up mineral substances from the earth into the root system. Etheric forces in the upper part of the plant bring forth the flowering process and the formation of seeds. While the life and chemical ethers support the tendency towards continuous growth in the plant, producing leaf after leaf in a repetitive pattern of growth, the light ether halts this process, thus leading over to the flowering stage and the formation of the blossom. It is then the warmth and life ethers which evoke the ripening processes of fruit and seed formation.[3]

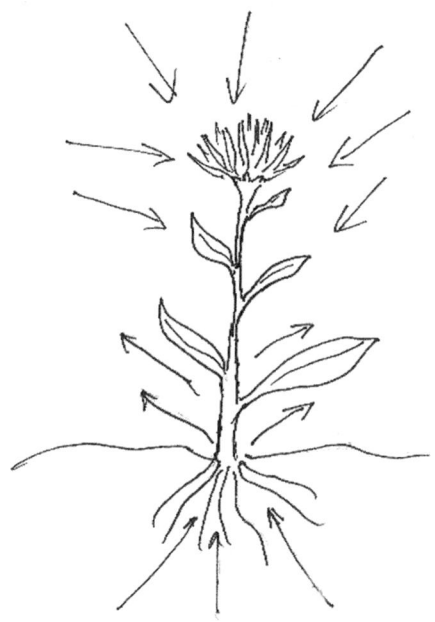

All four kinds of etheric forces exert an influence on the plant from outside, working together harmoniously to achieve the full cycle of plant life. The plant and its environment are one.

In contrast, more complex organisms develop a system of forces within themselves and are much more closed off from the environment. This is the case with human beings: their inner and outer environments are separated. Etheric forces act within the human being not directly from the cosmos, as with plants, but through the etheric body.

Steiner speaks of four such bodies within the human being: the mineral or physical body, which is formed from the earth, the etheric body, the astral or soul body and the ego, or I-organization, which are formed out of the cosmos.[4] The first two form the physical-etheric organization of the human being, the latter two the soul-spiritual organization.

These four bodies are active according to the conditions and needs of the human being as an independent organism. This means that initially the body of formative forces within the human being still receives into itself etheric forces from the cosmos, but these forces then become active in a much more independent way according to the various needs of such a complex organism. Because the human being is more closed to the cosmos than the plant, the centripetal, contracting tendency of etheric forces in the upper part, the head, is stronger than the centrifugal, dispersing tendency and the influence of earth forces in the lower part of the body. Through the dominance of the centripetal forces a new centre of etheric formative activity is created, enabling the development of an independent inner life. This process can be summarized as follows:

Through the physical organization of the human being, earth substances are taken in and excreted; in this process the 'Gestalt,' or wholeness, of the human being remains intact. The centrifugal tendency of the life ether in the metabolic processes is tempered through the influence of the I and the astral body, and does not lead to physical disintegration or chaos.

In the system of fluids, the dynamic, rhythmical, formative and repetitive activity of the chemical ether is halted by the light ether and by influences from the soul life of the human being, carried by the astral body.

In the function of breathing, the light ether and the influence of astral forces balance the centrifugal quality of the process of breathing out. With this the possibility of being conscious arises.

In the system of warmth, the human being maintains his own warmth level as separate from that of the environment. The warmth organization of the human being is highly differentiated within the body and also individually different between human beings. It can be characterized as the main field of activity of the I-organization.

In considering this, we realize that in the human being etheric forces do not act by themselves but in conjunction with soul-spiritual forces and their representations within the physical-etheric body: the astral body and I-organization.

The astral body supports processes of the light ether, especially in the human nerve-sense system. The I supports and moderates the activity of life and chemical ethers in the metabolic system. The I also supports the formative activity of the light ether in early development. It is therefore involved in both processes – working from the head down into the organs of the body, and working from the lower body upwards in the acquisition of walking, speaking and thinking.

At this stage we should turn to a discovery of Johann Wolfgang von Goethe, a German poet, writer and researcher/philosopher in the field of natural science in the 18th and early 19th century, and regarded by Steiner as one of the preparers of his spiritual science. What Goethe discovered in relation to growth activity within an organism[5] will also shed light on processes of growth and transformation in the young child.

Goethe found that there is a law of correlation or compensation governing organs within a closed organism – that is, an organism in which the outer and inner world are separated. He suggests that formative forces in such organisms are finite. This means that any concentration of formative forces and activity in a particular organ will make this organ stronger. However, if forces are used in order to fulfil a certain task within one part of the organism, then this will lead to a reduction of activity, or lack of potential, within another part of the organism.

Confirming and extending Goethe's findings through his own spiritual research, Rudolf Steiner states that this law also applies to transformations of formative activity in organ growth into activity within the soul life of the human being. He discovered that the etheric forces used in the activity of thinking are the same as are used in organ formation. Once transformed into soul forces, such forces are no longer available for the growth and physical development of the body. This is the spiritual insight which led Steiner to urge that the child's thinking be left undisturbed by adult intervention.

Steiner describes it thus:

> The forces that hold sway in the etheric body are active at the beginning of man's life on Earth, and most distinctly during the embryo period; they are the forces of growth and formative development. A portion of them, emancipated in the further course of earthly life from this formative activity, then becomes the force of thought ... It is of the utmost importance to know that the ordinary thought-forces of man are the forces of bodily growth and formation, refined and sublimated.[6]

The forces that have been building the physical body must be cared for and protected from depletion so as to be available and well functioning when they are needed at a later stage.

The role of etheric forces in the development of the young child

Cosmic etheric forces form the human body in embryonic development, then diminish gradually during the first seven years. During embryonic development the etheric activity is stronger than it will ever be in the subsequent phases of human life.

While sheltered from the direct influence of the earthly environment, the embryo is totally open to influences from the spiritual world, the zodiac and the planets. Steiner paints the following picture of the activity of the etheric body:

> It is of extraordinary significance that we, in our descent into earthly life, draw together forces from the universal ether and thus take with us, in our ether body, a kind of image of the cosmos. If one could extract the ether body of the human being, at the moment when he is uniting himself with the physical body, we should have a sphere ... containing stars, zodiac, sun and moon. These configurations of the ether body remain during embryonic

development ... Though they fade a little, they remain. Indeed, they remain right into the seventh year, until the change of teeth.[7]

Once the child is born and the physical body of the child has become a separate entity from the body of the mother, the etheric body of the child works independently of the mother's body, now within the child's physical body.

The specific quality of etheric activity during early childhood and the transformations that occur during this time can be better understood with the help of Hermann Poppelbaum.[8] He has described forms of archetypal activity of the etheric forces and he characterizes them as follows:

- *Connecting and repeating.* These are functions of the chemical and life ether.

- *Transforming,* such as happens in the plant process of assimilation. A function of the chemical ether and light ether.

- *Variation and enhancement,* such as in the flowering process. Mainly a function of the light ether.

- *Juxtaposition,* a function of all four ethers found in the entire life cycle of plants: in the above-below orientation, in growing-decaying, and in centripetal-centrifugal (contracting-expanding) activity.

When we reflect on the role of etheric forces in the first three years of a child's life, we begin to see the enormous importance of all of these processes.

A more vivid understanding of etheric forces in the human being arises if we begin to see the actual functioning rather than just the outcome.

Connecting and repeating

Connecting and repeating are characteristic for physical growth processes such as brain formation, but they are also present on a soul level in speech and thinking. One of the major findings of neuroscience over the last 20 years has been that most of the neural pathways and connections in the brain are established in the first years of life.[9]

The activity of connecting is not limited to brain development but extends into the processes of the entire nerve-sense system, as well as into the cooperation between the inner organs. Connecting is also the main process in the development of attachment in the first and second year of life, in the development of verbal communication, and in the development of structure and syntax in the third year of life.

A specific human form of connecting is the ability to imitate, a way of connecting and repeating based on the child's inborn urge to orientate herself towards human behaviour and human relationships. It is observable in the processes of learning to walk and speak. Imitation is also a major part of child's play, and it is the essential way of learning throughout early childhood.

The young child is a doer, keenly interested in the activity of adults. The art of education consists in bringing the work done by adults in the presence of children down to such a level that children can imitate it.

The first step of transformation of etheric forces: variation, refinement and enhancement

In the third year of life, at around age two and a half, a milestone is reached in the formation of the brain. Part of the etheric forces involved in brain formation are no longer needed and become available for other tasks.[10]

The consequence of etheric forces becoming free is a vivid memory. This is unlike the memory of older children and is described by Steiner as a kind of 'soul habit', based on imitation and repetition:

> If you watch a little child grasping something you will find that in this the concept of habit can be grasped ... A child imitates something one day. The next day, and the day following, he does it again, and the action is not only

performed outwardly but right into the innermost parts of his physical body. This is the basis of memory in the early years.[11]

At around the same time, the child becomes dimly conscious of her own inner space, and in saying 'I' to herself a consciousness of self begins to emerge. The child now expresses desire ('I want ... '), antipathy and hurt as if experienced in an inner space. Over time this space will become filled with more and more soul experiences. This event marks a new phase in the child's development, in which the role of the etheric forces may be characterized as variation, refinement and enhancement.

Whenever variation and enhancement occur in plant life – for example, in refining leaf shapes and sizes before the formation of the blossom – the light ether is especially active. Such a process of refinement occurs in the child between the ages of two and a half and five. Interestingly, books on child development[12] and checklists of developmental milestones consider all of the child's fundamentally important faculties to be present already in the first three years of life; subsequent phases of development are described as times for refinement and enrichment.

This applies to the capacities for movement, speech and thinking, and also to play. There is a difference between the rather scattered, 'peripheral' kind of the play in children under two and a half and the combination of inner and outer orientation in the play of children between three and five. The play of three- to five-year-olds has a feeling component, whereas younger children play more matter-of-factly with what they find around them.

The ability to express what comes from within can be understood as caused by the gradual release of formative forces that were hitherto active in fine-tuning the bodily functions of breathing and blood circulation. Rudolf Steiner characterizes the resulting new faculty as childhood fantasy or childhood imagination:

> The formative forces released from the head – acting now as soul and spiritual forces – join those which are being released in the chest region. This change can be recognized

outwardly by the emergence of an exceptionally vivid memory which the child develops between two-and-a-half and five, and also by its wonderful imagination.[13]

It is amazing to witness such enhancement and refinement of play during this time. If the child is given the appropriate environment and play materials, the age between three and five has the potential to be the most creative phase in life. If the child is able to practise and refine imagination through self-initiated play, the creative strength achieved in this process will stay with the child for years to come.

The activity of light ether brings forth the formation of blossom in the plant. It can also be found in the play activity of the child, albeit on a different level. Just as light ether pulls the plant upwards, so too does play lift everyday events up into the realm of imagination and transform them in the fantasy play of the child. Healthy play is never just imitation of what is, but an enhancement, a new creation.

The second step of transformation of etheric forces: juxtaposition, polarity

At the end of this period of refinement and enhancement a further step of transformation is under way. Steiner speaks about the child becoming receptive to admonition.[14] The child 'begins to listen to and to believe in what its elders say. Only towards the fifth year is it possible to awaken in a child the sense of what is right or wrong.'[15]

Whereas Steiner describes children under three as being closed to the will of the adult and solely following their own impulses,[16] the child is now able to perceive more clearly the intention of another human being and is therefore more willing to respond. This is not an achievement of the intellect. Rather, it is achieved through the maturation of the organs of the rhythmical system – breathing and blood circulation – and heralds a further step in the development of the child's feeling.

The growth forces that become free in this part of the body are different from those behind memory and fantasy, which have a connection to the realm of thought. Etheric forces of the heart–lung system carry the impulse for continuous exchange between the inner and outer world through the breathing system and through oxygen entering the blood stream. Transformed on the soul level, they bring about a different relationship between the inner soul realm of the child and the outer world – between the child's desire and the wishes of the adult. Yet there is still a long road ahead, from perceiving another person's will to the deeper understanding of another human being's feeling.

However, at the age of five a wonderful opportunity presents itself for deepening the relationship between the educator and the child because the child is more conscious of the soul moods and intentions of the adults around her. The child will start looking up to the adult as somebody who knows how things are done and what direction to take.

In the plant realm, juxtaposition or opposition of forces comes about at the moment when the tendency of the life and chemical ethers for perpetual growth of stem and leaves is arrested by the activity of light ether. This leads to the stage of blossoming. Where light ether combines with warmth ether, life and chemical ethers are pushed back. Formative forces will dominate and lead to further maturation but also to hardening processes, as is visible in seed formation.

In the sixth and seventh year the child goes through a period of development that is not harmonious. There is an abundance of life and growth in the lower body and a growth spurt in the limbs, leading to an urge for physical activity. The lower part of the body is now the centre of etheric growth activity. At the same time the influence of the light ether is visible in that thinking becomes more formed, more precise, but loses the fluidity of the previous fantasy stage. The child will speak and act after consideration rather than spontaneously. The child's features become more individualized, often appearing rather angular and bony compared to the softness of the younger child. Childhood fantasy and the ability to play recede and are replaced by a tendency to talk instead of act.

Appropriate pedagogy for this time is a difficult issue. How do we guide a child through a period that is dominated by the experience of polarity? While the potential to play imaginatively, gained in the previous phases, is still there, the child in the sixth and seventh year may feel that she has outgrown it.

Work carried out in the kindergarten appears in a new light if we consider the situation of the older child. Good handwork or domestic work requires that two opposing faculties – thinking and doing – be brought together. Idle talk and senseless activity, the two biggest issues for six-year-olds, have no place here. An opportunity is given to experience that opposites may balance each other. The manifold possibilities of the outdoors are also worth considering. Many work opportunities such as gardening and building, not to mention physical movement such as walking and climbing, involve dexterity and finding balance.

An experienced Steiner early childhood educator with considerable knowledge of the age group has told me that six-year-olds in the preparatory year for primary school thrive and become ready for school best if no intellectual demands are made on them, if there is no pressure but lots of opportunities to do things.

The third step of transformation of etheric forces: battle and balance. The birth of the etheric body

In the sixth and seventh year of the child the second dentition or 'change of teeth' is under way. Teeth are the hardest part of the body. According to Steiner, bringing forth the second teeth needs the forces of life ether and even the forces of the I. He describes this process as life forces pushing from below upwards, supported by astral forces and opposed by the form-giving and hardening forces of the light ether, working from the head down. They counteract and at the same time support the life ether forces by an action comparable to suction.[17] This interaction of different etheric forces, which have within themselves opposing tendencies, leads to a short battle of forces, during which the second dentition commences, usually with the loss of the lower incisors:

> Then whatever radiates upwards from the body is thrust back, whereas the forces that shoot downwards from the head are restrained. Thus, during the time the teeth are changing, the severest battle is fought between the forces striving downward from above and those shooting

upward from below. The change of teeth is the physical expression of this conflict between the two kinds of forces, those that later appear in the child as his powers of reasoning and intellect, and those that need to be used particularly in drawing, painting, and writing.[18]

Why a battle? As human beings, we carry within us forces of death as well as of life. Both groups of ethers have the potential for life and death within them. Life ether and chemical ether, if left alone, would continue growth until a collapse by over-growth occurred. If left alone, the light ether, bringing form and order, would effect a contracting, hardening process of such dimensions that life would become impossible.

Only if there is balance between the activities of both kinds of forces will growth be possible in the way described with respect to child development. The second teeth are formed out of the hardest substance (enamel) of the human body. Light ether activity is needed to facilitate the breaking through of the second teeth. Steiner describes how these forces of hardening have the tendency to continue their activity, not only in the head, but further down into the body as well. This would lead to a premature hardening of the entire body, which must be prevented if growth and development are to continue further. The forces that can arrest the light ether and prevent too much hardening are the life ether forces, primarily active in the lower part of the body.

This battle of forces, as Steiner describes it, is unique to human beings because it is a transformation process carried not only by the ethers but also by the higher members of the human being, the astral body and I-organization.

The battle recedes in the seventh year with the breaking through of the incisors. The etheric forces involved in the process of teeth formation are then freed and reappear transformed on the soul level as intellectual faculties. This is the moment of the birth of the etheric body.

> Supersensible contemplation of the human being will reveal to us apart from the physical body, another finer

body which we have called the etheric body or the body of formative forces. From this etheric body spring not only all the forces sustaining nourishment and growth, but it is also the source of the faculties of remembering and of making mental images, of ideation. It becomes an independent entity only during the change of teeth, at which time it is born in a similar way in which, at physical birth, the body is born from its mother.[19]

Protective layers. St. Kilda Pre-School, Melbourne. Photo by Paulene Hanna

Part 2: Nurturing and Protecting the Life Forces of the Young Child

Etheric forces play a crucial role in the growth and development of the child. Caring for them should be at the centre of educators' considerations for children in the first seven years. How, then, can we engender and maintain an environment and pedagogical situation in which the etheric forces of the child are appropriately cared for? This question will be addressed now by considering how the four etheric qualities, as wtell as the functions of the four ethers, could underpin educational practice.

How does a teacher or caregiver of young children engender a harmonious balance of the qualities of all four ethers in the organism of a kindergarten or childcare centre? The following suggestions relate to the overall task in Steiner early childhood education, which is to maintain an 'etheric' quality in all aspects of early childhood education.

Etheric qualities toward which the teacher will strive	Benefits for the child
An atmosphere of warmth, penetrating the entire organism of the kindergarten. The teacher's enthusiasm and love for her work carries this quality of warmth and expresses itself in joyfulness.	This atmosphere of warmth provides the conditions for strong activity of life forces in the child and for the healthy development of the physical body. Steiner indicates that joy hatches out the healthy forms of organs.[20]
Light makes visible, brings something to light. Here the ability of the teacher is required to 'see' the child, to observe and accept the child as an individual, in whom body, soul and spirit are unique.	Children feel perceived and appreciated for who they are. They then feel understood, and will open up inwardly rather than holding back and withdraw.
The qualities of chemical ether are differentiation, refinement, and order. These find expression in the teacher's devotion to her duty, in particular attending to rhythm, order and flow in the life of the kindergarten, paying attention to detail and to the quality of the atmosphere of the kindergarten. This is what Steiner means when he says that the kindergarten should be penetrated by a musical quality in all that the teacher does.	A rich and ordered environment will make the child interested in engaging in activity. In the way the teacher approaches her work, the child will have an example worthy of imitation. Imitation is the way in which the child connects to the flow of the life in the kindergarten.

Etheric qualities toward which the teacher will strive	Benefits for the child
The quality of life ether, of creating an entire organism, relies on the teacher's pedagogical intuition and will to create and maintain the kindergarten as a 'living entity'. The teacher's role is that of the I-being of this entity.	The child will experience harmony and feel safe in such an organism. Trust can develop, and leads to the feeling that 'the world is good'. Surrounded by harmony and order, the child can live in her dream consciousness and does not have to worry about what might happen next.

Considering these descriptions of the qualities and functions of life forces, we can now proceed to the question of their relevance in day-to-day living with young children. These functions or activities of the etheric forces can inform the teacher/caregiver about how to establish and maintain an 'etheric' quality when working with young children.

Connecting, imitating:

A precondition for effective education is establishing positive human relationships, relationships in which children feel recognized and appreciated for who they are. The child has a natural inclination to form attachments, which should be met by the adult with qualities such as reverence, warmth and genuine interest.

The young child is a doer and keenly interested in the activity of adults. Therefore, the act of connecting quite naturally finds expression in imitation. The art of educating young children consists in bringing the work that adults perform in the presence of children down to such a level that children can be part of it and imitate it.

> For the entire life of the kindergarten revolves around children adapting to the few people in charge, who should behave naturally so that the children feel stimulated to imitate whatever their teachers do ... . The task of the kindergarten teacher is to adjust the work taken from daily life so that it becomes suitable for the children's play

activities ... The whole point of a kindergarten class is to give young children the opportunity to imitate life in a simple and wholesome way.[21]

Repetition and rhythm:

Implicit in working with imitation are the elements of repetition and rhythm. Both are important for organizing life and work around children.

As previously mentioned, repetition and rhythm are essential features of etheric processes in nature. This is true not only in the life cycle of the plant, but also in processes within the human body such as breathing, digestion and blood circulation. A rhythmical way of living no longer occurs naturally in the modern family and society, and yet children need rhythm to maintain their physical and emotional health. As they cannot as yet establish rhythms for themselves, they need the adult to do this for them. In early childhood education the teacher/caregiver is responsible for bringing rhythm and order into the course of the day, the week and the year with their varied activities. At home a mother or father can do the same, giving structure and rhythm to family life so that there are times and routines for getting up in the morning, going to bed, and for 'how things are done in our family'. Rhythm allows the child to breathe, relax, and feel secure. The child knows how the day will unfold.

Refinement, enhancement:

It is important that life in the kindergarten contains possibilities for the child to refine and enhance her abilities herself. This is done in the child's free play, which is initiated and directed by the child, not by the teacher. Within this play activity the child will unfold a range of faculties by using her will, feeling and thinking, but most of all childhood fantasy and memory. The teacher can support this process by refining the environment, providing open-ended toys and materials that will stimulate the inner activity of the child. In addition, the richness and beauty of experiences of everyday life and festival celebrations will be the teacher's contribution to nourish and enhance the child's etheric forces. Most of all, the child's fantasy is enhanced by daily storytelling and the use of puppets and simple props to support the spoken word with images.

Refinement and enhancement should not mean putting demands on the child's intellectual faculties, as this would drain the etheric forces at a time when they are needed for the development of the physical body. Certainly, the child thinks naturally and expresses her thoughts in words. But this does not warrant trying to stimulate the verbal and intellectual capacities of a child through frequent dialogues, explanatory conversations or question and answer sessions, all aimed at providing information and stimulating her intellectual response. In children who are talked to in this way at a young age already the intellect detaches itself too soon from the unity of thinking, feeling and willing and becomes dry and clever. These children, who are proficient in reproducing the explanations and information given to them, often lack the ability to imitate because they respond primarily with their intellect and not with feeling and will.

Death forces in modern life and their impact on young children

As mentioned previously, life processes within the child develop through the polarity of life ether forces, which tend towards abundant life processes and growth, and light ether forces, which tend towards form, hardening and death. Steiner describes the polarity of life and death forces within the human body and the human soul, with will linked to life processes and thinking to death processes.[22]

In early childhood the activity of life forces must be predominant so that the child can build a strong and healthy physical body – hence the importance of will activity during this period. However, modern culture the world over places a high value on the intellect.

One could describe the computer as human thought captured in a man-made machine capable of performing complex thought tasks at high speed. The refinement of this machine over the last two decades is the outcome of the rapidly increasing intellectual capacity of modern human beings, especially those who spearhead technological development. Anyone who has to spend a considerable part of their working life in front of a computer will know the tiring, exhausting effect it can have: a warning sign for the depletion of life forces. The time that children spend in front of computers draws on the strength of their life forces and is therefore counterproductive to their health and well-being.

Life forces are also depleted through frequent television/video viewing. Here the child connects with a world of images that are illusionary and alienate the child from real life. In consequence the child's own imagination and will are not activated and the child may become passive and lose her natural desire to explore the world. There are many studies available that point to the dangers posed by TV and computers for the child's physical, mental and emotional health.[23]

In advertisements today the desirable child is the smart early achiever. However, the child's physical body is still developing according to the rhythms of life processes. Trying to accelerate this maturation process in one particular area such as intellectual development comes at a price in the form of a weakness in another area – lack of will and imagination, for example. At the time of the gestation of the etheric body – out of which the child emerges at the end of the first seven-year period of her life when thinking is supported by the now-freed etheric forces[24] – the child's emerging soul faculties need to be protected from damaging environmental influences just as the foetus was physically protected in the mother's womb before birth. However, even after this birth of the etheric body, the child's thinking develops best in imaginative rather than in dry intellectual activity for some years to come.

In the early years children should be allowed to be active with their will forces through movement, play and hands-on activities indoors and outdoors. Through play the child's thinking and speech develops holistically at a pace that is set by the child.

Young children love the rhythm and sound of poetry. Absorbing it deeply yet not intellectually, they build up a feeling for speech and thus a foundation for their later comprehension of content and meaning. Language education is possible through storytelling, nursery rhymes and poems rather than through lengthy explanations, conversations or question and answer sessions.

Young children are a wonderful gift. With each child new life forces are brought into the world. Teachers, parents and caregivers have the responsibility to care for these life forces in such a way that the child may have strong life forces available for an entire life span.

Endnotes

1. The use of the terms 'etheric forces' and 'etheric body' is explained in chapter 2 of R. Steiner's, *An Outline of Esoteric Science*, Anthroposophic Press, Hudson, NY, 1997. Steiner discriminates between the visible mineral substance of the body of living beings, plants, animals and humans, and the invisible, spiritual forces that keep the physical body alive and prevent it from disintegrating into its mineral compounds.

    For the spiritual researcher experienced in direct spiritual observation, etheric forces are a reality. For the non-clairvoyant, however, the notions of 'etheric forces' and 'etheric body' are initially thought-concepts. They become relevant when applied to find meaning and gain understanding of observations in nature and the human being.

2. Summarized from E. Marti, *The Four Ethers*, Shaumburg Publications, Illinois, 2011.

3. For a detailed description of the working of the etheric forces see chapters two and three in E. Schoorel, *The First Seven Years: Physiology of Childhood*, Rudolf Steiner College Press, Fair Oaks, CA, 2004.

4. For a description of these four principles or organizations see chapter two of R. Steiner, *An Outline of Esoteric Science*, Anthroposophic Press, Hudson NY, 1997.

5. Quoted from G. Wachsmuth, *Erde und Mensch. Ihre Bildekräfte, Rhythmen und Lebensprozesse, Vol. 1* (Third edition) Verlag am Goetheanum, Dornach, 1965, p. 311ff.

6   R. Steiner and I. Wegmann, *Fundamentals of Therapy: An Extension of the Art of Healing Through Spiritual Knowledge,* Rudolf Steiner Press, London, 1983, p. 8.
7   R. Steiner, *The Human Soul in Relation to World Evolution,* trans. R. Stebbing, Anthroposophic Press, New York, 1984, pp. 92–93
8   H. Poppelbaum, *The Etheric Body in Idea and Action,* Anthroposophical Publishing Co., London, 1955, p. 9.
9   A recent, easy-to-read summary of these findings appeared on the internet in October 2010 written by clinical psychologist Dr Regalena Melrose: *Why Waldorf Works: From a Neuroscientific Perspective.* See: http://themagiconions.blogspot.se/2010/10/discovering-waldorf-waldorf-from.html.
10 R. Steiner, 'The Child before the Seventh Year' in *Soul Economy and Waldorf Education,* Anthroposophic Press, Spring Valley, NY, 1986, p. 117.
11 R. Steiner, *The Roots of Education,* Anthroposophic Press, New York, 1997, p. 48.
12 This is very obvious in a widely used resource for mainstream training of early childhood educators. I am referring here to the three volumes by D. Nixon and K. Gould, *Emerging, Exploring, Extending,* Social Science Press, Tuggerah, NSW Australia, 2002.
13 Steiner, 'The Child before the Seventh Year', p. 117.
14 Ibid., p. 120.
15 Ibid., p. 121.
16 Ibid., p. 105.
17 Steiner has described this process again and again in his educational lectures, most notably in *Balance in Teaching.*
18 R. Steiner, *Balance in Teaching,* Mercury Press, Spring Valley, NY, 1990, pp. 16–17.
19 Steiner, 'The Child before the Seventh Year', pp. 110–111.
20 R. Steiner, *The Child's Changing Consciousness and Waldorf Education,* Anthroposophic Press, New York, 1988, p. 81.
21 One of the more recent books is by M. Large, *Set Free Childhood: Parents Survival Guide for Coping with Computers and TV,* Hawthorn Press, Stroud, 2003. Other authors such as J. Healy, D. Elkind and J. Ch. Pearce also need mentioning in this context.
22 See the next chapter on 'Thinking and the Consciousness of the Young Child'.
23 One of the more recent books is by M. Large, *Set Free Childhood: Parents Survival Guide for Coping with Computers and TV,* Hawthorn Press, Stroud, 2003. Other authors such as J. Healy, D. Elkind and J. Ch. Pearce also need mentioning in this context.
24 See the next chapter on 'Thinking and the Consciousness of the Young Child'.

2

Thinking and the Consciousness of the Young Child

Thinking as an inner process of developing one's own thoughts is not a favourite activity among human beings today. While there is an immense variety of products based on sophisticated human thought and created by highly trained engineers, programmers and designers, actually thinking for oneself is now experienced as stressful by many people.

Often tertiary students find pursuing a train of thought strenuous, and schoolteachers have trouble engaging their pupils in processes that require focused thinking activity. In adult learning more and more visual aids are being used, and the more they are used, the less effort is needed for directing the thinking process oneself. In student textbooks the content is presented in short paragraphs; the main ideas or research results are highlighted and framed so that one can take them in at a glance.

Steiner predicted that human beings would gradually lose the ability to think for themselves. This was of great concern to him as he regarded the human faculty of independent thought as an all-important human achievement with respect to the further spiritual development of the human being.

Against this background, understanding and helping the development of thinking and consciousness in young children takes on an added urgency.

What is this faculty of thinking in human beings?

This is an important question to start with if we want to approach an understanding of what thinking is in the first years of life.

Thinking is an activity through which the human being is able to make meaning of the phenomena of the sense world, as well as to enter into the sense-free realm of ideas. In this respect thinking is a supersensible faculty, as it does not derive its activity or all of its content from sense experience in the physical world alone.

In everyday existence, the faculty of forming mental images and interpreting experiences through concepts assists human beings in ordering, structuring and giving meaning to their lives. Through thinking we are able to orientate ourselves towards the highest ideals of humanity. At the same time, our thinking can be reduced to rationalizing our wishes, desires and actions in everyday life. If human thinking becomes too deeply and one-sidedly involved in issues of the material world, it is in danger of losing its connection with the realm of ideas and ideals.

The difficulty of maintaining a healthy balance in thinking in the modern world was a theme that Steiner returned to again and again in his lectures. In our time, many people find it difficult to develop for themselves the spiritual potential of thinking, thinking which is free from serving their own interests and desires. However, if we want to find the key to the thinking of the young child, we need to take as our point of departure the twofold nature of thinking: its spiritual as well as its earthly nature.

Child development and thinking

In his book *The Spiritual Guidance of the Individual and Humanity*, Rudolf Steiner speaks about the first three years of life and the evolving human being.[1] He describes how learning to walk, to speak and to think is a three-step process in which the incarnating child adapts himself to earthly conditions, and in which these fundamental human faculties establish themselves in the child under the guidance of higher spiritual beings.

As a result of his own spiritual research, Rudolf Steiner describes these faculties as creative forces in the spiritual world that are transformed and reappear as the human faculties of thinking, feeling and willing. He describes, further, how these faculties develop within the processes of growth and maturation of the physical body. The physical body is made up of three systems: the nerve-sense system, the rhythmical system and the metabolic-limb system. Within this threefold physical body, the three soul faculties of thinking, feeling and will are present in the process of coming into uprightness, forming the speech organs into instruments for the expression of language, and fine-tuning the brain into an instrument for human thought.

Through uprightness and subsequent walking at the end of the first year of life, the child establishes his orientation in three-dimensional space. Through the acquisition of speech in the second year, the child's soul attunes itself to a specific human community according to the individual destiny of the child. Through the development of thinking in the third year the child becomes part of humanity as a whole.

Steiner describes this three-step process of walking, speaking and thinking as a soul-spiritual activity guided by spiritual powers. It is a process of which the child has no conscious awareness because it occurs before the child becomes conscious of herself.

Here the following questions may arise: why does Steiner describe the development of thinking as primarily occurring in the third year of life? Is it not a continuous process from birth onwards? How do Steiner's indications fit in with recent neurodevelopmental research that interprets the baby's early responses to stimulation as intelligent behaviour? And if there is a major leap in the development of thinking in the third year, why then wait until the seventh year before addressing the child's thinking in education, as Steiner has advocated? What follows will address these questions.

The first and second year of life in relation to thinking

It is generally acknowledged that thinking develops in the young child in accordance with the maturation and differentiation of the brain, whose system of dendrites, neural pathways and synapses are hardly developed at the time of birth.

Steiner speaks about thinking as a spiritual as well as an earthly faculty. As a spiritual faculty it is linked to the activity of the etheric forces in and around the human being:

> These forces which function in the etheric body are active in the human being's life on earth – most distinctly during the embryonic period – as the forces of formation and growth. During the course of earthly life a portion of these forces emancipates itself from this occupation with formation and growth and becomes forces of thinking.[2]

In the very young child these etheric forces are working from outside, from the spiritual world, sculpting and fine-tuning the head and bodily organs without the child being conscious of them. Through this activity, 'connecting threads develop in the brain, and the forces which organize the connecting threads are seen by the clairvoyant during the first few weeks of the child's life as something that is forming extra sheaths for the brain'.[3] The etheric forces work from the head downwards, radiating their formative activity into the rest of the body.[4]

With respect to the earthly aspect of thinking, Steiner points out that during the first and second year of life the development of thinking is helped by movement and speech. All experiences of gradually mastering movement and speech will prepare the neural pathways which then enable the brain to serve as an organ for thinking.

I remember an eight-month-old boy in a restaurant, sitting in a high chair, enthralled with a spoon he held in his hand. He was moving it from one hand to the other. He licked it, turned it upside down and moved it faster and faster until the spoon fell to the ground. Of course, he did not say a word or show any emotional reaction, not even looking as to where the spoon had gone. It had gone and that was that.

Steiner states that in the very young child thinking is still hidden within the act of sense perception. The child is therefore not able to detach himself from the experience and to reflect on what has happened.

On another occasion a mother walks into the child's room one morning after experiencing an emotional upset. The moment the child perceives her, his facial expression changes. Instead of the usual joyous welcome he will have a more serious look on his face, and especially in his eyes, as he senses the disturbance in the mother. Sensing and knowing occur instantaneously and long before the child is able to give words to his experience.

An interesting question can be raised regarding the play of the baby and the very young child: does the baby think while playing? Again, in the intense exploration of objects, thinking is not explicit. But, as Georg Kühlewind points out, when young children are absorbed – however fleetingly – in the exploration of objects, they exhibit an amazing attentiveness, a total devotion, to the activity.[5] For an adult such a degree of inner attentiveness or heightened awareness is possible only after intense mental training. The young child is able to achieve this state naturally, due to an immensely strong inner willpower.

Such willpower and the child's resultant devotion to what he perceives and explores is also present in the child's ability to imitate, an ability which can be observed right from the very first days of life until around seven years of age. According to Steiner, imitation is intimately connected with the process of learning to think: 'The child learns to think because it is an imitative being, wholly given up to its environment. It imitates what happens in the environment under the impulses of thoughts.'[6] The child imitates and simultaneously is able to absorb into his body the thought quality underlying the actions being imitated.[7]

Imitating the teacher's hand gesture. St. Kilda Pre-School, Melbourne

An example of this is the kindergarten teacher who has worked with her thoughts, feelings and willpower to develop, learn and practise a morning circle for her kindergarten children. The moment she lifts her arms to perform it with the children, the children's arms will lift nearly instantaneously. Any adult who has tried to imitate another person's movements instantaneously will know how difficult this is, as adults tend to process sense perceptions through their own thinking before setting their limbs into motion. For the child, thinking is not yet separated from sense perception, and so the child imitates immediately in an act of surrender to the movements of the teacher.

There are more aspects to consider when looking at the emergence of thinking in the young child. Steiner speaks of the I as being involved in the moulding of the brain in the first three years. In the first year of life this spiritual individuality is mainly active in the development of uprightness and the ability to walk. Steiner uses the term 'bodily geometry' for the way in which the child practises movement and how it enables him to experience his place within the three-dimensional world. The brain and the ability to think are greatly stimulated through this activity.[8]

Thinking and movement, with their centres in head and limbs, form a polarity that organizes development during the early childhood years. The head pole is the centre of etheric growth forces working from the head downward. The limb pole is the centre of activity for the human soul-spirit, or 'I', establishing the fundamental human ability to be upright, then working from the limbs to the respiratory system and onwards to the head.

The I is the organizing principle behind the process of coming into uprightness during the first year of life, and the increasing capacity for movement has a positive influence on the healthy development of thinking. Steiner's spiritual research into this process is now confirmed by developmental research and the therapeutic practice of stimulating thinking through movement.[9]

As the child approaches the end of the first year of life, we may assume that the processes of intensive sensing, moving and exploring have left many impressions within his nerve-sense system and brain. With repetition, impressions will gradually form into mental images. These inner images, however vague they may be at first, will eventually be ordered and connected, leading to the forming of concepts. For this to happen it is necessary that the child can express mental images through words.

In the second year of life a new quality is added to these early inner pictures because the child can anchor them in inner and outer speech. As of this moment words become the vehicle for the development of thinking: thinking develops through talking.

> Just as speech develops from walking and grasping, in short from movement, so thought develops from speech … and since the child is one great sense organ and in his inner physical functions also copies the spiritual, our own thinking must be clear if right thinking is to develop in the child from the forces of speech.[10]

Karl König describes how the process of speech acquisition progresses from expressing physical well-being or physical needs to expressing the child's relationship to the outer world through words (naming) and, increasingly towards the end of the second year, through short sentences.[11] Speech mirrors the child's being in relationship to objects and people. It also links the child to the fine nuances of feeling that are inherent in the mother tongue.

How does thinking manifest at this stage of development? As the child is able to express himself through words and through connecting words, the adult catches a glimpse of the child's inner processes of thinking for the first time. It is interesting that this process is again helped by imitation. Children delight in repeating words and sentences they have heard being spoken by adults.

Here is an example of a 21-month-old child in a solitary play situation. He has built a simple shelter from building blocks and moves a car into it. 'There you go,' he says. He adds more blocks. As it gets higher, the structure becomes unstable and it gets harder to put on more blocks. 'Got it,' the child says after successfully placing another block on the wall. Then the whole shelter collapses. The child moves the car out and says, 'Build another one.' This sentence is repeated in the action of moving the car to a different place and making a new kind of primitive shelter.

It is quite obvious that these sentences are the comments of the carer, imitated in a new but similar context. The child's thinking appears in his ability to make this transfer from one situation to another and to use the sentences appropriately.

Recent developmental research has highlighted the increased ability of one- to two-year-old children to respond actively to sensory stimulation, and their increased interest in, and response to, verbal stimulation. Early childhood researchers have found that educators can stimulate speech and also memory in children between the ages of one and two-and-a-half years if, in the presence of the child, they verbally recollect recent events from the child's life.[12] Already in the 1920s and 1930s the Russian educational psychologist Lev Vygotsky suggested that the cognitive development of the child is enhanced if the adult's verbal communications are slightly above the child's current level of understanding.[13]

Besides words becoming a vehicle for thinking, thought activity can be observed in the child's solitary, outwardly non-verbal play. The child moves objects, covers them, puts them side-by-side or on top of each other. This serves the child in familiarising himself with the world of objects and finding out how they work. Through such interaction with the environment the child finds his way into thinking.

In this kind of play speech is present but is entirely inward. The child engaged in such play is a doer, an inventor even. If this play is nurtured, if the child is given sufficient opportunity for solitary play without disturbances, the child will develop inner attentiveness: the basis of all subsequent independent and original thinking.

Thinking in the third year of life

What is the gift of the third year of life? For Rudolf Steiner this is the time when the soul-spiritual forces[14] work specifically on fine-tuning the brain, the physical foundation of human thinking. At this stage the I of the child will be connected to all three systems of the physical body: the limb system, the rhythmic system, and also the nerve-sense system with its major organ, the brain. After this a portion of the etheric forces are freed. 'At the age of two and a half, the child's head organization is developed far enough for those forces of the ether body which have been working on it to become released ... acting now as soul and spiritual forces,'[15] which means they are working within the child's soul life.

What can we observe in the child at this age? A vivid memory is unfolding, and with it a more elaborate way of speaking and the ability to express thoughts and to form thought connections. The child enjoys playing with words and inventing new ones, and he can surprise us with his own original ways of arranging syntax and connecting thoughts.

The child's new achievements in thinking will have an effect on everyday life. It becomes easier for the child to follow routines because he can understand more of the meaning of what needs to be done. It therefore becomes easier to guide the child. When talking with the child, he seems more able to take in what is said.

It is fascinating to observe that children at this age are creative not only in inventing their own words but also in producing their own logic. It is worth noting that the very individual and unusual thought connections of a nearly three-year-old are not deliberate. They are not the outcome of conscious reflection, but rather seem to emerge unexpectedly.

Educators who witness these new faculties arising during the third year may be tempted to make use of the child's new thinking capacity, to accelerate the child's learning by way of instruction. The ability of the child to respond to structured learning after the age of two has been documented in developmental research and has been utilized in programme development for early childhood education. The third year is the time when many early learning programmes begin.

One can understand the motivation for using structured learning materials, such as sets of geometrical forms or picture and word cards, to enhance and accelerate verbalization and concept formation, to make use of the child's strong memory. The thinking potential is there in the child and can be called upon. But sustaining the gains from this structured learning process requires constant adult involvement. Otherwise the new abilities disappear again. What is learned at this age is not retained unless it is continually repeated, indicating that thinking and memory are still bound to objects and situations and are not yet independent inner faculties.

Steiner has warned of the consequences of early adult-directed learning that makes demands on the intellect and memory of the young child at a time when organ formation processes are still incomplete.

> What then will happen, if we make too great a demand on the intellect, urging the child to think, into thinking as such? Certain organic forces that tend inwardly to harden the body are brought into play ... This normal rigidity is over-developed, if intellectual thinking is forced.[16]

One of Rudolf Steiner's most significant discoveries is that the life forces in the human being are the spiritual force behind both physical growth and thinking, and that their balance can be disturbed by attempts to teach young children and accelerate their intellectual development. The forces used in growth and thinking tap into the same reservoir of etheric forces: what is used by the one is no longer available to the other. For this reason Steiner cautions against placing demands on thinking at a time when growth forces are still building the physical body – that is, in the first seven years of life.

Kindergarten teachers are able to observe at first hand the effects of early intellectual stimulation. Children who have been exposed to a lot of explanation and information at an early age are the ones who talk more than they play, who frequently lack the exuberance and liveliness of the young child. They appear to be over-alert, tense, with a tendency to fidget. It is important for those living and working with young children to be aware that hyperactive behaviour may stem from early intellectual stimulation.

However, the physical processes behind thinking, and its content which serves the purposes of everyday life, are just one side of the ability to think. The other is the aptitude for thinking, a quality shared by all human beings.

> When the child learns to think – well, in thinking we do not remain in the realm of the individual at all. In New Zealand, for example, people think in exactly the same way we do here today. It is the entire earth realm to

which we adapt ourselves, when as children we develop thinking out of speech ... In thinking, we enter the realm of humanity as a whole.[17]

This is true for all children, and it is in the third year that the foundations for both possibilities of thinking, the everyday and the universal, are developed by the child.

With this in mind, it is important that children not merely be familiarized with concepts relating to everyday life. Adults often take pride in the fact that a child can already express himself cleverly. Too much praise for children's intellectual achievements can fetter their thinking to the thought-forms prevalent in today's world. It can prevent them from connecting to the spiritual-universal world of thought as well as the thoughts that help to make sense of everyday life.

The next developmental step, around or shortly after age three, will bring the child's thinking closer to everyday life naturally. The child will become more conscious of himself as different from others and from the surrounding world. He will leave behind the dim spiritual experience of oneness and become increasingly interested in his earthly environment. From this time onwards, the child will experience himself more and more as the originator of his own thoughts. The child becomes able to say 'I think'.

It is important to note that I-consciousness is achieved only *after* the three fundamental human faculties of uprightness, speech and thinking have been developed. Some children today already use the word 'I' correctly at around the age of two or two-and-a-half, sometimes even earlier, but Steiner comments that merely saying 'I' does not yet signify the consciousness of self which appears after the age of three. In developmental psychology this phenomenon, observed around age three, is called 'the emergence of the psychological self'. Laura Berk describes this and related phenomena of 'metacognition' in the child, such as the use of the words 'think', 'remember', and 'pretend', and the child's realization that thinking is going on inside himself.[18]

There is a deep wisdom in the natural sequence of development as outlined above. At first the child does not experience thinking as a personal achievement. Thinking becomes personal only later, through the development of consciousness of self. This opens the possibility of reaching beyond the individual into the universal realm of thought. Stimulating consciousness of self too soon poses the danger that this dimension of thinking, which will lead to the experience of the universally human at a later stage, will not develop sufficiently.

Regardless of how tender and immature this consciousness of self might be, there is a general eagerness among educators to address it by encouraging the child to reflect, to review experiences, and to make choices and decisions.

Normally consciousness of self is a gift, yet it becomes a hindrance if it arises too early. It requires more maturity than can be expected of a three-year-old. In becoming conscious of their wishes and choices, some three-year-olds are overwhelmed by their own desires. They become demanding. They may also change their minds quickly and be swayed by emotion. In learning situations, some children are overwhelmed when made conscious of their achievements. They react with insecurity, lack of confidence in their abilities, and fear of failure. As early as three years of age, children can be known to say, 'I don't like my drawing,' or, 'I can't do that.' In a sense the early appearance of consciousness of the I may be regarded as a premature, untimely faculty.

Some educational conclusions for the third year of life

In early childhood education today the child's emerging ability to think has become the target for structured learning activities as of the child's third year. There will undoubtedly be more research identifying the potential of the child to think at an ever-earlier age. Programmes have been designed for stimulating such aspects of the young child's thinking as memory, colour and form discrimination, concept formation and verbal expression. Thus the child's thinking is being tuned to the prevailing intellectual aspect of our time.

Steiner was concerned about this early intellectual learning because of its abstract nature. More important than instructing the intellect is learning by imitation and the presence of adult role models. In 1906 he wrote:

> Children ... do not learn by instruction or admonition, but through imitation. The physical organs shape themselves through the influence of the physical environment. Good sight will be developed in children if their environment has the proper conditions of light and colour, while in the brain and blood circulation the physical foundations will be laid for a healthy moral sense if children see moral actions in their environment. If, before their seventh year, children see only foolish actions in their surroundings, the brain will assume the forms that adapt it to foolishness in later life.[19]

Steiner is emphasizing the moral quality of adults' thoughts and deeds as being the decisive influence on the young child. Therefore he regards the self-education of the adult as paramount. 'The education during these first two-and-a-half years should be confined to the self-education of the adult in charge who should think, feel and act in a manner which, when perceived by the child, will cause no harm.'[20] 'Why have so many people "nerves" today? Simply because in childhood there was no clarity and precision of thought around them during the time when they were learning to think after having learnt to speak.'[21]

Among Steiner Waldorf educators, and beyond, there is a growing awareness of the value of adult self-development, and the importance of children progressing from walking to speaking to thinking in the proper sequence and at their own pace. However, not enough attention is paid to the difference between educating the child before and after the third year. Instead of trying to stimulate cognitive learning by imposing structured activities at an ever-earlier age, early childhood educators should provide children under three with plenty of opportunities for solitary, self-initiated play.

If we return to the example of the boy and his spoon at the beginning of this chapter, we can see how his play expresses the activity of thinking before the emergence of consciousness of self. It marks an important stage in development and should be appreciated as a unique opportunity to explore the world while still in the consciousness of oneness. It is not just a prelude to, or a mini-version of, the complex yet often self-conscious play of older children.

In daily practice, early childhood educators need to appreciate the difference between the play of the child before and after the third year. When playing, the very young child is a kind of hermit, totally immersed in his own world. Through his play he weaves his own connection to the world before becoming conscious of himself and dependent on the suggestions and praise of adults.

Is it appropriate to interrupt children under three in play to make space for group activities such as the morning circle? What is the right daily structure for this age group? The educator needs to become sensitive to the state of consciousness of the younger child in order to create a balance between togetherness and the child's natural desire to follow his own inner impulses.

Thinking and the three- to five-year-old child

Around the age of three, children reach a new stage of development. While they may have been using the word 'I' for some time already, it is now that they become conscious of themselves as I-beings, as separate from others. They discover that there is an inner space within them that is not shared by anybody else. They become conscious of being different from others. Self and world are not one anymore, and at times this experience may cause pain. It is also a time of growing more able to interact with other children in a group, and becoming better prepared to separate temporarily from mother or father.

As already mentioned, the child's ability to remember increases in the third year in conjunction with this awakening of consciousness of self. Memory at age three is very vivid but it is still based on the habits of the body and is not yet a free inner activity. It needs to be triggered by events or objects.

When observing children at the beginning of the fourth year, it is plain that the new faculties can cause emotional imbalance. Outwardly the consciousness of self makes its appearance in the form of increased self-centeredness and a tendency towards egotism, which can throw child and family into turmoil. Often a leap in development announces itself with chaos, out of which new faculties will emerge, provided that adults are on hand to provide clear thinking, love and appropriate boundaries.

The child at this age learns best through imitation and example, experiencing the higher human faculties such as empathy and altruism in the adults around him. The example set by adults will leave its traces within the child. It will be imitated at a time when the three-year-old is not yet able to rely on his own intrinsic motivation to be social and considerate of others.

At the beginning of the fourth year children often display great mood swings, which usually abate within a few months. I have experienced this in connection with the enrolment interview for kindergarten. A child who is in the middle of crossing the three-year-old threshold is not in a good state to start something new.

The influence of the new consciousness of self on the child's feelings is palpable. The child now experiences emotions as his own, yet his I is not strong enough to master them. Such a situation can be managed by letting the child take a step back from being overwhelmed by the new situation to something familiar, like being held and guided. Most children are able to adjust to their newfound feeling of self if an adult takes the role of knowing the way and watching over a safe environment and a steady, predictable daily life. It is a relief for a three-year-old to be led away from 'I want' and 'I don't want', and to experience being part of a group with all its various activities and daily routines.

The emergence of the consciousness of I around age three should not be used to justify putting further demands on the child's ability to express his wishes and to self-reflect. Rather, it should be treated as the beginning stage of a new faculty, one that will mature only in years to come.

This is not accepted practice in education today. Instead, too much emphasis is placed on making children conscious of their wishes and feelings. This gives rise to irritation, expressed by frequent changes of wishes, strong desires, wavering when choosing and making decisions, a tendency to self-criticism when comparing their own achievements with those of others, and, in consequence a lack of confidence in their own abilities.

Between ages three and five, development occurs mainly in the rhythmical system, through the maturation of breathing and blood circulation. At this stage, according to Steiner, the etheric forces working in the rhythmical system of the body are gradually released. They become soul forces of memory and fantasy, active in the child's creative play. The most appropriate activity for this time is therefore free, imaginative play because it implicitly involves the child's thinking together with feeling and will.

Steiner paints a very complex picture of the spiritual processes underlying child development. He speaks about two kinds of etheric forces, *sculptural* or *growth* forces and *other* or *musical* forces, which work together harmoniously in the child up to the change of teeth.[22] These work in different ways.

The sculptural forces work on organ formation from the head downwards, in accordance with the main thrust of growth and formation in early childhood. After completing this task they will become forces of memory and thinking.

The musical forces work from below, from the metabolic-limb system upwards. While the sculptural forces are at work in processes creating form, the musical forces are active in bestowing life and vigour. They are seated in the metabolic system[23] and represent the less formed and potentially overwhelming creative power of the human being. These forces are not freed during early childhood, yet they make their influence felt in activities such as music, speech, drawing, and – later on – in writing. If these forces are left alone during early childhood, they will provide the right counterbalance to the formative forces.[24]

The change of teeth

At the age of three the first dentition is completed. At this time all second teeth are already present in the jaws in rudimentary form, waiting to grow and break through. One could say with some justification that the change of teeth is spread out over several years, from the fourth to the seventh year. And even then the second dentition continues, in a sense, until the appearance of the wisdom teeth.

Thinking and the Consciousness of the Young Child

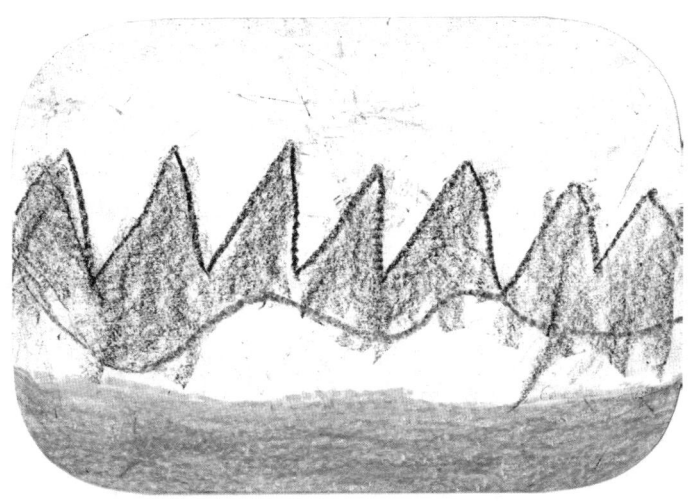

Drawing by a five-year-old: zigzag patterns appear around age four to five, which educators interpret as heralding the imminent breaking through of the incisors. Author's collection

Steiner uses the term 'change of teeth' in relation to the inner changes of the child in the seventh year. This is the moment when the hardening of the tooth enamel occurs and the incisors appear. Steiner describes this as a dramatic event, an outward sign for a huge change happening within. Spiritually it is the final liberation of the life forces that have worked in the hardest substance of the body, the tooth enamel, to complete the formation of organs culminating in the formation and breaking through of the second teeth:

> The change of teeth is a unique event. The forces needed to push out the second teeth existed prior to this event, but they are no longer needed afterwards. Once the second teeth have appeared, this particular activity of the etheric body becomes redundant. The final activity of pushing out the second teeth is an outward manifestation of the kind of working that is going on in the child's organism. Now, at the end of the first seven-year period, most of these etheric forces are released to flow into the child's soul and spiritual nature.[25]

From the change of teeth onwards the etheric forces no longer work in unison. The formative, hardening forces and the musical forces separate and a kind of 'battle' ensues:

> Then whatever radiates upwards from the body is thrust back, whereas the forces that shoot downwards from the head are restrained. Thus, during the time the teeth are changing, the severest battle is fought between the forces striving downwards from above and those shooting upwards from below. The change of teeth is the physical expression of this conflict between the two kinds of forces, those that later appear in the child as his powers of reasoning and intellect, and those that need to be used particularly in drawing, painting, and writing.[26]

There is much about the child in the sixth and seventh year that can be better understood if we take into account the battle raging within. The new, more acute way of thinking and forming concepts, the ability to memorize at will, do not emerge harmoniously. The child goes through phases of emotional imbalance – motivational passivity on the one hand and vigorous, often uncontrolled activity on the other. Childhood forces of fantasy are receding and the inner transition makes itself felt as experiences of emptiness and boredom. The ability to play may suffer or even come to a standstill. The child now represents in words or concepts what previously would have been acted out.

The fact that this crisis often coincides with the child's last months in the kindergarten has given rise to discussions about how to approach the special situation of these older children. It is beneficial for children at this time to engage their will by becoming part of the purposeful work of adults around them, or being given tasks, at first under adult guidance, then independently. Freya Jaffke has described working with engaging the will of six-year-olds in her book on *Work and Play in Early Childhood*.[27]

The educational challenge at this stage is to achieve balance with respect to the polarity of thinking and will. Thinking and will are brought into alignment if the life of feeling in the child is strengthened through nurture of the child's imaginative powers and his interest in the world. This is the task of the education of the child between seven and twelve years of age.

It may come as a great challenge to anybody whose thinking has been trained in the schools and universities of today to make sense of Steiner's indications regarding the connection between the change of teeth and the development of thinking. According to his spiritual research the birth of the second teeth represents on the physical level what the birth of thinking is on the soul level. Underlying this is Steiner's spiritual discovery of the transformation of etheric growth forces and their reappearance on the soul level as intellect.

Michaela Glöckler has offered some suggestions for understanding this enigma of the connection between teeth and thinking. There is a 'biting' quality to the intellect, the quality of analysing, which is also the function of the teeth. Moreover, the second teeth are the most lifeless part of our body: they do not regrow. In the brain cells, as well, there is very little life or regenerative activity.

Rudolf Steiner describes this relationship of teeth and thinking as follows:

- The young child is developing teeth for the purpose of thinking.

- The teeth are the most important organ of thought.

- Teeth 'grow in accordance with thought' before the age of seven.

- In the same measure as thoughts spring up in the child, the teeth do emerge.[28]

For today's readers these are enigmatic statements, which need to be put to the test in educational practice to establish their relevance. We could begin our search for meaning by picturing the spiritual activity behind the visible growth process, imagining the nature of such spiritual forces as are capable of producing something as hard as enamel-covered teeth. Thus we could get closer to a picture of the forces of thinking.

We could also study the process of the second dentition in different children and compare it to their individualized form of thinking, because the change of teeth and thinking are related not only to the processes of the etheric body but to the evolving of the human ego as well. Dentists with an interest in such questions are only now beginning to understand the second teeth as an expression of each person's unique individuality.[29]

Regarding the change of teeth, Steiner describes the I as working in the depth of the body together with other forces pushing out the teeth. The I pushes the hard substance of the teeth into the empty space created by the formative and musical forces. In this process, the I makes an impression on qualities of thinking such as wakefulness, the potential for independent judgement and consciousness of self.[30] However, these abilities will only develop gradually, coming to maturity finally after the age of 21.

If the child's ability to think is called upon too early, if thinking is not allowed to develop of its own accord, then the sculptural forces will overwhelm the child's creative potential. The ensuing hardening process will weaken the creative childhood forces prematurely.

> We must take the very greatest care that this intellectual thinking does not appear too early. For a human being can only come to an experience of freedom, if his intellectuality awakens within him of itself, not if it has been poured into him by his teachers. But it must not awaken in poverty of soul ... If he (the child) has nothing within him that he has acquired through imitation and imagery, which can rise up into his thinking out of the depths of his soul, then, when his thinking should develop at puberty he will find nothing within himself to further his own growth, and his thinking can only reach into emptiness. He will find no anchorage in life, and just at the time when he ought really to have found a certain security in himself he will be running after trivialities; in these awkward years he will be imitating all kinds of things which please him.[31]

Conclusion

The development of thinking and consciousness has been described here as an ordered, wisdom-filled sequence of events in child development. Observing this sequence, we see that it repeats the pattern of 'gestation' and 'birth' several times. We can identify critical points of development at the ages of three, seven and also at fourteen. There are three 'gestational' periods of thinking, each leading to a kind of 'birth' at these points in life.

At age three it is the appearance of consciousness of I at the end of a period of I-activity in the entire physical body of which the child is not conscious. At age seven it is the awakening of thinking as inner soul activity. At age fourteen, which is not discussed further here, the fully conscious and individualized power of thought will have emerged.

Up to then, the power of thinking is prepared through play from the age of three to five years, and through a pictorial approach to learning after the seventh year in connection with the development of the child's will and feeling. If thinking does not lose its connection to these soul forces too soon, it will appear at age fourteen as an independent soul faculty, ready to fulfil its mission as the highest of the human soul qualities.

Endnotes

1. The paragraph refers to: *The Spiritual Guidance of the Individual and Humanity*, Anthroposophic Press, Hudson, NY, 1992, Lecture 1, pp. 3–24.
2. R. Steiner and I. Wegmann, *Fundamentals of Therapy: An Extension of the Art of Healing Through Spiritual Knowledge*, Rudolf Steiner Press, London, 1983, chapter 27.
3. R. Steiner, *Understanding Young Children: Excerpts from Lectures by Rudolf Steiner*. Published in 1975, reprinted in 1994 by the Waldorf Early Childhood Association of North America (formerly the Waldorf Kindergarten Association of North America), p. 55.
4. R. Steiner, 'The Child before the Seventh Year' in *Soul Economy and Waldorf Education*, Anthroposophic Press, Spring Valley, NY, 1986, p. 112.
5. G. Kühlewind, 'Learning from the Child to be Human', *Kindergarten Newsletter UK*, Issue 36, 1999, p. 5.

6   R. Steiner, *A Modern Art of Education*, Rudolf Steiner Press, London, 1972, Lecture 4, p. 77.
7   I would like to mention here the recent discovery in neuroscience of the so-called 'mirror neurons' in the brain, which are now seen to be at the foundation of the faculty of learning by imitation, and are attributed great importance for deep learning, not only in the realm of cognition but also in the social realm. See J. Bauer, *Warum ich fühle, was du fühlst. Intuitive Kommunikation und das Geheimnis der Spiegelneurone* [Why I feel what you feel. Intuitive Communication and the Mystery of the Mirror neurons], Hoffmann und Kampe, Hamburg, 2006. See also the article by Chr. Rittelmeyer, 'The Human Body as a Resonance Organ' in: *Research Bulletin* Vol. 15 No. 2, 2010, published by Research Institute for Waldorf Education, Wilton, NH USA. Steiner in his time has pointed out that although the habit to imitate originates from conditions of pre-earthly existence, it still needs, like all spiritual abilities, a physical foundation in order to appear within the conditions of life on earth.
8   R. Steiner, *The Child's Changing Consciousness and Waldorf Education*, Anthroposophic Press, Hudson, NY, 1988, p. 19.
9   Mention should be made here the work of S. Goddard Blythe and the Institute for Neurophysiological Psychology. See S. Goddard Blythe, *The Well Balanced Child*, Hawthorn Press, Stroud, 2003.
10 Steiner, *A Modern Art of Education*, p. 112.
11 K. König, *The First Three Years of the Child*, Floris Books, Edinburgh, 1984, p. 16.
12 L. Berk, *Child Development* (Fourth Edition) Allyn and Bacon, Boston/Sydney, 1997, p. 277.
13 Vygotsky's ideas are outlined in Berk, pp. 247–250.
14 Steiner uses the expression 'soul-spirit' because he is referring to all spiritual forces in the human being: the I, active in becoming upright and able to walk; the astral or feeling body, active in the ability to speak; and the etheric body, which engenders all processes of growth and also of thinking.
15 Steiner, 'The Child before the Seventh Year', p. 117.
16 Steiner, *A Modern Art of Education*, p. 122.
17 Steiner, *The Child's Changing Consciousness*, p. 55.
18 Berk, p. 279.
19 R. Steiner, *The Education of the Child and Early Lectures on Education*, Anthroposophic Press, Hudson NY, 1996, p. 19.
20 Steiner, 'The Child before the Seventh Year', p. 115.
21 Steiner, *A Modern Art of Education*, p. 112.
22 Steiner, *Roots of Education*, p. 85.

23 For a detailed description of this process see chapter 3 in D. Klocek, *Knowledge, Teaching and the Death of the Mysterious*, R. Steiner College Press, Fair Oaks, CA, 2000. With his book Klocek has given a kind of commentary to Steiner's enigmatic lectures *Balance in Teaching*.
24 R. Steiner, *Balance in Teaching*, Mercury Press, Spring Valley, NY, 1990, pp. 18–22. Here Steiner describes the complex interactions of these two kinds of etheric forces.
25 Steiner, 'The Child before the Seventh Year', p. 111.
26 Steiner, *Balance in Teaching*, Lecture 2, p. 17.
27 More recently a task force of WECAN, USA, has published a handbook on working with six-year-olds, describing this time in the child's development in detail and discussing pedagogical ways of working with the older children in the kindergarten. See R. Ker ed., *You're Not the Boss of Me! Understanding the Six/Seven-Year-Old Transformation*, WECAN Publications, 2007.
28 Steiner, *A Modern Art of Education*, Lecture 4, pp. 77–82.
29 Reference is made here to the article by H. & J. Ruof: 'Dentition, A Mirror of the Child's Development' in *You're Not the Boss of Me!*, WECAN, 2007, pp. 23–31.
30 R. Steiner, GA 313, lecture of 14 April 1921.
31 Steiner, *Roots of Education*, p. 85.

3

The Development and Education of the Will

The development of the will in children is distinctly different from the processes of growth, refinement and transformation discussed previously.

Steiner gives the following picture: in early childhood the soul-spiritual and the physical-etheric forces work in unison *within the child's body*; and so, more than at any later time in life, the bodily experiences of the young child are also soul experiences.[1] But the soul-spiritual forces are also working through the spiritual sheaths which are formed around the child to protect the as yet unborn astral body and I. Through these sheaths the child is connected spiritually to other human beings who are close to her, and who therefore have a strong influence on the child's soul development. This holds true for the will, which is one of the three soul forces of the human being.

In the course of the first 20 years of life, all three soul forces – thinking, feeling and willing – will gradually become able to serve the conscious intentions and actions of the human being. The will takes the longest time to reach this stage. Steiner states that it takes 20 years for the will to become an independent soul force, a step which coincides with the birth of the I.[2]

It is surprising that although the will is the first of the three soul powers to be visibly very active, already in the early stages of babyhood, it is undeveloped, an instinctive action, totally bound to the body.[3] Even at the end of early childhood, at the time of the birth of the etheric body, the will is still held within the spiritual sheaths formed by the astral body and I-organization. Between birth and seven the child has neither the consciousness nor the ability to direct her will: will activity is completely under the sway of bodily functions and environmental influences.

The quality of will in childhood can be likened to a force of nature pouring out of the child. Only at the age of 14 does it take on a more personal quality. Only at age 20 does the young person become able to take the service of the I for – ideally – acting responsibly in the world. However, the will is never fully free; a compulsive element is always present. Therefore, the will remains the object of self-education all through life.

How does the will work within the human being?

Steiner describes two centres of will activity within the human being: one in the metabolic-limb system, the other in the brain.

The activity of the will in brain formation he characterizes as imprinting the results of will activity of the previous life into the brain structures.[4] Their quality will thus be determined by consequence of actions in previous lives. As a result, such brain forms will arise as are appropriate for the tasks of this incarnation. This will, flowing into the structures of the brain, sets the framework for developing memory, fantasy and logical thought.

In contrast, the will working in the lower part of the body is characterized by Steiner as 'new will'. With each incarnation this new will is given to the human being from the realm of the earth through heredity and through life experiences. It drives human movements and actions. The centre of activity of the 'new will' is the movement system and metabolism, with the blood circulation as its physical vehicle. The pulsating, circulating blood brings warmth to the organism through which movement and metabolic processes are activated.

Steiner's picture of the will is one of dual spiritual activity in the head and in the lower body. A similar duality is discernible with respect to the I. From below upwards, the I works together with this will. From above downwards, the I works together with the etheric forces in organ formation.

In this way the I supports the etheric body in growth and maturation processes and also the will in coming into uprightness. With respect to the perception of movement, the I works directly into the physical body through the nerve-sense system, but it has to work through the astral forces, the will, and the mediation of the etheric forces, to achieve truly humanized movement, which the will alone could not achieve.[5]

Thus the 'new will' is developed through all three spiritual members of the human being working together: the I, the astral body and the etheric body.

The stages of the development of will in the first seven years

In order to shed light on the nature of will and its education, Steiner outlined seven levels of will in his lectures to the teachers of the first Waldorf School.[6]

- Will on the level of the physical body appears as instinct.
- Will on the level of the etheric body appears as impulse.
- Will on the level of the astral body appears as desire.
- Will on the level of the I appears as motive.

Will also appears on three higher levels of further human development, which during life on earth are present in seed form only but will unfold in life after death. These levels of will – the wish to do better, intention and resolution – point to the further moral and spiritual evolution of the human being in the future. Educators will find them relevant as guiding principles for inner development and for reflecting on the future possibilities of children in their care. In early childhood, however, attention needs to be directed first and foremost to the lower forms of will.

The first stage of the development of will: between birth and age 2½

Will as instinct and impulse is already visible in the very young child. Instinct and impulse serve the fulfilment of bodily needs and urges –

not only basic needs such as food and sleep, but also the urge to move, to be active and explore.

Steiner describes the quality of will in very early childhood as strong and closed to the demands of parents or educators. He characterizes the child at this time as a 'hermit' and advises educators against interfering with the child's will, as the child is not yet perceptive to the will of people around her.[7] The child at this stage of life is entirely sympathetic to her own will, surrendered to her instincts, urges and resulting actions.

However, in the course of learning to walk, to speak and to think, the child is helped to become human. The instinctual will is partly overcome through coming into uprightness, and inborn primitive reflexes are gradually replaced with acquired postural reflexes. Here the signature of the individualized will shines through in the child's posture and gait. The ability to be upright is a gift of grace for the humanizing of the will force.

The means by which the child learns to be upright is imitation. When observing young children we are witnessing the immediate, natural impulse to imitate. The incentive for imitation comes from the environment. As already stated, the I and the astral body of the child work not only in the inner formative processes in the child's body but also from outside, through the human environment of the child. Without the model of other human beings the child would not learn to walk, to speak or to think. She would therefore stay animal-like.

The second stage of development of the will: between 2½ and 5

Around the age of two-and-a-half to three the desire-nature of will emerges. Desire-nature means that beyond the unconscious bodily will there is a *dim perception of will impulses by feeling*. Through being penetrated by feeling, the will becomes desire and does not remain just an instinctual will or urge in the body. Through the ability to speak, the child learns to express this soul quality of 'feeling in will'. This step manifests in the changing wants and corresponding fluctuating sensations and moods of the child, but also in the ability to express love and anger. Feeling in will still manifests mainly through physical gestures and actions rather than through words or purely inner feelings – as will be the case later on.

It has already been mentioned that two new faculties make their appearance at this time: memory and fantasy. What is the role of the will with respect to them?

Steiner compares *remembering and forgetting* with the process of sleeping and waking. Remembering is like waking up. The will is active in calling up memories, bringing them back to consciousness.[8] As the will in young children is very strong they remember easily, provided that a trigger has set the process in motion. Once the will is brought into action, children can recall sense experiences in great detail. The memories seem to just flow out of them.

With fantasy it is different. Fantasy becomes apparent in play and in the child's verbal comments from the age of two onwards. As mentioned previously, fantasy arises in the transformation of those etheric forces which are released from the rhythmical system to become the imaginative capacity of the soul. But were it not for the activation of the will, there would be only fleeting images, forming and dissolving again, lacking the possibility to manifest in action. Through her will the child is able to hold on to such images and to bring them to expression in her play. Children who are weak in their will forces may be affected in their ability to play imaginatively.

The third stage of the development of the will:
between 5 and 7

As already mentioned, children have a great need for physical activity at this time due to the limb system being the centre of growth and development.

The feeling-will of the previous stage was characterized by the child's self-interest. But now a quality becomes visible that is present in all children from birth onwards: *taking an interest in the world.* It is a new kind of desire, where the child is no longer mainly 'in love' with her own wishes and deeds and is instead eager to discover what is happening around her, independently of her own agenda. Desire appears to become less self-centred. However, there is great variation in what different children are interested in and how strongly this interest is aroused. What a child is inwardly drawn to will depend on individual destiny as well as the inherent strength of will.

Steiner says that the will and a part of feeling will 'wake up the head', that is, activate the child's thinking and prepare her for the next level of learning.[9] However, this process is just beginning in the last part of early childhood; it will unfold fully only after the seventh year.

At the beginning of the 'waking-up' process between age five and seven, we need to consider the situation – previously described as a 'battle' – of etheric forces during the change of teeth, after which the child's thinking acquires a more analytical, penetrating quality. Will, generally called 'motivation', is needed to use this new ability of analytical thinking effectively.

To get a picture of the role of the will at this stage of the child's development, we should bear in mind the extra mobility and physical strength gained in gross motor movement during the sixth year. Kindergarten teachers are familiar with the strong will forces that are unleashed in the limbs at this time. They can wreak havoc but they can also be put to good use.

There will be clashes between child and adult caused by the exuberance of will forces at this age. Each confrontation is like a waking up in consciousness for the child as to what has happened and how it can be avoided in the future. We do not have to look far in daily life for such waking-up moments of six-year-olds, when the will of the child meets a boundary or is confronted by a problem and the thinking process is set in motion. Adults have reason to be grateful here because they are witnessing the child take yet another step on the path towards independence.

The education of the will

What can parents and educators do to support children in taking charge of their will?

In mainstream early-childhood pedagogy the will is not recognized or acknowledged as a major factor in learning. The brain and the education of thinking are put before all else. Already in the early years the focus is on developing the child's thinking. Like an adult, the child is expected to implement acquired knowledge in various activities.

In contrast, Steiner states, 'We cannot really undertake much with the head. At birth the head brings with it what it is destined to become in the world. We can awaken what is in the child, but we cannot implant content into him.'[10] Rather, the educator should focus on the education of the will of the child.

Steiner suggests that, in the early years, thinking develops best by itself within an environment where there is enough opportunity for sensory exploration and for imitation. Will, on the other hand, *does* need educating because at the beginning of life it lacks conscious purpose and direction. The task of early education is to provide this direction through work with example and imitation: 'Through our words and actions, which the child imitates, we begin to work upon the child through his will.'[11]

This recommendation runs counter to the prevailing trend in early education today. Here the role of the adult consists in providing learning activities and extending the child's play through conversations designed to further her intellectual understanding.

Christoph Wiechert points out that Steiner's suggestions for the education of the will are a significant shift in the educational paradigm, the importance of which has not been recognized by mainstream education.[12] Yet teachers and parents of school-age children frequently complain about the weakness of will in children, their lack of motivation and inability to complete tasks.

There is little agreement as to the causes of this lack of will or ways to address it. For his part Wiechert suggests that in today's world the will lacks sufficient opportunity to anchor itself in the body – specifically the system of movement – of the child because the will is not sufficiently invigorated by physical activity. This becomes obvious to early childhood educators when they observe that children who have not gained dexterity and control over their limbs also have issues with play.

But there is yet another reason for the weakness of will in today's children. The difference between the nature of the will in the child and in the adult is not taken into account and, as a result, children's expressions of will are misinterpreted. People do not understand that a strong will is needed to support the child's interest in the world, or that stubbornness simply means the child is self-centred and focused mainly on her own agenda and not on anyone else's yet. Adults jump to interpret the child's strong will as a sign of a beginning power struggle between two wills, a battle planned or provoked by the child. Consequently, their reaction is either to enter into verbal negotiations or to impose their own will upon the child – neither of which does much to educate the child's will.

Education of the will means to *facilitate the child's learning to master her own will*. It is generally understood that the child cannot be made to 'will' or 'want' something. We can force the child to walk, to eat, to dress or tidy up. We can exert moral pressure through admonition or implement fear and/or reward tactics. In other words, we can suppress the child's will. But we cannot refine the child's will this way. Great difficulties are put in the way of children whose will has been crushed in early childhood.

Education of the will as self-education of the adult

Steiner states that the education of the will of children under three should consist first and foremost of the self-education of the adult.[13] He asks that adults apply themselves wholeheartedly to all tasks that may come their way and approach life with an open heart and mind. In dealing with the young child the educator should develop sympathy with the child and lovingly embrace the child's will. Lovingly accompanying the child's steps into life will create warmth around the child and in so doing create the optimum conditions for the will to become active.

Being an example worthy of the child's imitation is the best way to refine our own will as educators and to guide the will of the child. The child lives in a mood of sympathy and trust toward the world, which finds expression in her urge to imitate. Imitation works deeply on the whole being of the child. If surrounded by loving human beings, the child will be in sympathy with the innermost intentions of the adult and, in imitating

The child carefully watches the hands of her grandmother. Photo by author

them, 'slip' into the gestures of the adult. This is possible because the child's I-being and soul are still living in the spiritual sheath surrounding the child, which encompasses parents and educators.

Even though educators encounter the lower forms of will in children, they also need to be mindful of its higher forms: wish, intention and resolution.[14] These will become soul capacities in the future. Only in the light of such higher forces of will, present as seeds for the future, can the educator understand the nature of the will of the child and its future potential. Then the educator may find the right questions to ask with respect to educating the child's will, such as:

- How does the child place herself into life and what are the qualities of a particular child's will?
- What is the deeper intention behind the way in which the child uses her will?
- Do the child's actions reveal a future intention?

We can find the answers to these questions through observing the quality of the child's movements, gestures and play actions. Through inner work on our own will as adults we can strengthen our observational abilities. Then we can become aware of the finer aspects of a child's movements and begin to see the individualized spirit at work within the child's play activity.

Establishing habits

Another means of educating the will in early childhood is to establish rhythms and routines in the life of the child that will become habits. Regularly repeated activities, the rhythms of care and life, become patterns inscribed into the life body of the child.

Plant growth can be regarded as a habit of life as leaf after leaf develops in an ordered sequence. Similarly, the everyday life of the young child should have a rhythm and revolve around habits of when and how things are done.

Habits are alien to human thought processes. Nerve-sense activity does not create habits out of itself; it tends to shift quickly from one thing to the next. If adults want to take control of their thinking, they need to apply will in order to slow down and control the thinking process. If adults want to work well, they must direct their thoughts towards their deeds.

The very young child cannot do this as yet. And so the adult supports the ordering of the child's will by establishing habits that become part of the child's life in the same way that growth patterns rule the life of plants. Through these habits, which are established through rhythm and repetition, the will is held and supported at a time of life when children cannot apply their thinking to the will and direct their lives themselves.

Imprinting habits into the life body of the child begins within the first months of life and continues through early childhood and even the first years of primary education.

Educating feeling in will

To educate the will of children between the age of two-and-a-half and five, we have to pay attention to the emerging feelings that colour their actions.

In the early years, feeling develops through the acquisition of speech. The soul qualities of the mother tongue determine the mode of feeling in the child's soul life. During the middle years of early childhood the will is coloured by feelings. This new quality of will manifests in situations that trigger either the child's anger or sympathy. If the very young child has been hurt she will react by crying, seeking comfort or hitting the object or person she sees as the cause of the hurt. In the older child we can also perceive a reaction on the soul level – a being hurt inwardly – as well as an outer reaction. There are also situations where we can witness spontaneous expressions of compassion, such as hugging or caressing, towards a child in distress. The comforting gesture is accompanied by signs of inner sympathy, recognizable in the tone of voice, the quality of gesture and facial expression.

As already mentioned, the will at this time assumes the quality of desire. This may manifest in the increase of demanding behaviour, in insisting to possess or do something, and also in acts of frustration if wishes are not met. Then we experience a whole range of reactions in which feeling negatively aggravates the will action of the child, such as happens in tantrums.

While the adult has to find appropriate responses in such situations, the actual education of feeling in will is better helped through working with *example and imitation*, rather than mediation. Assistance in conflict situations is necessary, but it is less through the negotiating process than through the tone of voice and gesture that the educator will have an effect on the child's will.

Educating the will of the three- to five-year-old is enhanced through working with *guided movement* in the daily morning circle. Again, the example the adult sets is decisive. Steiner says, 'We guide the child's movements so that they become purposeful movements, penetrated with meaning.'[15]

Why is guided movement so effective for cultivating the will? The rhythm of verses and songs and the images they express, as well as the teacher modelling movements, provide a supportive framework that helps the child to hold her will and let it flow into action.[16]

Steiner makes an interesting comment: adults can educate children, even children who may be much cleverer than themselves, because the adult educates through will and the heart 'up to the stage of perfection, which we have reached ourselves'.[17] This holds true for working with guided movement. It is not a matter of intellect, it is a matter of how well the adult herself has been able to take hold of her will and how much she has perfected her own movement.

Educating the will at the time of the awakening of thinking

> When the child is seven years old, he has not merely been lying in his cradle all the time, he has achieved something, he has been helping himself forward by imitating grown-up people, and he has seen to it that his head spirit is *in some respects* awake.[18]

Also:

> The characteristic feature of this development up to the change of teeth is that the child is an imitative being. He imitates everything that he sees going on around him. He is able to do this owing to the fact that his head spirit is asleep.[19]

Steiner indicates that it is the child who wakes up the 'head spirit', that is to say the faculty of thinking. It is general educational practice today to stimulate the child's thinking in order to accelerate its development at an ever-earlier age. But this comes at the price of preventing the proper connection of thinking to the will of the child, the 'awakener of the head spirit'.[20]

Nowadays one hardly dares to say such things, let alone suggest that thinking should be left to children to develop themselves without adult instruction. Few educators today trust in thinking as a spiritual force within the human being, a force that will mature in due course given the right conditions. Nor do they trust imitation to be such a powerful means of learning that it supplants the need to provide explanations and additional information to extend learning during the early childhood years.

One of the reasons for this is the non-recognition of the vital role played by will forces in learning. If the importance of the education of the will were recognized, then the education of five- and six-year-old children would be based on educating through imitation and example, through establishing habits, and through providing an environment that supports children's transition from self-centered desire to interest in the world around them.

There is, however, an additional element to consider in the education of five- and six-year-old children: the spoken word becomes as important as the gesture in assisting the further development of the will. Through rhythmical language in poetry, rhythm in stories and verse, the will and feeling of children are aroused and brought into movement. They want to repeat, to speak themselves. Rhythmical speech, as well as the repetition of verse and poetry, stimulates the child's thinking 'simply through the very first words we say for him to repeat. Here we have a direct access to the will. For now what we release in the vocal organs through these first words will penetrate the sleeping head spirit as an activity of will, and will arouse it.'[21]

This last phase of early childhood presents the educator with a major challenge: to help each individual child find his or her specific relationship of will and thinking. How and when the will in each child wakes up the head depends on specific strengths and individual destiny; in some cases it is sooner, in others later. Thus the will appears as the most individualized of the three soul forces during early childhood and as the foremost vehicle for the incarnation of the I.

As mentioned previously, children between five and seven are often less balanced in their behaviour than they were between three and five. In addition, we often find that the order of the emergence of soul forces is not as recognizable as Steiner describes it. Just as, in very early childhood, some children speak before they walk, so too, in subsequent years, can speech and cognitive development speed ahead of the development of the will.

In this case the will would be weakened further by calls upon the child to judge herself and her performance and how she could improve. Such self-reflection and self-assessment is encouraged in mainstream kindergartens. From the perspective of educating the will this cannot improve the child's strength of will; on the contrary, it may adversely influence the child's confidence and self-image.

Engaging the will. Melbourne Steiner School Kindergarten.
Photo by Paulene Hanna

If the educator wants to help children to balance thinking and will, the field of practical work has proven to be successful. Children will observe the kind of work going on around them and may become interested and want to join in. Their will is then held within the activity of the adult and is less likely to become disoriented and fidgety. Also important are tasks that children can perform regularly, thereby serving the formation of habits through conscious repetition. No praise or judgements should be expressed as to how well the child has done since the sole aim is to bring the will of the child into activity without the child becoming self-conscious.

Will also helps to bring order to thinking, speaking and imaginative play.[22] This becomes obvious in the play of six-year-old children, where one often observes aimless chatting, repetitive actions or senseless noises instead of play in which the will is strong enough to give momentum to the child's thinking and fantasy. Often after a period of working alongside the teacher the play of the child becomes more ordered, purposeful and thus more satisfying for the child herself.

Artistic activity is the other important means of balancing thinking and will in the older child. More about this is said in the chapter on art experiences in early childhood education.

Appendix: Moral education in early childhood

Following acts of severe violence committed against schoolteachers and fellow students by school-aged children in several countries around the world, a public debate took place in Australia about core values in society. This debate led to a government decision to reinforce learning about values in education, and to provide schools and kindergartens with information as to how to do this.

It has been made compulsory for schools to publicly display 'value statements' and to discuss values with students. In state schools these values relate to appropriate social behaviour, respect for others, respect for property, fairness and striving for one's best personal performance. The display of value statements and the conversation about values extends down into kindergartens, pre-schools and childcare. The values deemed relevant to this age group are sharing, waiting one's turn, listening to others, gentleness, tolerance and non-discrimination.

There is nothing wrong with supporting forms of social behaviour among children. Of course, depending on the world view of adults, there could be many other values. The values endorsed by the government are those which are regarded as neutral with respect to religion and are acceptable to people with diverse world views. The question is whether this purely cognitive approach to reinforcing values is an effective way of achieving the acceptance of, and adherence to, such values by children.

The issue of moral education is important in Steiner education as well. However, a very different approach is taken. It is based on the following principles derived from Steiner's insights into child development:

- Morality is experienced by the child through the actions of adults. It is learned and not intrinsic to the child at the early stages of development up to the age of eight or nine. Which values will become relevant to the child will depend on which values are lived by adults in the child's proximity.

- In order to have an effect on the young child up to age nine, moral education cannot rely on intellect and understanding – or therefore on verbal reasoning and exhortation – but has to be directed to the will and feeling of the child.

- Morality is an ideal that has evolved during the course of history in accordance with the evolution of human consciousness. Each child repeats the process of evolution of consciousness during the time of growing up.[23]

What, then, is morality? The answer will depend on a person's world view. Some might define morality as a societal agreement to hold in check the antisocial impulses of the human being. Others might see it as the individual's striving towards, and adherence to, the highest ideals of humanity. In the latter case morality is defined by the individual and may not necessarily be in accordance with the values of a society at a given time. According to Steiner this form of morality of the individual has only become possible in recent times, as humanity has begun the development of what he calls the 'consciousness soul'. That is to say, consciousness has been refined to such a degree that human beings have become able to reflect on the impact of their behaviour in the light of the needs of fellow human beings and humankind as a whole rather than focusing on personal gain.

A child is born neither moral nor immoral.[24] Morality has to be acquired in the course of life. Whoever observes young children will notice that the little ones are egotists to start with – and rightly so – at this time of their lives. The will for life and the instinct to survive are strong in young children, and need to be. It would make no sense to judge this behaviour as moral or immoral because it is part of the child's unconscious urges. Strong and selfish as the will appears at this stage, it needs to be educated, to become more and more social.

The child brings with her a precondition for becoming a social human being: she is totally open and positive toward the world, as the trusting gaze and smiles of a baby might suggest. The egocentrism of the young child is partly a consequence of not yet being able to discriminate between 'mine' and 'yours'. The experience of oneness between self and world brings about a natural inclination to take from the world whatever the baby or very young child can get. This gesture of 'the world is mine' is not directed against anybody, and in that respect it is different from egotism as it appears in later stages of childhood.

Internalising morality is part of the education of the child's will. Steiner states that the will is the only soul force within a young child that needs to be educated. We have to do this educating by influencing the child from outside, in full recognition that the will is initially in a state of 'sleep'. Therefore, direct attempts to train the child's will by reasoning and stimulating reflection are futile.[25] It is better to abstain from trying to reach the inner being of the young child through reflection and judgements about good and bad.

As Steiner describes morality as belonging to the realm of will rather than thought, the approach taken towards moral education in Steiner early childhood education is the same as towards education of the will: learning by imitation and example. What is done again and again and imitated by the child will become part of the child's habits. Whether the child develops habits or behaviour based on what is moral or not depends on the adult.

The acquisition of good habits is a form of deep learning, which can in part be summed up in the axiom that children want to please adults. It works because young children, in their naturally positive openness to life, 'believe in the morality of the world and therefore believe that the world may be imitated'.[26] Therefore adults are naturally accepted as good, their deeds as moral and their words as true.

Steiner states that moral quality has to flow into the deeds of adults in order to reach the child; it remains ineffective if only grasped by the child's intellect. 'Those who are exhorted to be good become only weak, nervous human beings,'[27] a consequence of addressing the thinking of the child instead of the will.

Among other things, moral education is helped by the human upright posture. The vertical posture connects the human being to the cosmos and opens the human being to higher spiritual influences. Steiner points out that in the process of learning to walk a moral force streams into the child.[28]

The opportunity arises to approach moral education through guiding the child's movement. Especially when the movement of the teacher is artistically formed – such as in eurythmy – and the child is able to participate through imitation, the moral qualities inherent in these gestures and forms can be absorbed by the child. If the teacher's gestures and actions depict truthfulness and purposefulness rather than an arbitrary arrangement, then they can help to lay the physical foundations for a healthy moral sense in the child.[29]

For children under three, moral education is totally contingent on the morality expressed in the deeds of the people around them because, according to Steiner, the education of the very young child is the self-education of the adult.

From age three through to puberty, as the child's feelings become more visible and the will impulses are coloured by feeling, it is the task of education to harmonize feeling and willing in the child, that is, to educate not only the will but also the life of feeling.

There are three kinds of feeling which relate to developing morality: the feeling of gratitude, the feeling of love and the feeling for one's duty.[30] As we shall see below, each one links to a particular phase of child development: developing gratitude to early childhood, developing love to middle childhood and developing a sense of one's duty to adolescence. They are not moral postulates for children to follow, but should be present in each of these phases as essential experiences:

- *The world is good*: this experience is essential for early childhood and will lead to the feeling of gratitude.

- *The world is beautiful:* this experience is essential for the primary school years and will lead to the development of love for the world.

- *The world is true:* this experience is essential to adolescence and will lead to a feeling for one's duty.

Becoming a moral human being is connected to living through these essential experiences in the right way.

The world is good

It is important that the deeds the young child witnesses bear the quality of goodness. This goodness shines through in the love and care with which adults perform their work and the positive thoughts accompanying it. For the young child, adults engaged in their various activities are personifications of morality. This shows in the complete trust with which young children look up to adults and imitate what they are doing. Verbal admonition has a place after the age of five, but even then it is less effective than the living image of morality that the working adult provides. Experiencing the moral quality in the deeds of adults leads to a feeling of gratitude in the child: gratitude for food, for a wonderful day, for being alive. The child expresses it through joy and the desire to be active.

However, a mood of gratitude can only prevail in the child's environment if educators and teachers experience gratitude themselves. Gratitude becomes especially visible in the teacher's love for nature, in the way plants, animals but also human beings are lovingly cared for. The child participates inwardly in the soul experience of the adult, as she is not yet able to develop such an inward relationship to nature herself. In early childhood the adult is the gateway to the world.

The world is beautiful

With this Steiner characterizes the next stage of development from the seventh year onwards. We might ask what morality has to do with beauty. Adults are used to separating aesthetics from questions of good and bad.

Experiencing beauty, if stirring the feelings, leads to awe and wonder, the foundation for a respectful relationship with nature, with the world. Thus the experience of the beautiful and resultant feelings of wonder can stimulate the child's interest in the world and also her reverence towards the living. Children are able to feel intensely the beauty of a sunset, the wonders of the ocean or the animal world. And even when intellectual understanding prevails in later years there still remains an undercurrent of feeling, connecting the child with the world and human beings for life on a deeper level. Then the tendency to hurt and destroy may be overcome through love, which develops out of interest in the world, thus enriching gratitude with the ability to extend one's soul to embrace other human beings and nature.

The class teacher's task is to present the lesson content in such a way that interest is awakened and wonder is aroused in the child. This has a much more powerful and long-lasting effect on the development of morality than admonition or punishment. The latter should only be used in the management of acute crisis situations, and are inappropriate for the development of moral impulses in the child.

The world is true

In adolescence the intellectual quest for truth begins. Meaning is sought beyond the happenings of everyday life, and when none can be found teenagers start to detest this everyday life and the adults who have created it or are trapped in it.

A sense for one's duty or mission in life can arise only if the young person can meet somebody who represents ideals through her whole being. The adolescent is looking for ideals worth striving for. The will to do one's duty arises as a result of having found something to live for, and this opens up a meaningful perspective on life and a sense for one's individual path within it. Unless they meet adults who represent through their lives truthfulness and devotion to their tasks, it is difficult for young people to find their way to moral action. Adolescents are a living question to the worldview of their parents and teachers, and to the direction they pursue in their lives.

Through cultivating these three soul moods, morality as an inner disposition will gradually develop in the child. It is a repetition of a process in human evolution wherein different cultures have developed certain moral qualities which are then passed on to future generations, albeit often in a new form. The contribution of early Asian cultures was to develop and nurture wonder and devotion. The achievement of the Greek and Roman age was to develop an intense interest in understanding and mastering the world. It is the task of the time of the consciousness soul to intensify this interest into a sense of duty for developing relationships based on love among human beings and love for the earth.[31]

Endnotes

1. R. Steiner, *Menschenwerden, Weltenseele und Weltengeist, Part 2* (GA 206) R. Steiner Verlag, Dornach, 1991, p. 103.
2. Steiner states that in our time the human being is in the process of developing the will as the youngest member of the inner life. Thinking and feeling have been developed in earlier times. In: *Cosmosophy Vol 2* (GA 208) Completion Press, Moorooka, Australia, 1997, p. 114. He also states that in our time the egotistic element of the will has permeated human beings' relationship to the world and egotism has permeated their will. See *Education as a Social Problem,* Anthroposophic Press, Hudson, NY, 1984, p. 100.
3. R. Steiner, 'The Emancipation of the Will' in: *A Modern Art of Education,* Rudolf Steiner Press, London, 1972, pp. 91–92.
4. Steiner speaks about the two streams of will in GA 205, Dornach, 1987, p. 124 (Lecture 7, given on 15 July 1921).
5. Steiner mentions that the will of the human being at birth is not yet truly human; it lacks morality. Morality needs to be acquired gradually during life and the I is the main factor in this process. See *Curative Education*, Lecture 3, given on 27 June 1924.
6. R. Steiner, *Study of Man* (second edition) Rudolf Steiner Press, London, 1966, Lecture 4.
7. R. Steiner, 'The Child Before the Seventh Year', *Soul Economy and Waldorf Education*, Anthroposophic Press, Spring Valley, NY, 1986, p. 105.
8. Steiner, *Study of Man*, Lecture 8, p. 113.
9. Christof Wiechert says that teaching needs to take into account what children want to do from within. He names three conditions for learning in the early years or primary schooling: 1. Children like doing what is in accordance with their being. 2. Children are enthusiastic about what they are doing; this is in accordance with their being. 3. Gradually through the first two steps children will awaken to learning which makes demands on their thinking, the head. In: *Journal of the Pedagogical Section at the Goetheanum,* No. 32 (2007).
10. Steiner, *Study of Man*, Lecture 10, pp. 154–155.
11. Ibid., p. 154.
12. Chr. Wiechert, 'Awakening the Spiritual Powers of the Head, Educating the Will', *Journal of the Pedagogical Section at the Goetheanum,* No. 29 (2006) p. 5.
13. Steiner, 'The Child Before the Seventh Year', p. 107.

14 Steiner, *Study of Man*, Lecture 4.
15 Ibid., Lecture 12, p. 178.
16 More is said about morning circles in Chaper 6 of this book, 'Moving with Soul'.
17 Steiner, *Study of Man*, Lecture 10, p. 152.
18 Ibid., p. 155. My emphasis.
19 Ibid., p. 150.
20 'Let us consider what we have now discovered: that the human being enters the world with a sleeping spirit and a dreaming soul, as far as his head is concerned: that hence it is necessary right from the beginning, from birth onwards, to educate him through his will, for we can only approach his sleeping head spirit by working upon his will.' In: *Study of Man*, p. 152.
21 Ibid., p. 153.
22 R. Steiner, *Menschenwerden, Weltenseele und Weltengeist, Part 1* (GA 205) R. Steiner Verlag, Dornach, 1987, p. 156f.
23 Further information on this can be found in A. Mazzone, *A Passionate Schooling*, Griffin Press, South Australia, 2010, Part 2, chapter 5.
24 Given that Steiner's view of the young child includes the spiritual life of the child before birth, we can ask: why does the child not bring moral impulses into life from her spiritual existence? Steiner states that all will-impulses from the past have been incorporated into the child's body, foremost into the formation of the brain. In each incarnation a 'new will' is acquired which needs to be developed through education to a level which is in accordance with the possibilities of a human being's destiny and ideally includes the achievement of high moral standards. See *Menschenwerden, Weltenseele und Weltengeist* (GA 205) p. 124.
25 Steiner, *Study of Man*, Lecture 8, p. 113.
26 Ibid., Lecture 9, p. 134.
27 Ibid., p. 70.
28 GA 224, (Third edition) Dornach, 1992, p. 118. See also R. Steiner, *The Spiritual Guidance of the Individual and Humanity*, Anthroposophic Press, Hudson, NY, 1992, Lecture 1. And GA 221 (Third edition) Dornach, 1998, pp. 112–113: Uprightness makes it possible for the human being to take in moral impulses, which come from the cosmos. This vertical position discriminates human beings from the animals, in which the horizontal direction prevails and which are therefore bound by instinct and drive.
29 R. Steiner, *The Education of the Child and Early Lectures on Education*, Anthroposophic Press, Hudson NY, 1996, p. 25.
30 Steiner, *Soul Economy*, p. 290ff.
31 Reference needs to be made here to a lecture series by Steiner on 'Theosophical Morality' given in Denmark in 1912, published in GA 155. Here he develops in more detail the contribution of cultural epochs to the development of morality.

4

Relationships in Early Childhood: Attachment, Separation and Individualization

The theme of establishing and maintaining supportive relationships with young children in education has received much attention in early learning frameworks in recent years.[1] The formation of positive attachment relationships is crucial for the healthy physical, social, emotional and cognitive development of young children. The issue of relationships and, especially, of attachment and separation in early childhood will be discussed here in connection with fundamentals of Steiner early childhood education.

Attachment and separation

How does the young child form his first relationships with other human beings?

The process of attachment – particularly during the first year of life – has been investigated.

Visual discrimination of human faces and the development of object-permanence in the child have been identified as prerequisites for attachment behaviour.

From a different angle, the phenomenon of attachment in the first year of life and the experience of loss have been investigated by the psychoanalytically oriented psychologist John Bowlby. While classical psychoanalytical theory regarded the baby's focus on oral satisfaction and the relationship to the mother through breast feeding as pivotal for successful bonding and positive emotional development, Bowlby broadened this view on the basis of observations by pointing to the importance of a number of additional factors.

Bowlby writes:

> The act of bonding is defined as any form of behaviour which results in the fact that one person establishes closeness to a distinct and preferred other person. As long as this person remains available and willing to respond, this behaviour may only consist of an occasional looking or listening to identify where the person is ... The process of attachment leads to the establishment of emotional bonds and to ways of behaviour which remain present during the entire life.[2]

He continues by stating that intimate bonds are the source of joy and strength for the human being during an entire lifespan.

Bowlby points out that there is nothing pathological in a strong attachment to another human being as such, not during childhood or later. The decisive factors for the development of bonding are to be sought in early childhood.[3] He discriminates four different phases in the process:[4]

1. The pre-attachment or non-specific contact phase (birth to six or eight weeks).

2. 'Attachment in the making' phase (six weeks–eight months).

3. The phase of attachment to one person, usually a parent (eight months to two years). During this time nearly all children develop some kind of separation anxiety. This

peaks at around one-and-a-half to two years of age, after which it usually eases off.

4. A gradual increase of acceptance of substitute caregivers takes place from the third and fourth year onward.

There are similarities and differences between these four phases and Steiner's description of the process of incarnation. Steiner describes four stages in the evolution of the earth, which are repeated in the incarnation of each human being. These four conditions of incarnation of earth and human being are the adaptation to the conditions of warmth (the evolutionary stage of Old Saturn); of light (the evolutionary stage of Old Sun); of water (the evolutionary stage of Old Moon); and finally, the condition of earth existence or existence in the mineral realm.[5]

All are fundamental for the coming into being of the human body and for the processes of sustaining life. The four elements of warmth, light/air, water and earth are also reflected in the inner life of the human being – in the temperaments, for example. The implication here is that warmth, light/air, water and earth are qualities that also exist as gestures of the human soul. As such they are pivotal in forming human relationships, including with young children.

In the process of attachment and separation during the first years of life we can find all four qualities in an ordered progression: in the stages of non-specific attachment, bonding and then the steps of developing independence:

Phase 1: Indiscriminate attachment (first 6 weeks)

Warmth is the fundamental quality of relationship at the beginning of life. Being in warmth is an experience of oneness for the child in which boundaries do not exist. So intense is the relationship between mother and child that there is no experience of separate beings on the side of the child. Breastfeeding is such an experience. The communication between mother and child is described in modern terminology as 'interactional synchrony', in which mother and child match emotional states. This early symbiosis is one of the great mysteries of human existence.

Relationships in Early Childhood

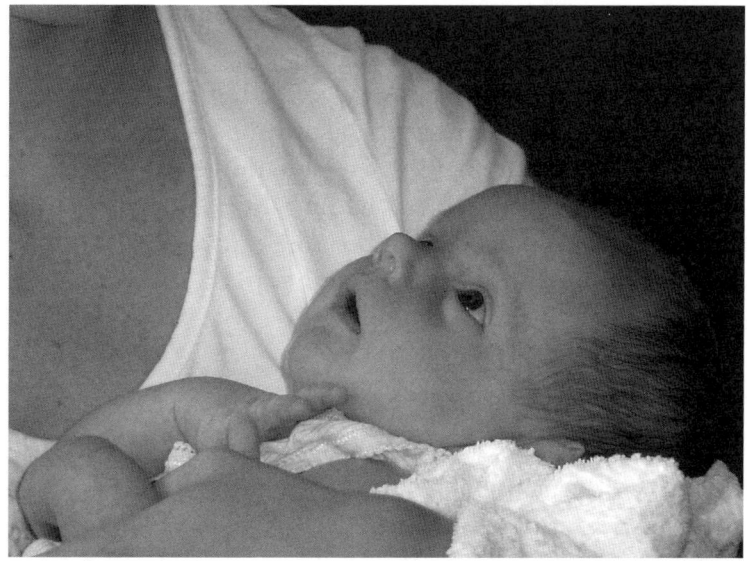

Baby aged four weeks: the gaze plays an important part in the transition from early symbiosis to specific attachment. Photo by author

Phase 2: Specific attachment (6 weeks to 8 months)

This is the phase of light, of seeing/perceiving the other human being. Now the experience is one of intimate communication between two beings perceiving each other. A unique relationship, a 'bond', is formed: the child makes contact, the mother responds and vice versa. It is a time of great joy and harmony. Bonding is established not just through the acts of feeding and care in response to basic needs. The feeding and touching experiences in baby care are filled with subtle processes of recognizing one another as human beings. Most importantly it is through eye contact, smiling and speaking to the baby, and touch, that a positive bond between the mother[6] and the child is established.

Phase 3: Exploring (8 months – 2½ years)

The relationship is extended to include part of the world. The mother now becomes the secure base from which to explore the environment. The close relationship continues, yet the child temporarily forgoes closeness in order to get to know the world around him. This is the gesture of water: of flowing, moving on. New challenges arise. The child wants to do things by himself, yet he relies on the presence of the person who provides security. The existing bond between mother and baby has to adjust to this new situation. The mother has to transform her attachment to the 'cuddly baby' into a relationship that accommodates the child's need to be more independent at times. For the child it is natural to expect the mother to be always available as a 'secure base', the place to return to.

Phase 4: Separation (2½ years onwards)

As the child approaches the end of the third year, he moves into a new phase – of separation. The child acquires a certain degree of independence. The new qualities of the child's thinking lead to a clearer perception of self and world. This experience can be related to what Steiner calls the 'earth stage' of human evolution, or the experience of the solid element. Contours become sharper; things, events and people can be observed more clearly.

With clearer perception of the environment and people, a sense of time also develops. Now the temporary character of being separated from the mother can be understood and more readily accepted by the child. Consequently it is easier for other caregivers to assume the role of mother substitute, and the child will form an attachment relationship with them. Interest in other children also grows at this time, and child-to-child interactions become more frequent and stable.

Why consider the four phases of attachment in early childhood in connection with the four conditions given by Steiner in the context of understanding the evolutionary processes in earth existence? We do this because looking at such archetypal transformational processes of warmth, light/air, water and earth can deepen our understanding of the development and forming of relationships and thus lead to a better understanding of the role of the educator and her pedagogical task.

'In the beginning there was warmth.' This is a sentence for meditation on receiving the child into the world as an act of giving warmth, of sacrificing one's own interests to serve the well-being of a child and of giving unconditional love. This meditation can help to establish the right relationship to a newborn child.

Consciously moving into the experience of 'light' – the 'seeing' of each other as two beings in relationship – can help us to understand 'secure attachment' as a deeply human experience. It adds another dimension to the research findings on attachment, the majority of which were originally gained by observing behaviour of higher animals.

Then the 'moving away' gesture of the child needs to be understood as a spiritual necessity for becoming an individual and meditating on the qualities of 'water' can help with an accepting response to this gesture of the child, rather than wanting to hold on to the bliss of the oneness of the baby days.

Finally the bond between mother and child needs to be transformed to allow for independence. Looking at the increasing physical and mental faculties of the child we can develop positive thoughts about the breaking of the ties of the earlier stages of bonding and joyously see the child who now becomes an 'earth' citizen in his own right.

Bonding, imitation and secondary attachment

How does secondary attachment between young children and educators come about?

For Steiner, imitation and example are the 'magic words' for education in early childhood. Imitation is an important way of establishing and maintaining attachment relationships between educators and children. For the adult, being an example worthy of imitation requires an inner gesture of devotion and love for one's work. For the child, imitation is a process of merging with the gestures and deeds of the adult in a mood of trust and surrender. According to Steiner, the ability to imitate is already present at birth as a legacy from prebirth existence in the spiritual realm and it remains the major form of learning throughout the time of early childhood, including with respect to relationships.

The recent discovery of the ability of newborn babies to imitate different expressions of a human face, if the face appears at a certain distance from their eyes, has changed attitudes towards the infant. No longer do psychologists and educators see the baby as a passive, helpless being, imbued by the adult with everything he needs to learn. Steiner has pointed out that the child comes to earth 'instructed', that is, bringing abilities from the spiritual world in which the child has lived in communion with other spiritual beings. This spiritual experience is the archetype of relationships on earth, especially of those in the early years, when the urge to imitate is still strong.

Anyone who has worked with young children will know that imitation is not one-way communication but always a mutual giving and taking, a process initiated by the child as much as by the adult. So rather than regarding forming relationships as a process initiated by the adult, we should see it as a process to which the child actively contributes. The child integrates himself into the conditions that he finds in his environment at a given time. The role of the adult here is that of a facilitator rather than an initiator.

Secure and insecure attachment

Achieving a secure attachment in the first and second year of life is of great importance for the further development of the child. Not only is it easier for the securely attached child to make contact with adults and engage in play relationships with other children, secure bonding also has benefits for the future cognitive and social development of the child.[7]

From observations in Steiner kindergartens we know that difficulties in establishing a secure attachment relationship between child and teacher often coincide with a weakness in the child's ability to imitate and to play intensely. There is no systematic research from Steiner kindergartens beyond such observations. However, mainstream research into separation anxiety gives the following descriptions of forms of attachment:[8]

Secure attachment

Already at the age of six months the child has active ways of getting the mother's attention. Once mobile, the baby will keep within eye contact of the mother, even when moving away from her.

Children with secure attachment can show separation anxiety. Crying when the mother leaves is not a sign of being too strongly attached but an expression of a preference for being with the mother. Characteristic of securely bonded children is their happy and immediate contact when rejoining their mother. The strength of protest at being left in the care of others depends on the specifics of the situation and the temperament of the child.

Children who have a secure bond with their primary caregiver enter more readily into relationships with others as they get older. The time of this step can vary greatly. Some children with a secure bond to the mother are only ready to let go at school entry age. Most achieve the natural separation stage some time between three and five. It is important for the kindergarten teacher to accept these variations without labelling the 'late' children as having a problem.

Research based on 'Adult Attachment Interviews'[9] has shown that mothers who are in a secure attachment relationship with their children share some features in common, seemingly related to the way in which they have come to terms with attachment experiences in their own childhood. Mothers who have gained a certain objectivity and balance in dealing with their own childhood experiences, be they positive or negative, are significantly more likely to have a secure attachment relationship with their children. Their children, in turn, show more affectionate interactive behaviour.

Insecure attachment

1. Avoidant attachment:

These children do not seem to seek closeness with the mother. They do not react with signs of distress when the mother leaves. They react to strangers much in the same way as they react to the mother. On the mother's return they do not interrupt what they are doing and they are slow to greet – and even avoid greeting – the mother. There are many degrees of avoidant attachment, from temporarily ignoring the mother to an attitude of total disinterest, passivity and absence of protest behaviour.

In the above-mentioned research, mothers of such children devalued their own relationship experiences as a child. They discussed their experiences intellectually, with little emotion.

2. Resistant attachment:

These children show their insecurity by clinging to their mother when she wants to leave. They may do so to such a degree that they are unable to play or relate to anybody else. When the mother returns they show signs of anger, sometimes hitting or pushing. This may be accompanied by crying, which continues long after the reunion has taken place.

When interviewed, mothers of these children showed highly charged emotions in relation to their own childhood experiences. They expressed anger towards their parents and seemed overwhelmed and confused by their own experiences.

3. Disoriented attachment:

In the case of severe attachment problems children show insecurity through contradictory behaviour on the return of the mother. They may respond to the mother only weakly and even try to pull away from her while being held. They may appear confused, cry at odd intervals without apparent reason, or show no reaction at all.

In the research interviews mothers of these children did not seem to have a definite way of dealing with past experiences. They were confused and disoriented when it came to discussing difficult experiences from their own childhood.

In all three forms of insecure attachment the parent had an unresolved emotional issue that was seen as adversely affecting the mother and child's ability to form a secure relationship.

It seems highly likely that the above-described 'mother's internal working model' has a significant impact on her ability to enter into an attachment relationship. It is important that a mother answers the needs of a baby readily and willingly and that she understands these needs well.

Equally important is how she responds to the baby's attempts to make contact and how she builds up a quality relationship in caring for the child.

Rudolf Steiner points to the importance of the inner life of the adult during the entire time of early childhood and to the impact of the soul life of the caregiver on the young child. These may have lifelong consequences, he says. Especially during the first three years the adult's inner qualities of clarity of thought and purposefulness of action are vital for the development of a healthy nerve-sense system and a healthy metabolic system in the child. Steiner also advises us to maintain a joyful and loving relationship with our children, and to refrain from sharing with them unresolved emotional issues from our own past or present.

Some examples to illustrate issues of child–teacher relationships which relate to bonding, separation and the emerging individuality of the child

Early attachment experiences between children and parents seem to affect the child–teacher relationship and child–child interaction in early childhood education. Not having experienced a secure attachment relationship may be the cause of emotional and social problems, experienced once the child enters into a group situation. In any such case it is important to consider whether signs of separation anxiety may be the expression of a secure attachment relationship or not. It is normal for the young, securely attached child to show distress when the mother leaves. Separation anxiety normally peaks around the age of 18 months to 2 years. But this also means that up to this age bonding may be disturbed by a traumatic event in the child's life. In addition, the transition into institutional care can upset the child and lead to temporary or permanent insecurity in attachment. Destabilising secure attachment in children as they enter childcare is one of the potential dangers and biggest concerns in providing care for babies and toddlers.[10]

The following examples are based on experiences in Steiner early childhood settings and are presented to highlight the issues discussed above:

The anxious child

'Jessica', aged six

> *Brief history:* Jessica was breastfed until six months. Described by the mother as crying a lot and being most content in her mother's arms. Jessica's birth was followed two years later by the birth of a sister. After the birth of the second child the mother suffered from severe postnatal depression, which was treated and healed. Jessica, now six years old, shows signs of separation anxiety which abate when she has settled into the familiar routine of the kindergarten. She has not developed an attachment to the teacher.
>
> *First observation:* A new assistant has started work today and is sitting at the table helping children to make paper butterflies.
>
> Jessica enters with her mother. She looks at the assistant with wide eyes and does not respond when greeted. She takes hold of her mother's dress, not wanting to let go when her mother tries to take it from her hands.
>
> The mother suggests that she sit down and make a butterfly. Jessica sits down, with one hand still on her mother, and keeps looking at the assistant.
>
> At first Jessica does not engage in making a butterfly, indicating this by shaking her head. Then, after she has watched the other children for a while, she too starts to make one.
>
> When the mother attempts to leave, Jessica wants to sit on her lap and get a hug. Then she walks off to play.
>
> *Second observation, two weeks later:* Jessica has found a child with whom she likes to play. The two girls run off together, perch themselves on a high rail and chat to each other about

their past holiday. They roam the room holding hands, dragging or pulling each other along. They run out of the door then back inside. They return to the high perch on the pole and chat and giggle together in quickly spoken words.

They get a blanket, put it over the pole; it is their house. They talk about the possibility of someone stealing their house.

When the teacher asks for helpers, they run over to help move a table, and as they go past the drawing table they both sit down to do a quick drawing. Their chatter continues as they draw. Then they both run over to their house once more, making a short excursion to where other children are playing. They cause a brief disturbance then go back to their house.

Jessica needs time and a sensitive approach on the part of the adults to form a relationship with either the teacher or the assistant. At age two the process of primary bonding was severely disrupted and the behaviour in kindergarten at age six may well be a consequence of this. While on the one hand she clings to the mother and is anxious about the new person in the room, she is able to go and play without further signs of distress. This may be a good sign that she is overcoming her anxiety. It could also be a gesture of warding off strong emotions – such as separation anxiety – that she has yet to overcome.

The description of the two girls' play situation offers a glimpse of the solution the child may have found for herself. Their play could be characterized as superficial and unsettled. The children change activity in rapid succession but nowhere are they really engaged. Jessica has built a relationship with another child who is capable of sharing and enjoying the same kind of 'butterfly activity' that she does. In itself, this type of play is not necessarily a cause for concern. But given the previous experiences of this child it might be.

Her teacher needs to take into consideration why Jessica did not connect with her. It is possible the child has moved into an inner space of avoiding close relationships with adults. The child–child relationship cannot be regarded as an emotional substitute for bonding with an adult; it is a different experience. The teacher must draw on much empathy, sensitivity and patience to look out for, and respond to, any signs that Jessica may wish to come into a closer relationship.

Attachment relationships to caregivers and teachers play an important role up to the age of nine, when the child has outgrown the stage of imitation. We should always be aware of those children who somehow 'disappear' in their group of play friends and do not establish a relationship with their teacher or caregiver.

The dependent child

'Betty', aged six

> *Observation at playtime:* Betty is asked to tidy a particular corner of the room in which she had been playing with two other girls. She begins by collecting the larger objects in the area and returning them to their proper place. She begins to pick up the cloths that she and the two other girls had used in their play. Betty then notices that the other girls have wandered off and are not tidying up.
>
> She approaches the teacher with her arms full of cloths and says, 'They are not helping.' The teacher responds by saying that she, the teacher, will help her and that she will also ask the two girls to come and help. When the girls are asked they come over and Betty smiles. The smile changes into an expression of annoyance when one girl starts playing. 'We will never get this done, stop playing and help,' she says in a stern voice.
>
> The girl walks away and Betty approaches the teacher again, saying, 'Susan is not helping.'

This example illustrates a fairly common situation in which a child, often a girl, wants to do exactly the right thing and be seen to be following the rules. She wants to please her teacher. She expects that the teacher will ensure that everybody has to follow the rules and help to tidy up. Here we have a six-year-old who is in a secure relationship with the teacher and who has reached the stage in her development when rules and fairness have become important. Her problem is not attachment, it is separation and independence – the next step.

Because Betty has to learn about doing things she wants to do, regardless of how others behave, it would not help the child here to affirm and reinforce her insistence on the rules. Instead, the teacher should indicate that while the rules are correct, and while the teacher herself follows them, there are times when things are different. It may be appropriate to point out for the six-year-old that the important thing is that she herself is doing what needs to be done to make the room tidy again.

Becoming conscious of being an individual and being able to express this in a social context is an important step in the growth of human relationships. Usually this theme is not considered in the context of attachment and separation. However, it should be, as we witness more and more children who struggle with bringing themselves as individuals into the right relationship with being a member of a group.

The consciousness of I emerges around the age of three. Ideally, by this point, the child has experienced the stages of secure attachment, of being part of the family group, of exploring the world and extending social experiences in contact with other children. Ideally, this has been a gradual path into independence.

Yet today's children have to tread the path to the consciousness of self early on and often reach this stage prematurely. Many toddlers are expected to dress, feed, wash themselves and make choices about everyday life, at home and in childcare situations. In the kindergarten, and also in families, we meet children who have lost their sense of being part of a group. They want things to be done their way. They find it hard to fit in with other people's needs, and also to accept rules.

Early independence can be overwhelming for the child. This can show in abrupt and challenging behaviour, like the following:

The 'defiant' child

'Christian', aged six

> *Observation:* Christian's behaviour becomes very boisterous during the morning indoor playtime. When the teacher calls his name, he stands up, turns to face the teacher and gives her a penetrating stare. Christian opens his mouth, puts his index finger vertically across it, and proceeds to repeatedly run his finger down his mouth. The teacher says, 'Christian, come here,' three times. He continues to run his finger down his mouth and does not move towards the teacher. When the teacher physically approaches Christian he throws himself to the ground, face to the floor. He remains in this position for a few seconds. The teacher then says, 'Christian, come to the table.' He raises himself up and walks towards the table. When he reaches the table he puts his bottom on it and slides along it before sitting down beside the teacher. Christian's entire attitude changes as soon as he sits at the table. He shows interest in the teacher's handwork and instantly initiates a conversation about the nature of the project.

Based on this brief observation we cannot say whether he has experienced a secure attachment relationship before in his life. But it can be concluded that this child, in spite of his defiance, has some attachment to the teacher and does what she asks him to do, albeit hesitantly. The teacher is able to reach the child by her calmness, her presence of mind and her consistency, otherwise the situation could have turned out to be difficult.

In order to really know what caused such a situation we would need to work on forming a deeper relationship with the child. To support him, we would have to ponder over the nature of his play – which in this case had turned 'boisterous' – and we would have to identify the good and the difficult aspects as they are part of the child at this time. It would also be fruitful to explore what kind of conversations he enjoys and may be interested in conducting with the teacher. Hidden behind the outer defiance and the questions about the teacher's work may be a deep wish for a different kind of relationship with his teacher. Being six years old he may well see himself as the teacher's equal, who has somehow outgrown the kindergarten, and therefore reacts with resistance when the teacher addresses him in a way that clearly expresses that she is in charge.

The child who does what he wants

'Thomas', aged five

> *Observation:* Thomas has found a long cardboard tube and fiddles with it during candle lighting and verse. The teacher asks him to put it down. He continues. The teacher asks again. He puts the tube on the floor, briefly, then takes it up again. The teacher walks over and takes the tube away. Thomas jumps up and leaves the circle, speaking angrily. He starts crying, leaves the room and goes to the bathroom. After the morning greeting is over, the teacher goes to fetch him and he comes back into the room without further difficulty.

At story time Thomas says, in the middle of the story, that he wants to tell something. The teacher replies that he can tell it after the story has finished. She continues telling the story. Angrily, Thomas says, 'She never listens to me!' He gets up and goes to a corner of the room. He drops himself on a big cushion. He stays there until the end of the story, then walks over to the teacher. He comes very close and whispers something into her ear. The teacher responds with a quiet voice.

The teacher's comment: Thomas gets easily upset when things do not go as he wants. His father is strict, his mother soft. The teacher tries to be consistent.

The mother's comment: one cannot make this child do anything he does not want to do. At home Thomas often plays by himself, never with his younger sister, sometimes with his older brother.

We could diagnose this child very quickly as hyperactive, unable to wait and unable to take into consideration the social aspect of situations and routines or the needs of other children. We could also look at the situation another way: as being confronted with a child who, through his reactions, questions the validity and appropriatenesss of how things are done. In this case it is the ceremony of candle lighting and the way of telling a story.

This child may have received mixed messages in his primary attachment relationships. He may therefore be insecure and react with anger towards the adults who care for him. He does, however, have a stable relationship to his teacher. She is able to bring him back into the group and he is eager to tell her something, even though he did not get his way.

But he demands, and may well need, more attention than other children in the group. 'She never listens to me,' is the key sentence that may lead to a deeper understanding of the child's inner life.

How can the teacher be with him in such a way that he feels listened to and appreciated? The teacher is confronted with the conflicting demands of being consistent and of giving this child what he asks for. How can she respond to an individual child who expresses himself so strongly and in such a demanding way? Would it be feasible to interrupt the story? Should there be the occasional story that allows for more active participation of the children? Whatever steps are taken, the main task in this as well as the other cases is to nurture and to deepen the relationship between teacher and child.

Henning Köhler[11] has written about the fundamental importance of warm and supportive relationships when working with difficult children. He names four principles that the adult should follow when developing a relationship with the child. These are protecting, accompanying, consoling and healing.

While Köhler's considerations and examples stem from his work in child therapy, his four principles are valid for early childhood education as well. Each directs the attention of the educator to the question: *'What kind of relationship do you (the child) want to have with me (the teacher)?'* On the basis of such reflections the teacher is able to determine what the child or the group currently needs and what rhythm and form should be given to the life in the kindergarten at this time.

For example, going back to working intensely with imitation and example is a valid response that provides flexibility with respect to the teacher–child relationship. It is a mode of working in which the child is offered a situation that is emotionally secure and yet leaves the child free in his response. It offers the experience of working in a meaningful and fulfilling way for the adult and invites the child to form a bond with the teacher in doing things together in a warm, emotionally non-demanding relationship situation.

Endnotes

1. In the Australian National Childcare Accreditation Council's 'Quality Practices Guide' for quality areas in childcare, relationships with children feature as quality area number one. Early childhood centres are described as 'communities of learners' and children as active and competent communication partners.
2. Quote translated from the German edition: J. Bowlby, *Verlust, Trauer, Depression*, Frankfurt am Main, 1983, p. 57. A comprehensive overview of research into attachment and separation issues is given by L. Berk, *Child Development*, Allyn and Bacon, Boston/Sydney, 1997, pp. 405–409.
3. Regarding the notions of attachment and bonding: 'bonding' stands for the establishment of a close mutual relationship between two persons, while 'attachment' describes more the feeling of closeness of one person towards another, regardless of whether there is a positive response or not. However, both notions are very close in meaning.
4. This summary is given in L. Berk, *Child Development*, p. 407.
5. R. Steiner, 'Cosmic Evolution and the Human Being', *An Outline of Esoteric Science*, Anthroposophic Press, Hudson NY, 1997, chapter 4.
6. I use 'mother' in the sense of a person who is not only the main caregiver but also the human being willing to provide the possibility for a close emotional attachment relationship.
7. Berk, *Child Development*, p. 416.
8. For details of the research report see Berk, pp. 408–410.
9. In structured interviews mothers were asked to remember and describe attachment experiences in their own childhood. There was a statistically significant correlation between the mother's attachment experiences in

childhood, her reaction to this as an adult and the attachment behaviour of the child. See Berk, pp. 413–414.
10 Berk, pp. 417–418.
11 H. Köhler, *Difficult Children: There Is No Such Thing,* AWSNA Publications, Fair Oaks, CA, 2003, p. 125ff.

5

Children in the Modern World

Working as a kindergarten teacher in the 1990s I became aware of changes in children's behaviour. It was before the time that the phenomenon of change in children was discussed in public. At this stage I summarized my observations in describing two types of children. According to my observations there were children who loved the rhythm and the habits of life in the kindergarten. They settled well into play and were imaginative. Then there were children who were fast, always on the move, keenly interested in and eager to explore the world. But they were quick in assessing what was going on around them and easily distracted from their own endeavours. They had difficulties finding their way into their own play and often disrupted the play of other children. I felt that my way of working somehow fell short of meeting the needs of these children and providing them with opportunities that would engage their interest.

A few years later – in 1999 – Jan Tober and Lee Carroll's book *The Indigo Children*[1] appeared, and around the same time Eugene Schwartz published *The Millennial Child*.[2] Both books address the question of change in modern children, yet in very different ways. Schwartz investigates the causes of the increasing number of children diagnosed with ADHD. Tober and Carroll's subject is the 'Indigo Children', their name for the new type of children observed in their counselling practice.

Other authors joined the discussion[3] around the question whether a new type of children or even an evolutionary shift was emerging, or whether the unusual, often defiant, behaviour observed in these children was caused by growing up under the conditions of modern life.

Indigo Children received so much attention because it presented interviews with mostly older children speaking about themselves and their experiences of being different. Some of these children show a consciousness advanced beyond their years.

In recent years the subject of these 'new' children, as well as of ADHD children, has faded from view, even though teachers experience on a daily basis that the phenomenon has not gone away. Since the turn of the millennium another issue has attracted public attention – that of autism and Asperger syndrome. But while unusual behaviour and disciplinary problems are part of the picture, the underlying causes are very different. Therefore autistic spectrum disorders have not been included in the following considerations about the new generation of children.

There is general agreement among those who have investigated the question as to the main characteristic of these children, namely their high sensitivity and awareness of self and others, which appears to be developed in advance of their age and differs from the consciousness of most people today. Every year, teachers meet children who match the characteristics of 'Indigo children' and for whom current educational methods do not work. These characteristics are summarized below.

According to Henning Köhler there are three types of 'new' children:

1. 'Caring, compassionate souls': already at a very early age gifted with extraordinary social awareness. They are sensitive and need security.

2. 'Searcher souls': adventurous children, constantly on the move, gifted with a strong vitality, sometimes over-active, eager to communicate with others, flexible, often technically interested, willing to take risks.

3. 'Fairyland travellers': introvert, shy, dreaming children with strong imaginations. They often have 'invisible friends'. They have difficulties maintaining attention

and remembering. They are often gifted in the practical aspects of life.

Tober and Caroll also list three groups:

1. The intellectual children who are drawn to technology.
2. The children strong in will, who are fiercely independent and risk-taking.
3. The artistic children, who are often gifted in the social field.

We can recognize that the special giftedness of these three groups of children corresponds to the three powers of the human soul: thinking, willing and feeling.

Generally the following characteristics are mentioned in the literature:[4]

- The children's gaze is deep and serious, described as 'wise' already at birth. Later on it can turn into a look of utter defiance.

They:
- say 'I', often as early as 18 months of age;
- display an early consciousness of self and may appear to others as overly confident or even arrogant;
- seem to see through people and comment on people's hidden thoughts and feelings;
- are interested in evil at an early age;
- react to lies or false pretence through adverse behaviour;
- accept some people immediately, others not at all;
- often choose as friends children of a similar kind;
- want to discuss things and be involved in decision-making;
- respond positively to truthfulness in relationships;

- surprise through unexpected, deeply thoughtful remarks;
- reject rituals, especially those which have become devoid of meaning;
- may disrupt festival ceremonies, candle lighting and morning circle: this antipathy is unexplained and does not appear to be a reaction to bad experiences;
- express great determination at an early age and are not easily distracted from what they want;
- are only attentive to what interests them;
- oppose guidance and authority;
- like to invent their own toys rather than using ready-made ones;
- have an abundance of energy, but difficulties in controlling their movements;
- appear to be fearless or unaware of danger;
- resist currently-used methods of education, including punishment, which they interpret as a weakness of the adult;
- seem to react badly to the stresses of modern life, such as hectic lifestyle, lack of warmth in human relationships, fear and anxiety and the pressure to achieve;
- show unusual developmental profiles: in some areas they may be advanced beyond their age. In other areas, such as the control of movement, they appear to be years behind their age.

It is tempting to attribute the majority of these to the effects of modern life, which could have been avoided through a different kind of education or by shielding children more thoroughly from the influences of modern civilization. However, this falls short of explaining many of the characteristics listed above.

Often, when dealing with such children, the teacher's attention will be focused on inappropriate or hyperactive behaviour that is difficult to handle. Consequently the new generation of children may appear to the teacher to have ADHD.

ADHD symptoms are present in some, but not all, of the 'new' children. The difficulty lies in the diagnosis of what constitutes ADHD. The main symptoms are lack of attentiveness, restlessness and lack of impulse control, and many therapists question their validity for diagnosing a psychological disorder. Questions such as the following arise:

- What is attention? How short is a 'short attention span'? Is attention any less intense because it is short? At what age should we intervene, given that short attention spans are normal in children under three?

- Who draws the line between a child being unable to keep still and the diagnosis of a behavioural disturbance? How much is a diagnosis influenced by the people – parents, caregivers – who have to cope with the behaviour on a daily basis? What are the criteria for a medical/psychological assessment and the subsequent prescription of medicine?

- Lack of control of movement is normal during the first and second year of life; usually control will be achieved by age three. But there may be conditions in the life of the child which may slow down this process or make the child fall back into early movement patterns.

Much depends on the viewpoint and the judgement of the observer. More and more doctors and psychologists question whether the diagnosis of ADD or ADHD expresses a reality or whether this diagnosis, given to 30–40 per cent of children today, is a label for conditions with similar symptoms but very different causes. Köhler, among others, suggests that rather than concluding that nearly half of today's children are seriously disturbed, it may be the case that our understanding of these children is sadly lacking. We have not provided them with an appropriate environment or a suitable education.[5]

Köhler suggests that we are witnessing an evolutionary shift which necessitates a corresponding adjustment of current developmental-educational theory and practice. His argument is supported by recent medical research into changes in developmental patterns in children. Below is a summary of these findings:

- Many newborn babies sleep less than they used to. Many are alert and awake for extended periods of time right after birth.

- The newborn communicates and imitates immediately. Babies make eye contact; they imitate from day one.[6]

- Children's developmental patterns are more diverse than they used to be. The Swiss paediatrician Remo Largo[7] worked on a longitudinal study of children and their development from birth to adulthood over more than 20 years. He states that individual developmental patterns vary by up to two years in an increasing number of children. Largo does not classify these children as developmentally delayed. Rather, he uses the notion of 'developmental originality' or individual developmental history.

- More children than previously noticed show a polarity of being very advanced in some areas of development but behind in others.

- Many children say 'I' to themselves in the second year of life instead of the third year.

- Changes in brain structure have been identified and new faculties observed in children, along with the disappearance of others. These phenomena have been the subject of much discussion in recent educational psychology literature.[8] Healy and Hüther state that the formation of synapses in the brain depends to a large degree on the use of the brain and the life choices that an individual makes. We can no longer infer that reduced synaptic activity in the brain is the cause for a reduced ability to think. The opposite seems to be true as well: reduced thinking activity causes the synaptic structure of the brain to change.

- Even though the current culture prizes the cognitive faculties that are related to the left brain hemisphere, there are more and more older children in whom the right brain hemisphere and imaginative faculties predominate. This can either lead to an inclination towards visual learning and a dependency on visual stimulation or cause giftedness in imagination and creativity.

- There is an increase of 'difficult' children without obvious environmental causes or obvious miseducation. Even parents who have supported and educated their child with love and dedication report that the child remains 'difficult' and has been so since birth or early age.

Georg Kühlewind[9] suggests that we are witnessing a new generation of children who herald a shift in human consciousness, but who at present are met by an environment and general consciousness that is very much oriented on the past. This causes friction, clashes and suffering. Similarly, Henning Köhler[10] describes these children not as damaged but rather as 'strange' in relation to the expectations and educational measures they are exposed to. Köhler has observed and studied such 'unusual' children in his practice over many years. He says that it makes a huge difference to them if we change our attitude and perspective and start to see them as competent in their world but not fitting into the current world.

The question remains unanswered as to whether there is an evolutionary shift heralded by a new generation of children or whether there is an increasing diversification of individual developmental patterns in all children.

Eugene Schwartz argues for the existence of an evolutionary shift[11] by pointing to three characteristic steps of transformation of the human soul life in the 20th century which he considers to have been evolutionary shifts as well. He characterizes the first as a shift in thinking, the second as a shift in feeling, the third, occurring at the end of the millennium as a new impulse in the will.

In the years after the First World War, and all through the 1920s, there appeared in Middle Europe the so-called 'youth movement', characterized by a rejection of the lifestyle and values of the society of the time by the younger generation. Steiner warmly welcomed the ideas of these young people. He addressed the youth movement in a series of lectures and pointed to ways in which their legitimate concerns and ideals could be reconciled with the best part of the cultural past. He was very clear that if these young people did not find in the thoughts of the older generation what could meet the longing of their souls, then this unfulfilled longing would become destructive.[12]

In the 1960s a second 'youth movement' appeared: the student protests and following them the peace and 'flower power' movement, with alternative forms of lifestyle and of raising and educating children. Schwartz interprets this movement as being centred in longing for deeper transformative processes in the realm of feeling.

For our time Schwartz suggests that the phenomenon of the new generation of children could be interpreted as a third wave of longing for the spirit. This time it is appearing in the very young and manifesting in the way in which these children express strength in the area of will.

We could include into this third wave the appearance of 'Indigo Children' since the late 1980s. This would mean that we are witnessing a shift of the human capacities in the realm of will. There are children who come into the world already determined about what they have to do, who are not easily deterred. Even they themselves may be overwhelmed by the strength of will forces rising up within them. At the same time they long to be met with spiritual understanding.

Children today need parents and educators who have gained some wisdom through life and are flexible in thought. If they do not meet such adults, their strong will forces and distinct consciousness of self and others, albeit immature, may lead to desperate and destructive actions. If we are not to lose these children we have to form a sympathetic and supporting relationship with them based on the continuing effort of gaining a spiritual understanding of these children.

What justification is there for suggesting that children today are leading the way towards a higher consciousness? Has it not always been so that children are able to bring something new from the spiritual realm into our world? Surely the next generation is always ahead of the previous one?

Rudolf Steiner[13] indicated that human beings born after 1930 would have a different consciousness than those born before. They would have the following characteristics:

- A strong imaginative ability, which, if not cared for, would become socially destructive.

- A loosening of the etheric body and with it the capacity for a more extended consciousness and a higher sensibility.

- An ability to feel and connect with the environment more intensely. This, however, may express itself only as a feeling of disquiet or discomfort in relation to their surroundings.

About children, Steiner says:

> When the human being today descends from pre-earthly existence into the physical body, he experiences something similar to the instructions in the Old Mysteries ... Things are different today. What I said was valid for human beings who had lived through fewer earthly lives than is the case with human beings today, who have already absorbed a lot in previous lives. This enables them to

undergo a certain instruction by spiritual beings in pre-earthly existence.

This one has to assume, if one meets children today. It is not the task anymore to somehow pour into the child what in old times needed to be instilled. Today we have the task to say: The child is already instructed, and now he puts his physical body around his knowing soul and this sheath has to be penetrated in order to call forth what was pre-earthly instruction by the Gods. Thus we have to think today pedagogically.

He continues:

If we think in the direction of anthroposophically oriented Spiritual Science, it becomes clear that all education does nothing else than removing hindrances, which hide what the child brings with him.

Therefore in Waldorf Education it is immensely important that the teacher really looks at the child as somebody who presents a riddle to him, which the teacher has to solve … The emphasis is not on what the teacher has intended to bring to the child; he never should proceed in a dogmatic manner. He has to regard the child as his teacher and he has to observe the child. The child will disclose through his behaviour how the sheaths should be penetrated so that the instructions of the Gods may stream forth from the child himself … [14]

This is our task in respect to the modern child: to acknowledge by the ways of education the spirituality dormant in each child; and, as teachers, to become able to perceive in the child's behaviour how the bodily conditions can become permeable for this spirituality, and how hindrances can to be removed in each individual case.

We could, for example, look at the strong wish of many children today to do everything by themselves. Because this is not yet possible, we witness the frustration it causes. If we think of the child as being instructed in the spiritual world, it is not so strange that children cannot discriminate between knowing spiritually-intuitively and not knowing as yet here on earth. They will overestimate themselves in relation to the lessons to be learned on earth because they remember the spiritual wisdom in which they participated.[15] And if the adult cannot acknowledge the spiritual wisdom of the child, then this hinders the spiritually conscious child from entering into a relationship of imitation and example with the adult.

Does it really make a difference for the educational and therapeutic process whether we speak of removing hindrances that block the spiritual intentions of the child, or talk in terms of malfunctions or developmental delays?

The difference is this: the answer of how to remove hindrances blocking the way of the individuality comes from searching for a spiritual understanding of this individuality through observation and meditation. The assessment of specific functions and delays can play a part within this understanding of the child but is not the foundation for educational intervention. The observational findings have to be related back to the fundamental insight that the child is spiritually instructed and may disclose herself to the educator if the teacher is able to meet the child in her essential being. Carried by a deep interest and tolerance towards the difficult aspects of these children, the teacher is able to tune into the meaning of unusual behaviours and pathways.

There are good examples of this attitude in the descriptions of the therapeutic relationships which Henning Köhler gives in his books.[16] His work is based on an exceptional interest in these unusual children and the ability to build relationships with them. Relationships, including those with the parents, are at the core of education and therapy. All other therapeutic or educational means fulfil a supporting role for the fundamental pedagogical relationship.

Is there a new generation of children with a spiritually more evolved consciousness and a new strength of will? Without aiming to present a final answer, it seems that there are many relevant observations and experiences which support this assumption. However, we could conclude that what we are seeing, so obvious and outstanding as it appears, may only be the tip of a state of being which all children who are born today experience to a greater or lesser degree. It is important for day-to-day educational work that we include all children in any considerations of change in educational practice resulting from the phenomena described above.

Why does Steiner education have the potential to meet the children of today and provide what they are needing and looking for? An answer is attempted for the early childhood part of Steiner education in the following description of qualities which are essential to this approach and which are directly derived from its spiritual foundation.

Education is based on forming authentic relationships with the child

The teacher strives to meet the child in a genuine way. She observes and respects the child's response and leaves the child free in the realm of creative activity. In early education this means that a relationship based on working with imitation and example leaves the child free to choose what to take up or leave aside. Thus working with example and imitation can become the ideal basis for human relationships, as it creates closeness without denying the differences between the work commitment of the adult and the various ways in which children will or will not participate in this work.

Joy is an essential quality of living and working with young children

In its objective form, that is, freed from self-feeling, joy carries the qualities of levity and light. Children thrive in a light-filled environment, both physically and spiritually.

The quality of relationships depends on self-development and the schooling of perception of the educator

Steiner early childhood educators are on a continuous path of self-development and self-reflection. Part of this path is a schooling in perception. 'Learning to see' is one of the foundations for meaningful interactions with children and for effective intervention.

Preparing programmes and plans serves the teacher by bringing consciousness to her actions, yet programmes need to remain flexible with regard to their application.

'Learning to see' is also fundamental to acquiring a perception of the four members of the human being working together in the child, and whether or not they are in harmony. Steiner reminded teachers that it would become increasingly necessary to understand such preconditions for health in each individual child.

Early childhood educational practice is based on the principle of enhancing life processes through providing the time and space for the child to breathe out and be active without pressure and haste

Space is created for the young child to play and explore freely. Programmes are adjusted to individual needs and developmental stages. Rhythms and routines are handled flexibly, taking into account the nature of the individual child or the specifics of a group of children.

Educational intervention in respect to developmental difference will depend on the presence of movement or stagnation in the progress of the individual child

Interference is refrained from as long as the child makes progress by herself, be it ever so slowly. Developmental plans are used in order to become conscious of and monitor individual developmental patterns and progress. Underlying such plans is the picture of the whole child.

Education supports the child's mastery of her will and the development of self-trust in her abilities

The realm of self-initiated and self-directed movement and play is respected and nurtured as the foundation for the experience of freedom and self-confidence.

The six aspects listed above are offered as indicators for detecting hindrances that may arise through educational practice. They are also meant as a guide for establishing an educational environment that will assist in removing hindrances caused by the conditions of modern life in children of today.

Endnotes

1. J. Tober and L. Caroll, *The Indigo Children*, Hay House Inc., Carlsbad, CA, 1999.
2. E. Schwartz, *The Millennial Child: Transforming Education in the Twenty-First Century*, Anthroposophic Press, Great Barrington, MA, 1999.
3. In 2001 Georg Kühlewind published a book with the title *Sternkinder* [Star Children], followed by a flood of articles pro and contra Kühlewind's book specifically in relation to Steiner education. Henning Köhler joined the debate in 2002 with his book *War Michel aus Lönneberga aufmerksamkeitsgestört?* [Did Emil of Lönneberga have Attention Deficit Disorder? *subtitled* The ADHD Myth and the New Generation of Children]; and also in 2002 Siegfried Woitinas published his book *Wer sind die Indigo-Kinder?* [Who are the Indigo Children?]. Köhler's and Woitinas' books are published in German only.
4. This list is a compilation of attributes as found in the publications by Tober/Carroll, Schwartz, Kühlewind, Woitinas and Köhler.
5. More recently than Eugene Schwartz (*Millennial Child*), Thomas Armstrong has pointed to environmental factors for the increase of ADHD, such as the appearance of technology in education of young children and the disappearance of play. See S. Olfman, ed., *All Work and No Play: How Educational Reforms are Harming Our Preschoolers*, Praeger Publishers, Westport, CT, 2003.
6. M. Dornes, *Der kompetente Säugling* [The Competent Baby], Fischer Verlag, Frankfurt, 2001; also research summary in: L. Berk, *Child Development* (Fourth Edition) Allyn and Bacon, Boston/Sydney, 1997.
7. R. Largo, *Kinderjahre*, Stuttgart/Zurich, 1999.
8. J. Healy, *Endangered Minds*, New York, 1991; G. Hüther, *Bedienungsanleitung für ein menschliches Gehirn* [Instructions for Using a Human Brain] Göttingen, 2001. More recently: J. Bauer, *Das Gedächtnis des Körpers* [The Memory of the Body], Frankfurt, 2005; and *Prinzip Menschlichkeit. Warum wir von Natur aus kooperieren* [The Principle of Humanness: Why We Cooperate Naturally], Heyne, Munich, 2008.
9. G. Kühlewind, *Star Children: Understanding Children Who Set Us Special Tasks and Challenges*, Temple Lodge Publishing, Forest Row, 2004, pp. 69ff. and p. 77.

10 He describes his work in: *Difficult Children, There is No Such Thing,* AWSNA Publications, Fair Oaks, CA, 2003; but also in his already mentioned book on ADHD.
11 See his book *The Millennial Child.*
12 R. Steiner, *The Younger Generation: Educational and Spiritual Impulses for Life in the Twentieth Century,* Anthroposophic Press, Spring Valley, NY, 1967, Lecture 11.
13 R. Steiner, *Die Verantwortung des Menschen für die Weltentwickelung durch seinen geistigen Zusammenhang mit dem Erdplaneten und der Sternenwelt* (GA 203) R. Steiner Verlag, Dornach, 1989, Lecture of 22 January, 1921, p. 100.
14 Ibid. The quotation is my translation from the German.
15 S. Woitinas, *Wer sind die Indigo-Kinder? Herausforderungen einer neuen Zeit,* Verlag Urachhaus, Stuttgart.
16 Not only in this recent publication but also in Köhler's earlier work about anxious and depressed children can one sense the deep understanding with which these children are approached.

6

'Moving with Soul': Supporting Movement Development in the Early Years

Significant research has been done on the importance of movement in the development and learning of children. Sally Goddard Blythe's work on the understanding and treatment of retained primitive reflexes in the movement patterns of children with learning difficulties should be mentioned here.[1] Audrey McAllen, a Steiner teacher, created 'The Extra Lesson', a remedial program which combines aspects of research into sensory-motor integration with parts of the Steiner school curriculum, and condensed it into a program of learning support which is used in many Steiner schools around the world for school-aged children.[2]

Also influential in this context is Karl König,[3] anthroposophical medical doctor, embryologist and founder of the worldwide Camphill Movement serving people with cognitive disabilities. König contributed to the understanding of the spiritual dimension of movement and forms of disturbances in the realm of movement. Like McAllen, his work is deeply rooted in the understanding of the human being given by Rudolf Steiner. König points to the archetypal gestures behind the ways in which human beings approach the world. In discovering and understanding these archetypal gestures he then developed methods of treatment. In the following considerations the archetypal gestures of relating to the world through body, soul and spirit are the key with which we can unlock the secret of movement development in young children.

Part 1: The development of movement in the young child

Karl König has given three images as a help for understanding the incarnation process. They provide a good foundation for the understanding of the first three years of life. These images relate to developing a relationship to the spatial dimensions of earth existence, to making judgements related to the earth environment, and to the development of thinking and I-consciousness. Movement is essential to all three. It is not confined to movement of the body alone, but is also an inner process expressing an individual human being's feeling and thinking.

1. Uprightness and the incarnation into the earth realm

Incarnation is described by Rudolf Steiner as the process of finding one's place in the world, of becoming conscious of and at home within three dimensional space – the vertical or frontal plane, the horizontal plane and the sagittal plane.[4]

For the young child the frontal plane is all-important. It is grasped when the upright, vertical posture of the human being is achieved, so that the upright human being is now able to have different experiences of the front space and the back space. The child experiences the space in front quite comfortably, as the eyes can see what is there. The back space causes slight uneasiness in young children. While the front is explored through all forms of moving forward, movement into the back space is undertaken cautiously, or not at all, because in moving backwards one has to rely on the sense of hearing rather than vision. However, the child will eventually learn to trust in moving backwards. If the child does not succeed in finding a balance between both the front and the back space, insecurity and a fearful attitude towards life can develop.

In the process of incarnation many steps are already taken in the womb when the embryo and then the foetus practise elements of what will eventually be the complex posture of uprightness. According to Steiner, incarnation is a process of the spiritual human being descending and taking abode in the material substance of the body. Some of the primitive reflexes that are already present in the womb are images of the incarnation process, of contracting from the expanses of the cosmos into the small space of a body. The withdrawal reflex, which is activated when the foetus is touched, leads to the foetus curling up in a gesture of contraction. In contrast, the Moro reflex, activated when support under the head is withdrawn when holding the baby in a supine position, is a gesture of expansion or surrender, when both arms are moving sideways and outward.

The tonic labyrinthine reflex expresses contraction in bending forward and expansion in arching backward. The symmetrical tonic neck reflex expresses expansion in the wonderful upward stretch of head and arms while the lower body is crouching, contracting. Conversely, when the legs are extended and the bottom lifted up (expansion) the head is lowered towards the ground and the arms are bent (contraction), conveying an image of reverence.

Primitive reflexes supersede each other in sequence within the healthy development of movement and are steps towards achieving uprightness.[5] These unconscious, instinctive gestures are gradually replaced by willed movements. Yet on the level of the soul they will remain as the archetypal gestures of contraction and expansion, of withdrawal and openness, of devotion and surrender and as reactive gestures within the psychological repertoire of the individual. They are gestures of the incarnating ego filled with a mood which Steiner calls 'bodily religion'.

Sally Goddard Blythe's research into the phenomena of 'retained reflexes' and her therapeutic approach are based on the observation that all children go through the same sequential patterns of primitive reflexes. While these reflexes have an important role at a certain point of development, they become a hindrance for the healthy development of the postural reflexes and the mastery of willed movement if retained beyond their time.

Goddard Blythe has designed a developmental movement programme with the aim of helping to overcome these retained reflexes. In this therapeutic movement programme the sequence of reflexes is repeated through exercises in the order in which they would normally occur. The expected outcome is that these exercises cause the retained reflexes to disappear – as they would have under normal developmental circumstances.

Many therapists working in Steiner education use a programme of exercises – the so-called 'floor exercises' – which repeat the sequence of primitive reflexes as part of the Extra Lesson remedial programme for school-aged children, and sometimes also for kindergarten children. However, Audrey McAllen herself cautions that this remedial/therapeutic work should only be done with children older than seven years in order to allow the etheric forces the full seven-year period of early childhood for the completion of the development of the physical body and its organs.[6]

Through her work with learning difficulties in children Goddard Blythe has made some important discoveries about the superior role of the sense of balance and the vestibular system for the prevention and therapy of learning difficulties. As the sense of balance is part of the brain stem it is fundamental to any movement development leading to deliberate, purposeful movement. Therefore, in her therapeutic program, Goddard Blythe emphasizes the stimulation of the vestibular system, hearing and balance. She, as well as others, has been able to show clear benefits of music therapy programmes for children with movement disturbances and resulting learning difficulties.[7]

In 2004, Wibke Bein-Wierzbinski,[8] a former co-worker of Goddard Blythe, published a PhD thesis in which she could prove the effectiveness of a movement therapy that does not repeat the sequence of primitive reflexes. It is based, instead, on specific movements only, which according to her research play a key role in normal movement development. Bein-Wierzbinski questions programmes that build on the theory of repeating all stages of primitive reflexes. She suggests that a child may have overcome the primitive reflexes initially anyway, but at a later time and possibly under stress he may have returned to primitive reflex patterns. She suggests that all primitive reflexes may be present in an inactive state within the human being and that they can 'flare up' under certain circumstances.

Bein-Wierzbinski proposes that rather than repeating the whole sequence of primitive reflexes in therapeutic programmes, only certain key developmental movements should be practised. This is to avoid reinforcing movements other than those healthy movements that play a key role in achieving uprightness. She points out that these key movements reach a critical stage at around the age of four to six months. If they are mastered they will set the child on the track of subsequent normal development. Bein-Wierzbinski suggests that these particular movements should be practised and strengthened through therapy.

They are as follows:

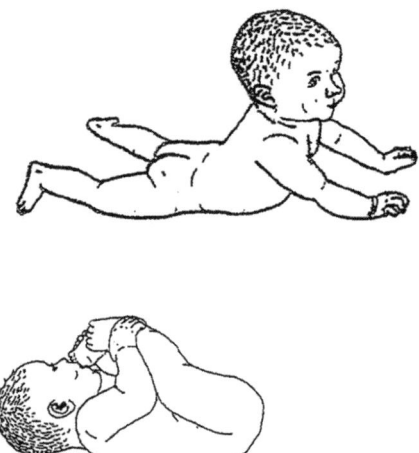

Extension–contraction movements around five months of age

1. First, the full body stretch as occurring naturally between four and six months of age. The back is straight, and legs and arms are straight as well. The head and the upper body are supported by the hands and by the legs from the hips downward.

2. Second, a movement with the opposite quality to the full body stretch: bringing both feet to the mouth with the help of the hands. The entire body is curled up.

Both movements together convey the image of an expansion–contraction polarity.

Bein-Wierzbinski was able to show that if these two movements are performed correctly and frequently then the process of becoming upright proceeds normally. She confirmed through her research the validity of a movement therapy program called 'Rota-Therapy', which has been developed by Doris Bartel and others in Germany. It is based on certain key rotational movements and avoids the repetition of reflexes.

Rota Therapy focuses on achieving relaxed movements of the spine, overcoming the arching of the back that signals retained reflex patterns. The critical step for the development of free deliberate movement is the shift from the head in leading rotational movement to the region of the lower spine and hips. This results in a rotational movement that makes the head free and independent from the movement of the rest of the body.

Rotational movements around six months of age

In Bartel's interpretation, retained reflexes are caused by a disturbance in the regulation of movement in the central nervous system, which leads to increased muscle tone and therefore limits the child's range of movement. In her therapeutic approach Bartel uses rotational exercises in all three dimensions of space. Her patients' histories show that these exercises lead to a change in the central regulation of the muscle tone and consequently to normal movement development.[9]

A set of movements is used which is based on variations of turning sideways and rolling over as they occur naturally in movement sequences of children in the first year of life – crawling, rotation, sitting, rotation to change direction, crawling in a new direction, rotation, sitting, and so on. According to experiences with Rota Therapy, the practice of rotation will lead to the alleviation of a whole range of developmental and learning disturbances. Rota Therapy is mainly done through enabling parents to practise movements regularly at home in consultation with the therapist. Currently there are movement therapists working with Rota Therapy in Germany and Austria.

Ingrid Ruhrmann[10] combines treatments derived from anthroposophical therapies with Rota Therapy for children who display retained reflexes among various other disturbances. She uses anthroposophical therapies to strengthen the etheric forces of the child – through water applications, nutrition and rhythm, for example – and complements these with the Rota approach for retained reflexes. It is worth noting that Rota Therapy for younger children can be given with the child sitting on the mother's lap. Thus the child experiences these exercises in close contact with the mother. Only the older child will practise the movements on the floor. Existing reflex patterns are diagnosed but are not part of the movement patterns of the therapy, as they are seen as hindrances to normal development.

Ruhrmann suggests indicators for normal development. At age two and a half the child should have achieved the following milestones:

- Upright posture; the child is able to stand still (balance).
- Free head rotation without causing either arms or legs to move.

- The head does not tip to the front nor is the neck extended towards the back.
- The arms swing freely while walking.
- Movement is intentional.
- The hands can be brought together at the vertical midline by will.
- The hands move freely in the horizontal plane, above and below the horizontal midline (butterfly).
- The speed and force of movement can be varied at will and adapted to different situations.
- The centre of gravity and the rotation point of the spine are in the hip area.
- The face is relaxed while moving, which means that the child does not spend extra effort in maintaining posture and balance.[11]

Uprightness and the ability to control and balance the movements of one's body are the foundation for all further differentiation and refinement of movement, including the work the kindergarten teacher wishes to achieve during morning circle. If uprightness and balance are not yet achieved at the time of starting kindergarten, the child will still be absorbed in gaining control over basic movements of the body. He will find it difficult to engage in imitating the gestures of the teacher and to take hold of all spatial dimensions in movement.

2. Movement in the realm of feeling: forming an active relationship to the world, discriminating and making judgements

Karl König links the ability to form an active relationship with the world to the development of movement of arms and hands, through which the child learns to discriminate what is around him. The arms and hands are freed from carrying the body and can thus be used to explore the properties of the world of objects. In exploring the space above and below, the arms act like wings, moving on both sides of the body above and below the horizontal midline, sensing the different qualities of the space above and below of the region of the limbs and head. Hands assist the child in making sense of the world through touching and identifying objects, through forming concepts and through responding inwardly to this experience with sympathy or antipathy. This discriminating faculty develops at a fast pace from the second year of life onwards, particularly in conjunction with the development of speech and play. Speech therapists have long known the important role which movement in general – but the movement of the hand in particular – plays in the process of the development and differentiation of speech.

However, speech development is dependent not just on the successful development of movement but also on the integration of movement with the activity of the senses – specifically with vision and the auditory system. The acquisition of speech needs the model of the speaking human being: the tone of voice, the colour of a particular language and the rhythm of speech. Goddard Blythe describes the link between speech development and the development of auditory capacities through the practice of music, such as choral singing. She indicates that music can play a decisive role in overcoming speech- and subsequent learning problems.[12]

In the context of the integration of sensory experiences and movement Wilma Ellersiek's work needs to be mentioned. Her rhythmical-musical hand gesture games arise from a spiritual understanding of the young child and provide an excellent educational and therapeutic tool for the development of speech and movement.

In her hand gesture games Ellersiek pays special attention to the integrating, balancing role of the rhythmical system and the development of the life of feeling in the child through the harmonious union of speech, singing and gesture. All her hand gesture games are of such a rhythmical-musical quality that they speak to the child's soul – not in an emotional way, but by allowing the child to experience the archetypal quality behind the natural world through the images created by gestures and words.

Ellersiek has distinguished three areas of activity:

1. The touching hand: touching games for limbs, body and head.

2. The playing and dancing hand: hand movement. Finger and thumb games, sometimes including word games and simple musical instruments.

3. The showing and telling hand: hand games through which little stories are told. The hands may take different roles and move to rhythmically spoken verses or song.

Ellersiek has emphasized the importance of the artistically precise performance of the hand gesture games by the kindergarten teacher. Rhythmical, harmonious movement is nourishment for the child's soul and should pervade all aspects of movement education in the life of a kindergarten.[13]

3. Right–left discrimination and the emergence of dominance

The third aspect in the development of movement is related to the sagittal plane – the axis of symmetry of the body or 'midline' – and to gaining awareness of right and left.[14] König names three preparatory steps for this achievement:

1. The first step is taken when the eyes of the child begin to look at an object and the gaze of both eyes meets in the act of focusing in the frontal plane.

2. The second step is achieved when both hands of the child are brought together at the midline of the body or sagittal plane and the child becomes able to grasp an object.

3. The third step occurs through the alternating forward movement of the left and right leg/foot when the child begins to walk. Initially this is a parallel action of both legs, alternating the movement of the feet in the right

field and the left field of the sagittal plane. Both feet and legs perform the same movements, yet with a time difference caused by the requirements of walking. Here we can perceive how the child enters into the frontal plane and the sagittal plane at the same time.[15]

The description of this three-step process can help when considering whether, when and how to work with the sagittal plane and right–left discrimination in the education of the young child. All through early childhood the child still continues to move both hands in a parallel manner. The independence of the hands from each other emerges very slowly. As this independence is a prerequisite for the crossing of the midline, a certain maturity of the action of both hands needs to be achieved before we can expect the right–left discrimination to emerge. This may be as late as the end of early childhood, or the first grades of school.

The final aim in relation to mastering movement in the sagittal plane is dominance,[16] in right-handed children usually defined as preference for the upper, right, front option within the three planes. Dominance is fully achieved only around the ninth year. This coincides with a major step in becoming conscious of oneself as an individual. At the age of nine, the child has reached the adult proportion of body height being the same as the width of the outstretched arms. In eurythmy lessons nine-year-olds can for the first time comfortably perform the exact cross-position, the gesture of the ego.[17] It is interesting that the child progresses from the pentatonic to the diatonic musical experience at the same time.

In early childhood right–left discrimination should be prepared gently. The child's consciousness should not be focused on which hand or leg to use. Most of the guided movements in the morning circle should be based on parallel movements of both arms and hands. Some parts of the circle for the older child can be directed towards preparing independent movement of the hands by using such images as nest and bird, pot and stirring spoon, cradle and baby, and so forth.

Part 2: Working with Movement in Early Childhood

1. Self-directed movement for the child under three

The development of movement, speech and thinking in the first three years of life is guided and protected by spiritual beings. In the early years the child seems to be guided 'from inside' and seems to 'know' intuitively what he needs to do: an endless and rich variety of movement combinations. Rudolf Steiner describes that the child needs to be left undisturbed at this early stage of development.[18] The unhindered exploration of movement is the precondition for the development of a sense of freedom in the human being.

The situation changes in the third year of life. At this time in the child's development, when the foundations for thinking have been laid and I-consciousness is stirring, Steiner recommends the benefits of eurythmy for gently guiding the child's natural inclination towards rhythm and movement. The child has reached a level of development where he not only unconsciously absorbs what lives in the environment but is eager to follow an adult who leads a movement sequence through example.

It needs to be emphasized that in work with children under three there is no need for the kind of structured movement programme used with three- to six-year-olds in Steiner kindergartens and preschools. Whenever one experiences circles in playgroups for toddlers, the circle seems mainly to serve the mothers' enjoyment and learning. In a group situation with children under three, be it in childcare or in toddler groups, the play area is the space for free movement and the child's playtime is the movement program.

The space needs careful preparation nonetheless, with provisions made for climbing, for exploring different heights, and ways to get up and down. It is a space for practising a variety of movement skills. The adult accompanies the child's explorations with warmth and love and, as much as possible, without interference with the child's will.

The previously-mentioned research of Goddard Blythe on the importance of vestibular stimulation in the very early years should be taken seriously in work with young children.

Intuitively, mothers have always stimulated the baby's vestibular system through rhythmical, soothing movements. Later the child is rocked on the lap to the rhythms of nursery rhymes.

On achieving the upright position the child delights in being rocked more vigorously backward and forward, sideways or up and down in a seesaw-motion. Swinging up and down or being whirled around will stimulate the organ of balance. As of the third year of life the child will find pleasure in rolling in the grass, in jumping and sliding, sitting on a swing, or turning and spinning in the upright position. Many of the traditional outdoor games are beneficial for vestibular stimulation. It seems that being outdoors for part of the day is conducive for gaining control over the movement system. The outdoor environment also seems very suitable for adapting the rhythm of times of activity, play and rest to children's individual needs. The first three years is the prime time for children to become confident in their bodies and to develop a healthy sense of self. However, self-directed movement has a place in the child's play throughout the time of early childhood.[19]

Movement play. St. Kilda Pre-School. Photo by Paulene Hanna

2. Guided movement with children from the third to the seventh year

From the age of two and a half the child displays an increased natural desire to participate in group activities. The child is filled with interest in what happens around him, enjoys social experiences and imitates the teacher out of an innate desire to do so.

Kindergarten teachers work with this natural desire. Steiner indicates that adults imprint their way of doing things into the malleable physical organs of the young child by way of imitation. Hence he attaches great importance to the quality of the gestures that adults perform in the presence of young children. In the early years these gestures enter into the physical body of the child more deeply than the spoken word or singing.

We can observe several stages in the process of imitating movements: from the purely inward movement that may show itself only in the facial expression, to the small, occasional hand movement, and then to movement that involves the whole body of the child. The impulse to move lives much more strongly in children than in adults. It is an expression of the strength of the child's will forces and of his healthy etheric forces.

Yet despite this activeness in movement the consciousness of the child is still dreamy and the healthy young child is not yet self-conscious of the quality of his own movement. The three- to four-year-old child naturally has no desire for self-expression but moves in an attitude of sympathy for his surroundings. Therefore his movements have a devotional quality. By participating in guided movement, the element of devotion and sympathy can be strengthened in children and counteract the tendency towards becoming self-conscious too early. For when the child becomes self-conscious of his movements, it can stifle his natural vitality and will forces. A self-critical element creeps in. The child compares his own achievements with those of others and may say: 'I can't do it.'

Kindergarten eurythmy, as well as the daily morning circle based on imitation, lead the child away from self-feeling towards an interest in and a feeling for what is happening around him. This can be supported by working with the feeling quality of language, of vowels and consonants, and with the rhythm and the musical quality of words and sentences. This will lead the child into the realm of feeling as well – but this time into feeling for the beauty of language, which frees the child from being centred on his own feelings.

Today there is an increased interest in working with children through speech, following on from the work with movement described previously. Stephen Spitalny has presented some preliminary thoughts on this.[20] In early childhood education the deliberate use of the sounds and rhythms of language is still in its beginnings.

Wilma Ellersiek has done pioneering work in this field. Her work makes a wonderful case for supporting the development of the ability to discriminate in the child which Karl König has described in connection with hand movement and the development of feeling (see Part 1 of this chapter). Ellersiek's hand gesture games carry the cultural impulse of refining speech and movement, of becoming sensitive to the subtle variations in rhythm and tone of speech in unity with appropriate movements of arms and hands. Thus movement and speech become helpers in developing the fine aspects of humanness, in 'moving with soul'. The child can develop a strong will and confidence through self-directed movement, but thinking and feeling, which refine movement and bring it into relationship with archetypal forms of nature and of human action, have to be brought to the child through the example of the adult and through imitation.

In addition, the hand gesture games can assist incarnation into the body, as described previously. Many hand gesture games are based on the archetypal movements of expansion and contraction and will be of help to the incarnation process of the ego into the body. Eurythmy, in its educational and curative form, has always worked with the harmonizing and balancing quality of the archetypal movements of expansion and contraction.

In educational work, expansion and contraction movements can be practised in a variety of games based on the opening and closing of the hand. Later on, the entire body can be involved through movements such as curling up and stretching high, or through moving between the centre and periphery. Wilma Ellersiek's hand games are a wonderful help for working with the young child towards a harmonious interplay between these two poles of human existence.

3. Archetypal movements and their relevance in movement with children

Experiences of archetypal movement remain relevant for movement work with children up to the end of early childhood. They are 'archetypal' in that they evoke the experience of the essence or quality of an object, process or being within the human soul. All 'expansion and contraction' movement variations are archetypal, as is the experience of breathing in and breathing out. For spatial dimensions there are the archetypal experiences of 'above and below', 'front and back' and 'right and left', which evoke very different sensations within the soul.

The most important archetypal experiences in early childhood are those which relate to the front space and the polarity of above and below. To support the exploration of the front space the kindergarten teacher can work with different ways and paces of walking, running, skipping and coming to stillness. A cautious, occasional step into the back space may be taken to encourage the child's use of his sense of balance and hearing.

When working with the modes of breathing in (tension), breathing out (release) and the polarity of contraction–expansion, there are manifold images that lend themselves to express this polarity: opening–closing (performed with hands or as a group in a circle); going out–coming in (flying birds); lifting–pressing (the different walks of fairies or giants); jumping up and down (connecting with the earth's gravity); sleeping–waking, growing–withering, hiding–reappearing, and so on. The teacher must bring these experiences to the child in such a way that they speak to the soul.

In addition, more and more images are used that belong to the natural world and to human life and work. We can discover archetypal gestures in all realms of nature, the seasons, the weather, the plant world, the animal world. In the realm of the human being we can work with the gestures of care and love for other human beings, plants and animals.

One of the great benefits of guided movement is the way it can bring the rhythmical element back into a child's movement patterns. Children of today do not find their way easily into rhythmical, lively movement. Modern life has lost its rhythmical quality and children are surrounded by mechanically generated movements. They are drawn into imitating mechanical movements and get easily trapped in repetitive patterns. Through guided movement, through the images that speak to the child's soul, it is possible to invite natural liveliness and soul participation back into the movement of children.

Movement as activity of the human soul and spirit

Steiner describes movement as a spiritual process, which involves the three spiritual 'bodies' of the human being before movement becomes visible in the physical world: movement originates as intention in the I, is willed by the I, yet generally this intention remains unconscious in the act of moving. Steiner states that the I cannot convey the intention to move to the limbs directly, even though the I should be regarded as the final 'mover'. He goes on to say that movement appears first as inner movement through the activity of the astral and etheric bodies, which are the 'transmitters' of movement into the body. Through the astral body the intention of the I will take on the quality of interest in the soul. Through the activity of the etheric body, intention and interest receive the quality of life. In the act of becoming outer, visible movement the intention of the I is fulfilled and will as a process of inner and then outer movement reaches completion.[21]

When searching for an understanding of the origin of movement we need to take into account all four aspects of the process – the activity of the I, the astral, etheric and physical bodies. In modern psychology of movement this is not recognized.[22] The discovery that physical movement is preceded by the movement of the soul is Steiner's contribution to a spiritual psychology of movement.[23]

According to Steiner it is possible to move only physically, without the participation of the soul-spiritual members of the human being. In such a situation movement takes on a lifeless, mechanical character.[24] Kindergarten teachers can strive to protect the child from this tendency by imbuing their own movements with soul and life so that the child is able to absorb these qualities through imitation.

Karl König compares the activity of moving with that of performing music: the I is the musician playing the instrument of the body, and movement is the music that comes out of this process.[25] König's musical analogy describes the soul-spiritual quality of movement well and is the key to unlocking the mystery of movement. It is the soul and spirit who move the limbs and thus enable the individual signature of a human being to be imprinted onto the body. Learning to recognize this individual signature in the movement of children is both a task and a challenge.

In his lectures to teachers Steiner also characterizes the soul experience of moving as musical. What he means here is not the preconditions for movement to arise but its consequences for the soul. He indicates that the soul belongs to the realm of stillness and does not experience physical movement directly, but rather reflects movement as 'tone' in the soul. The movement that is in harmony with nature and the cosmos creates the most harmonious experience for the soul.

What is 'cosmic movement'? It is the rhythms and patterns of the movements of the stars and the earth. They are expressed through gestures and movements in order to let archetypal cosmic qualities be experienced by the human soul.

> Our purpose is to imitate, to absorb the movement of the world into ourselves through our limbs. What do we do then? We dance … All true dancing has arisen from imitating in the limbs the movement carried out by the planets, by other heavenly bodies or by the earth itself. The head rests and the soul, being related to the head, must participate in the movements while at rest. It begins to reflect from within the dancing movement of the limbs. When the limbs execute irregular movements, the soul begins to mumble. When the limbs perform regular movements, it begins to whisper. When the limbs carry out the harmonious cosmic movements of the universe, the soul even begins to sing. Thus the outward dancing movement is changed into song and into music within.[26]

Endnotes

1. *Reflexes, Learning and Behaviour*, Fern Ridge Press, Oregon, 2002; and *The Well Balanced Child*, Hawthorn Press, Stroud, 2003.
2. *The Extra Lesson: Movement, Drawing and Painting Exercises to Help Children with Difficulties in Writing, Reading and Arithmetic* (Fifth edition) Rudolf Steiner College Press. Fair Oaks, CA, 1998.
3. *Being Human: Diagnosis in Curative Education*, Anthroposophic Press, NY, 1989.
4. R. Steiner, *The Child's Changing Consciousness and Waldorf Education*, Anthroposophic Press, Hudson, NY, 1988, Lecture 2.
5. For more on this amazing sequence of primitive, transitional and postural reflexes see S. Goddard, *Reflexes, Learning and Behaviour*, chapters 1 and 2.
6. Originally Audrey McAllen's programme did not include these floor exercises. Neither did she recommend starting the Extra Lesson programme in the first seven years of life. 'Birth to Seven Years', in M.E. Willby (ed.) *Learning Difficulties: A Guide for Teachers*, R. Steiner College Press, 1999.
7. S. Goddard Blythe, *The Well Balanced Child*.
8. See www.paepki.de for references to available therapy and to the PhD thesis.
9. These few sentences do not give a full picture of Rota Therapy. There is a very informative article on Doris Bartel's website called 'Grundlagen' [Foundations], now available in English, see www.rota-therapie.de; Bartel has also published a book: *Der gesunde Dreh* [The Healthy Turn] (2009), which contains an overview of developmental disturbances, the principles, aims and areas of application of Rota therapy, as well as case histories. The actual exercises are not described as they need to be adjusted to a child's specific situation and can only be given by a trained therapist.
10. I. Ruhrmann, 'Examples for Remedial Support', in M. Glöckler, S. Langhammer and C. Wiechert, *Education – Health for Life*, Kolisko Conferences Publication, Dornach 2006.
11. For more detail see Ruhrmann 2006.
12. See Goddard Blythe, *The Well Balanced Child*, 2004, chapters 5 and 6.
13. W. Ellersiek, *Giving Love – Bringing Joy: Hand Gesture Games and Lullabies in the Mood of the Fifth, for Children Between Birth and Nine*, trans. K. Willwerth, WECAN Publications, 2003. In the meantime three more volumes have been translated and published by the Waldorf Early Childhood Association of North America.
14. See K. König, *Being Human*, chapter 4.
15. Like König, Goddard Blythe identifies three steps for mastering movement in the sagittal plane: focusing of the eyes; the ability to bring both hands together in the middle; and the ability to walk rhythmically (left/right swing).
16. König, chapter 4.

17 R. Bock, 'Gestalt und Gestaltwandel im 9. Lebensjahr' [Changes in the 'Gestalt' in the 9th Year of Life], *Medizinisch-Pädagogische Konferenz,* no. 28, 2004.
18 R. Steiner, *Soul Economy and Waldorf Education,* Anthroposophic Press, Spring Valley, NY, 1986, p. 105f.
19 I would like to acknowledge at this point the work of Helle Heckmann, who has pioneered the outdoor kindergarten in Steiner early education and has documented in publications and video presentations the importance of self-directed movement for the healthy development of children. See H. Heckmann, *Nøkken: A Garden for Children,* Nøkken, distributed by WECAN. There are recent DVDs available about the work of Heckmann, specifically also on the theme of movement.
See: www.waldorfearlychildhood.org.
20 S. Spitalny, 'Ringtime as Pedagogical Opportunity – Some Thoughts', *Gateways,* no. 30, 1996.
21 R. Steiner, *The Foundations of Human Experience,* Anthroposophic Press, New York, 1996, Lecture 4.
22 Goddard Blythe describes the superior role which music can play in alleviating learning difficulties, but she does not make the link to music as a soul experience, or to the spiritual dimension of movement. See *The Well Balanced Child* chapters 5 and 6 on music and the overcoming of learning difficulties.
23 Steiner on the child becoming upright and learning to walk: 'It is the soul who sets itself into relation to space and makes the body be upright.' In: *Spiritual Guidance of the Individual and Humanity,* Anthroposophic Press, Hudson, NY, 1992, Lecture 1.
24 Steiner indicates that the etheric body cannot participate in movement which is derived entirely out of the physical body. Then the movement of the etheric body does not occur and thus is unable to accompany physical movement. This will have serious consequences because the normal human condition of the etheric body mediating between the soul-spiritual human being and the physical organization is then disrupted. See *Curative Education: Twelve Lectures for Doctors and Curative Teachers,* Rudolf Steiner Press, London, 1972, Lecture from 26 June 1924.
25 König, *Being Human,* chapter 1.
26 Steiner, *Foundations of Human Experience,* Lecture 12.

7

Self-directed Play in Early Childhood: A Chance for the Child, a Challenge for the Educator[1]

Self-directed play is disappearing fast from early childhood all over the world. It is being replaced by 'play-based activities' that are initiated and directed by adults.

One or two generations ago, many children still lived in rural or suburban areas where they were able to play outside, away from the watchful eye of parents or teachers. They directed their play themselves, exploring the natural environment, collecting treasures, immersing themselves in their own world of imaginative play. Over time, and with increasing dangers and fears related to playing unsupervised outside, children have become more dependent on entertainment and activities that adults organize for them, be it within educational settings or at home. Today many early years educators observe an increasing inability in children to self-initiate play and to sustain it. A Swiss Steiner kindergarten teacher has spoken of a 'play famine' spreading all over the world: children cannot find their way into play and yet they are longing for experiences that are deep, nurturing and self-empowering.[2]

More than 80 years ago, Rudolf Steiner pointed to the importance of self-initiated play in young children, especially between the ages of three and six years: 'The way a child plays, especially at ages four, five and six, goes down in a certain way into the depths of the soul as a force.'³ However, such play is disappearing. Many children are unable to activate within their innermost being this truly individual activity. This play has to be facilitated by adults: adults who refrain from taking the lead or making suggestions, and who, through their calm presence, encourage children to let play arise out of themselves. Becoming a 'play facilitator' is a path of learning. The qualities of a play facilitator may be described as wonder, curiosity, sense of belonging, attentiveness, open-mindedness, trust in the child's abilities, listening and acceptance.

Self-directed play – more than learning about everyday life

The child takes play themes and sequences of play action (such as family play, animal play, shopping, cleaning) from everyday life. However, each child is unique and there are individual differences in the way a child reproduces what she has absorbed from her environment. Actions may be taken out of context. Sequences may be changed at any moment and thus appear as somehow not fitting into space and time. They seem to have arisen out of a dreamlike state of consciousness, as if following an invisible script from within. The young child is able to switch between everyday consciousness and this 'dream' consciousness. Whenever such dreamlike play is happening, the child will emerge from it with deep satisfaction.

Children's play in its original quality is characterized by:

- timelessness and presence 'in the moment';
- the phenomenon of 'flow', that is, the ability of changing play themes and transforming objects in the child's imagination without interrupting the play process;
- the absence of premeditated purpose and set goals in the child under five;
- the quality of attentiveness and the ability to live fully within the current activity/situation;
- a state of deep satisfaction at the end of the play situation.

A century ago, Rudolf Steiner pointed to the importance of self-initiated play for young children. He warned of the consequences of replacing such play with activities that are planned according to pedagogical intentions and influenced by the intervention of adults. His reasons for suggesting non-interference by the adult in respect to child-initiated play are based on a deeper understanding of play in relation to:

- the specific nature of play of children up to age five;
- the role of play in the development of the child;
- the role of play in the biography of the human being.

The nature of play

The urge to play occurs in young children up to the age of five with an elementary force comparable to the urge to eat and sleep. Rudolf Steiner likens it to the flow of a river. In the younger child play is not premeditated but arises out of the moment. The release of will through play action is a source of joy for the child. This joy is not linked to the achievement of a specific purpose. The child's satisfaction results from the process of playing, not from the end result.

The incentive to play derives from observations of people, objects and occurrences in the child's surroundings, and is carried by the child's innate faculty of imitation.

> Let us look at the kind of play that occurs in the youngest child from birth until the change of teeth. Of course, the play of such children is, in one respect, based upon their desire to imitate. Children do what they see adults doing, only they do it differently. They play in such a way that their activities lie far from the goals and utility that adults connect with certain activities ... The usefulness in and connection to everyday life are left out.[4]

Play is a form of wrestling with the material world, exploring its properties and learning about the effects one's actions can have on the environment:

In play the child experiments with external objects in order to find out whether or not they respond to his own activity, he generates an act of will. Through the way in which the external objects respond to the operation of the will, the child learns from life ... in a totally different way than normally follows from the influence of another personality and his pedagogical principles.[5]

Play and child development

On several occasions Steiner makes a distinction between the child's play before the age of five and after. Around this age a developmental milestone in the child's intellectual and verbal abilities is reached which enables the child to plan and direct her play more consciously. Play becomes premeditated, carried by certain ideas or themes. It therefore appears to have purpose, and loses its non-intellectual, more spontaneous quality:

> The way a child plays is most characteristic of the individual child before the age of approximately five. Of course, children also play after that age, but all kinds of other things will be mixed in and play no longer flows as completely from inner arbitrariness, if I may call it that.[6]

In consequence, there is less free exploring and experimenting and more orientation towards imitating the activities of adults, their social roles and social situations.

Steiner describes play before age five as intensely creative. This creativity is based on the inner mobility of the child in effortlessly changing and transforming play objects and situations. But this inner mobility will only come to full expression if the child's toys and materials allow multiple uses and thus lend themselves to the child's transformative activity. In this context Steiner speaks about the importance of providing suitable 'open-ended' toys, and the stifling effect of many commercial toys on the free flow of the child's imagination.

All through early childhood the child's play actions are based on imitation. However, it is more the gesture and the outer form of an activity that is imitated. The images and content appearing in play are usually not 'original' inventions of the child, but are triggered by experiences. It may seem surprising, but Steiner does not attribute an imaginative quality to the play of the young child in respect to themes and content. These are derived from influences working on the child from the outside. A close analysis of children's play will confirm this. The creativity of the child expresses itself in the characteristics of the sequencing in the play of a particular child, in transformational processes rather than in the play themes.

We can summarize Steiner's view on the developmental aspect of play by saying that he is realistic and unromantic about the themes and content of child's play. In his view, play is not an original creation, such as a work of art. This applies to the areas of story play and floor play in Steiner early childhood settings as well, the themes of which are often mistakenly attributed to the child's inner imaginative faculties. However, even though the content of play is taken from the environment and is not original, the quality of play being self-directed is the foundation for later creativity and also a source of present and future physical and emotional good health: 'What is gained through play activity stems fundamentally from the self-activity of the child, through everything that cannot be determined by fixed rules.'[7]

The role of play in the biography of the human being

According to Steiner the value of play has to be viewed in the context of an entire biography. Play, in early childhood, receives its deepest meaning through the fact that it is an expression of the spiritual individuality of a human being.

Using the image of the river once again, Steiner compares the role of play in the biography of an individual to the phenomenon of a river which, after its initial stages, disappears underground, continues to flow there, and reappears flowing above ground again further downstream. The flowing water in the riverbed he likens to the individuality of the child, which shows itself in self-directed play, but then, after the sixth or seventh year, disappears in this form to be replaced by other forms of activity. These serve the development of the child's intellect, social abilities and integration into society rather than being a direct expression of the child's individuality:

> The urge to play, the particular way in which a child plays, disappears and sinks below the surface of life. Then it resurfaces. But as something different, as the skill to adapt to life. There is an inner coherence in life throughout all its stages. We need to know this in order to teach children in the right way.[8]

> The child has a spiritual-soul activity that, in a certain sense, still hovers lightly, etherically over the child. It is active in play in much the same way that dreams are active throughout the entire life. In children, however, this activity occurs not simply in dreams, it occurs also in play, which develops in external reality. What thus develops in external reality subsides in a certain sense. In just the same way that the seed-forming forces of a plant subside in the leaf and flower petal and only reappear in the fruit, what a child uses in play also only reappears at about the age of twenty-one or twenty-two, as independent reasoning in gathering experiences in life.[9]

It is fair to say that Steiner was one of the first who, through his spiritual research, identified play as a spiritual activity and recognized its benefits for a human being's later life. The connection he drew between a childhood of play and subsequent skills to adapt to adult life appears ever more relevant in the light of increasing evidence linking the absence of self-directed play to an inability to cope with life and to an increased risk of delinquency.

The following model for understanding play, suggested by the author, may be helpful in recognizing and appreciating the extraordinary variety of children's play.

The six dimensions of play

Standing upright on earth, the human being is poised between six directional forces in space, each of which evokes a corresponding soul experience:

Above–below: Through uprightness the human being experiences the forces of thinking as being above, in the head; the forces of will activity and movement as below, in the lower part of the body.

Back–front: In the activity of standing or walking, the human being is taking hold of the front space; we can see what is ahead and confidently take the next step into the future. The back space is the direction from which we come. It is related to the past and therefore less accessible.

Right–left: Right-handed people experience the right side of the body – and specifically the right hand – as being more active and outward oriented, whereas the left side conveys more of an inwardness.[10]

The human being enters into these dimensions at birth, and, on completing the first seven years of life, is more or less well adapted to the conditions of spatial existence.[11]

In children, six different types of play are observable which can be related to these qualities. We might assume that the presence of all these types indicates a balanced development of play. However, in studying them we may also find that children's preferences and inclinations for one or the other type of play express their individual differences.

1. There is play in which the child actively explores the environment and forms mental representations of these experiences. The child develops thinking through the activity of the limbs *(direction: from below up)*.

2. There is play that specifically develops the coordination and dexterity of the limbs and the mastery of the body. The child's mental activity gradually gains control over movement and will activity *(direction: from above down)*.

3. There is play in which the child reproduces the roles and events of everyday life and in replaying social experiences builds an understanding of the social world *(direction: right–left, from the outer realm to the inner realm)*.

4. There is play in which the child expresses her inner life and sometimes also traumatic experiences. She balances her life of feeling through the release of such experiences in play *(direction: left–right, inner becomes outer)*.

5. There is play in which the child enters the world of images and archetypes, which are the heritage of humanity, and unconsciously reproduces those images in play *(experience of back space: what comes from the past is made present)*.

6. There is play in which the child invents something new, often in the area of constructing *(experience of front space: the future is brought into the present)*.

Play Type 1: Exploring, finding out about the world of objects

This is characteristic of very young children but retains its importance all through childhood. It influences the development of the brain as the physical foundation for thinking through coordination and refinement of the movements of limbs and hands. According to Rudolf Steiner this type of play is especially typical of the young child:

St. Kilda Pre-School, Melbourne.
Photo by Paulene Hanna

The child tries out, experiments with objects, tries whether this or that effect can be provoked by his own activity ... The child educates himself through life itself, not through another person. Nothing intellectual should be mixed in this play. The more the play is happening in the realm where things are perceived in their living quality rather than being intellectually understood, the better the play will be.[12]

Play Type 2: 'Physical play' involving the whole human body as the realm of experience

St. Kilda Pre-School, Melbourne. Photo by Paulene Hanna

This begins with the very first experiences of young children as they explore their bodies and play with hands and feet. Later it turns into the practice of developing physical skills. It is crucial for gaining self-confidence. Feeling good in one's own body is important for the later development of loving relationships with other human beings. In children between three and six years this play is known as 'rough and tumble'. Often there is not enough opportunity for positive and safe physical play experiences that are free from competitive elements. Not only does this type of play contribute to the development of movement and the mastery of the limbs, it also promotes a positive feeling towards self and others.

Play Type 3: Play as rehearsing roles and playing out themes of social life in family and society

St. Kilda Pre-School, Melbourne. Photo by Paulene Hanna

This is well known and documented in early childhood education as 'role play' or 'make-believe play'. All children engage in this kind of play if allowed the time and space to do so. It continues beyond early childhood into the early primary school years. It is a kind of preparation for the conventions and demands of life at a given time. What the child observes and experiences in her environment, she plays out and thus digests. Roles are imitated, rules negotiated, social skills practised. Educators value this play because it facilitates understanding about how everyday life works.

Play Type 4: Play as a healer

St. Kilda Pre-School, Melbourne. Photo by Paulene Hanna

Ever since the beginning of play therapy in the early twentieth century, play has been recognized and used for its self-healing capacity. It is one of the blessings of early childhood that children have an innate urge to play out what troubles them. Thus play can help to prevent children from developing a long-term emotional disturbance. This play 'from inside – out' needs time, a quiet space and an adult who can listen, accept and support whatever the child releases from within.

Often it will be possible for this play to happen in a group situation. However, children with severe trauma and attendant behavioural difficulties might need the opportunity for individual play in a one-to-one setting, be it at kindergarten, in a therapy room or at home, supported by the presence of an understanding adult.

Play Type 5: Playing stories

Human beings live in three different states of consciousness: in day-consciousness, dream-consciousness and sleep-consciousness. In young

Samford Valley Steiner Pre-School, Brisbane. Photo by author

children these states are not yet clearly separated. During storytelling, in play, or at other times when the child is more open to inner experiences than to sense impressions, children may slip into a state of dream-consciousness. Steiner states that children still partly live in the memory of their spiritual home. They are like travellers between two worlds. They possess an ability which adults can only know from the moment of going to sleep at night to waking up in the morning.

Because of this dream-consciousness children are drawn to stories of all kinds, and particularly to fairy tales, which preserve memories of soul experiences from times long past and images that match the child's dream-consciousness.

In Steiner kindergartens children experience the world of archetypal images through the fairytales they are told. These stories and their imagery reappear in the children's play. In the child's inner life they are transformed according to the child's individuality so that no two children ever hear the same story.

'Story play' does not feature as a play type in research on children's play. Either it is not seen to happen at all, or it is regarded as identical to role play and consequently not worthy of mention.[13] In Steiner education the inner connection of the young child to the cultural past is valued, and stories and fairy tales are an essential part of the curriculum and the daily rhythm. And so, on a daily basis, children re-tell stories in puppet plays using props, or they create their own variations of stories they have heard from the teacher.

This type of play is of great significance for language development as it lets children use speech creatively. It is also vital for the child's soul development because it allows children to experience and act out archetypal human situations beyond the limited range of everyday life experiences.

Play Type 6: Creating landscapes, places, patterns

St. Kilda Pre-School, Melbourne. Photo by Paulene Hanna

Creating out of nothing, inventing something new, is a superior human faculty. Children should be given the space and undisturbed time to create freely: to make landscapes and places where people or animals can live; to construct bridges, build towers or invent unusual devices, vehicles and tools.

Sometimes arrangements are created that resemble patterns found in ancient cultures. While they are not 'new' in a cultural sense, they are new for the children who create them, as they are unlike anything they have seen before. Creating rhythmical patterns with spiritual meaning is an ancient art form. Children delight in this activity. They create on the spur of the moment, using whatever they can find: pebbles, leaves, flowers, sticks, shells. In Steiner early childhood education these natural materials are readily available.

This type of play happens mostly on the floor and can become quite complex. At times it can involve large groups of children all creating a 'whole world' together, as a six-year-old boy once put it.

The aim here has been to bring to consciousness the many dimensions of play and to suggest that play is at its most human, individual and beneficial if all of its six aspects are acknowledged and nurtured equally.

> It is truly remarkable to see how the child's soul and spirit are active in free play. The element of thought has not yet been absorbed. And it is a kind of play which comes into being without any notion of use or practicality; it is the kind of play in which the child only follows what comes from within ... The way the child lives into play originates in the freedom of the child's soul, but only seemingly so. For when one observes more exactly, one will see how children incorporate everything they experience in the world they live in ... When one has sharpened one's powers of observation in this respect, one will no longer look upon play of this kind as something interesting, something which just happens in a certain phase of the child's life. One will put playing in perspective and view its character in the context of a total biography.[14]

Facilitating Play

The ability to facilitate self-directed play is not a natural gift but something that can and must be learned. Play facilitation is nothing new to Steiner early childhood educators. Steiner speaks about 'well-guided play' – not in the sense of directing, redirecting or extending play, but as the involvement of the teacher in her own work alongside the playing children. This leaves them free to either imitate the teacher or follow their own inclination in play. Play facilitation is a more recent term for accompanying children through observing and listening, and the endeavour to understand each individual child. This empathy has always been at the heart of the teacher–child relationship in Steiner early childhood education and finds expression in the practice of working with imitation and example. In this sense, early childhood educators who are trained and working within Steiner education are play facilitators and very conscious of the importance of allowing a child 'free rein' in play.

Observing and understanding play are the prerequisites for play facilitation. When speaking with teachers who practise play facilitation in Steiner early childhood education, what stands out is the reverence with which they approach the play of the child and their certainty that the process of play unfolds through its own momentum.

Even though play in which the child's inner being is active must be self-initiated and self-directed, there is still a role for the adult in providing an appropriate space and time for this play to unfold undisturbed. Just as a river needs the riverbanks in order to flow properly, so too does play need facilitation or, to use Steiner's word, guidance. The adult sets the conditions, but what is gained from play is achieved through the self-activity of the child. It is important to understand that 'guidance' does not mean that play becomes an adult-initiated or adult-directed activity.

What should educators do to guide children's play? Steiner's advice can be summarized as follows:

1. *Follow the child's lead*: 'The first great essential is to learn to deal with them [the children] lovingly, and lovingly give them only what their own beings demand.'

As the child follows the impulses from within her being, the play facilitator should attempt to find out what interests her then be inventive as to what toys and materials are offered for free use, and how.[15] These toys should be offered as possibilities only. They should be open-ended and suitable for multiple uses in play.

2. *Make an effort to understand* children's play as an expression of their individuality. How children play in the fourth, fifth and sixth year will sink down into the depth of the soul and become strength for later in life.

Look at children and try to understand what is individual in their play: try to understand the individuality of children playing freely until the change of teeth, and then form pictures of their individualities. Assume that what you notice in their play will become apparent in their independent reasoning after the age of twenty.[16]

3. *Do not intervene* in children's play unless there is a risk to the child or to other children. Steiner states that 'the real educational value of play lies in the fact that we ignore our rules and regulations, our educational theories and allow the child free rein.'[17]

4. *Work actively* in the presence of children at domestic and artistic tasks, and thus set examples for skilled and devoted working. What the teacher does is purposeful and useful for life in a particular educational setting.

5. *Trust* that children will, with open senses, absorb the nourishing, supporting qualities of the environment and the educator's work, and that they will meaningfully transform these qualities through their own will activity.

If self-directed play is nurtured and guided well, it will become a source of joy and satisfaction for the child and thus contribute to the child's physical and mental health both now and in the future.

Endnotes

1 This essay arose from lectures the author had given in the context of a research project on play in Steiner early childhood education, conducted by the author between 2003 and 2006. The full process and findings were published in 2010 by WECAN in the book *Supporting Self-Directed Play in Steiner/Waldorf Early Childhood Education*, New York, 2010.
2 M. L. Nüesch, *Spiel aus der Tiefe: Von der Fähigkeit der Kinder sich gesund zu spielen*, K2 Verlag, Schaffhausen, 2004.
3 R. Steiner, lecture from 24 February 1921, quoted in F. Jaffke, ed. *On the Play of the Child: Indications by Rudolf Steiner For Working with Young Children*, WECAN Publications, Spring Valley, NY, 2004, p. 26.

4 Steiner in *On the Play of the Child*, p. 22. For the aspect of play as a river and the urge to play see p. 25.
5 Ibid., p. 20.
6 Ibid., p. 21.
7 Ibid., p. 19f.
8 Ibid., pp. 25–26.
9 Ibid., p. 24.
10 It is not the place here to discuss left-handedness, where this experience is slightly different, but not totally the opposite.
11 Rudolf Steiner speaks about these dimensions of existence in *Mystery of the Universe: The Human Being, Image of Creation*, Rudolf Steiner Press, London, 2001, Lecture 1.
12 R. Steiner in *On the Play of the Child*, p. 19f.
13 It is interesting to see how different authors categorize play. Role play came to the attention of educationalists through Sarah Smilanski's work. Often play is described according to developmental phases and kinds of activity. Recently a publication by the Alliance for Childhood has named 12 types of play: large-motor play, small-motor play, mastery play, rules-based play, construction play, make-believe play, symbolic play, language play, playing with the arts, sensory play, rough-and-tumble play, and risk-taking play. It is unclear from the context what kind of considerations led to this classification. The 12 types of play seem to have been arrived at from three different viewpoints: from the developmental viewpoint related to motor skills, language and sensory development; from the nature of play activities such as constructing, make-believe, rough and tumble; from specific features of play such as making use of symbols, using art materials, taking risks. See *Crisis in the Kindergarten: Why Children Need to Play in School*, Alliance for Childhood, College Park, MD, 2009, chapter 7, p. 55. Available online at www.allianceforchildhood.org.
David Elkind (*The Power of Play*, Da Capo Press, 2007, p. 103.) has suggested a different way of looking at types of play. He suggests four types: mastery play which serves the building of concepts and which would resemble type 1 in this publication; innovative play, which resembles type 6; kinship play with focus on social learning, similar to what is called role play elsewhere; therapeutic play, which is similar to play 'from inside out', as it is called here. It is interesting that story play receives no specific mention in any of these publications, that it is not perceived as different from make-believe play or innovative play.
14 Steiner in *On the Play of the Child*, p. 57.
15 Ibid., p. 40.
16 Ibid., p. 24.
17 Ibid., p. 19. This relates only to the time set for 'free' play, not for the art experiences or domestic activities.

8

Art Experiences in Early Childhood Education[1]

Some general considerations

Following on from the considerations on the role of self-directed play and imitation, the question arises of how to transition from this way of learning in early childhood to learning based on instruction in primary school education. This is the step out of the dream consciousness of early childhood into the more awake state of consciousness of the child, taken in the seventh year.

Many educators observe with concern how modern society and the demands it places on the intellectual capacities of the child seem to wake children intellectually at an ever-earlier age. Steiner describes a developmental progression leading from the stage of imitation through the stage of imagination to abstract thinking. The time needed for this process is twice seven years, a period of growth and development which extends to the fourteenth year. However, none of the three abilities – imitation, free imagination and abstract thinking – arise suddenly on the completion of a seven-year cycle. Each step is prepared in the preceding cycle and arises through a process of gradual transformation:

- *Imitation* is already observable at the beginning of a child's life. According to Steiner, it is a gift which the child brings with him from pre-birth existence.

- The beginnings of *imagination* can be seen in childhood fantasy, in the transformative power of play.
- The beginnings of *thinking* are observable in the play of children and in their verbal communication long before the stage of forming abstract and independent thoughts.

What is the role of the arts in this process?

Artistic experiences such as music, sculpture, painting and drawing can be part of the life of the child as of the age of two or three if the child is given the opportunity to engage in them. Here the following questions arise:

- How should art experiences be introduced to the young child?
- What is the educator's role in this process? Should artistic experiences be a regular feature, or should the educator wait until the child begins to express himself artistically on his own initiative, similar to how the child begins to play?

Steiner early childhood settings generally have programmes that include painting, drawing, music, modelling, offered at certain times during the week. Even though self-initiated or self-directed play is valued as the most vital activity for the physical, soul and spiritual health of young children, the actual programme in Steiner early childhood centres is based on the duality of self-directed play of the child on the one side and teacher-initiated, guided experiences on the other.

In a recent publication from the Alliance for Childhood in the USA,[2] 'playing with the arts' is listed as one of 12 kinds of play in danger of disappearing. But is painting or drawing play? Is modelling play?

In the publication mentioned above, 'playing with the arts' is explained as follows:

> Children integrate all forms of art into their play, using whatever materials are at hand to draw, model, create

music, perform puppet shows, and so on. They explore the arts and use them to express their feelings and ideas.[3]

Is using art materials in play an artistic experience? How does one determine whether play becomes an 'artistic experience'?

In the recently-introduced Australian Early Years Framework (birth to five), the aspect of communicating through the arts is emphasized. Through the use of art materials (crayons, brush, paper, paint, clay, etc.), we are told, the child explores media through which he communicates his ideas and feelings.[4]

In Steiner early childhood education, offering artistic experiences would follow the principle of learning though imitation and example and thus include a role for the educator. As one of the 'Essentials of Waldorf Early Childhood Education'[5] Susan Howard includes 'creative, artistic experience'. But here artistic experience is described not as the child communicating ideas, but as the adult's endeavour to bring an artistic quality to the work she is doing in the presence of children, so that this quality can be imitated in the child's own activity. The adult's artistic creativity and aesthetic sense are seen as pivotal for preparing the way for the child's artistic experiences.[6] It may manifest in the aesthetics of the environment and play materials, in specific artistic endeavours, and in the aesthetic quality of domestic work.

Steiner describes what is required of the teacher in the following words: 'In order to become true educators, the essential thing is to be able to see the truly aesthetic element in the work, to bring an artistic quality into our tasks … . If we bring this aesthetic element, we then begin to come closer to what the child wills out of its own nature.'[7] Based on this, Susan Howard formulates the following key questions:

- Is the teacher engaged artistically in the domestic arts and work processes?
- Is the teacher herself engaged in creative artistic endeavours?
- How is creative, artistic experience of the child fostered through the furnishings and play materials of the kindergarten?[8]

When, in 1924, Rudolf Steiner was advising Elisabeth Grunelius on setting up the first Waldorf Kindergarten, she asked him about how to prepare for the task of being a kindergarten teacher. He replied that it was of vital importance to regularly practise some form of artistic activity.[9]

Anyone who has tried it will know the replenishing and balancing effect of practising an art. It is beneficial for both teacher and children if the teacher's forces are not drained and feelings are balanced. Steiner states that it is important for the teacher to cultivate an aesthetic sense and that we will soon notice how this enlivens the children.[10]

> By awakening an all comprehensive feeling for beauty, we can nurture their free development ... We ought to do everything to awaken and cultivate the sense of beauty, especially during the time between the second dentition and the coming of puberty.[11]

Moreover, it is good for children to observe the teacher not only engaging in domestic work but also practising and striving in the realm of the arts. They will then experience in real life situations how an adult wrestles with materials, form and colour, how an adult perseveres in playing an instrument or creating a piece of textile art.

The teacher's artistic striving and wrestling with materials has an effect on the child's exploration of materials in play. For example, a kindergarten teacher may have scheduled a woodwork project such as carving a boat or making wooden bowls for the doll's corner. Soon children will be imitating the teacher's chiselling, using sticks for tools. They imitate the will aspect of the activity, working away at their piece of wood with their sticks with the same serious engagement as the adult.[12]

> By watching how in children's play human nature pours itself in complete seriousness into the treatment of external objects, we can direct the child's inborn energy, capacity and gift for play into artistic channels. These still permit a freedom of inner activity while at the same time forcing children to struggle with outer materials, as we have to do

in adult work. Then we can see how precisely this artistic activity makes it possible to conduct education so that the joy of engaging in artistic activities can be combined with the seriousness of play, contributing in this way to the child's character ... Art will lead from the child's liberating play activity to the stage of adult work.[13]

This process begins with imitation. As Steiner points out, we need to recognize that in imitation, in all sense-directed activity, artistic impulses are at work that allow the child to respond in an entirely individual way.[14]

This holds true for teaching in the primary years as well:

The more joy the teacher can experience in beautiful forms, in music, the more he longs to pass from abstract works into the rhythms of poetry, the more of the plastic-musical there is in him, the better will he be able to arrange games and exercises that offer the child an opportunity for artistic expression.[15]

The process then reaches the final stage of engaging the will in life and work on the basis of the experiences of goodness and truth, mediated through the sense for beauty. These future stages are prepared in early childhood through observing the teacher who is able to incorporate an artistic element into her work, and imitating her actions.

Even though there is, according to Steiner, an unspoilt sense of beauty in each child, young children orient themselves on their parents' or teacher's sense of beauty with total trust in their aesthetic judgment. This applies as much to the choice and qualities of toys and materials as to artistic creations.

Aesthetic judgment and aesthetic preferences develop during childhood. They are influenced by the people close to the child, then modified later through other influences. Teachers will have developed their own subjective aesthetic sense of beauty, but this can in no way be the sole basis for decisions on the aesthetics of toys or the environment. Far more is involved in choosing toys and equipment than personal experiences of what is beautiful, pleasant, cute, pretty, satisfying and rewarding.

Therefore it would be wrong to give a child one of those exquisitely made, detailed 'beautiful dolls', even though they may well satisfy a teacher's subjective sense of beauty. A doll with lots of detailed features may prevent a child from setting his own inner powers to work. An unspoilt child will be much happier with a piece of wood, or with anything that gives his imagination a chance to be active.[16]

Simplicity in toys is what the child needs to engage his own power of fantasy. Simplicity in setting up a kindergarten room provides space for the child to create freely. Simple creative activities such as fluffing up wisps of wool, or making an animal from a ball of raw wool simply by pulling out ears or beak, will not only satisfy children's urge to make toys for themselves, but also engage their power of fantasy.[17] From a fairly young age onwards, children long to make things to play with, and in this way, too, we can bring the element of art into their play.

Simple toys ... Shan Mei Zhen Kindergarten, Taiwan

To lead play gradually over to the creation of artistic forms and then to work is to act in complete harmony with the demands of human nature. And it is interesting to find that the children's plastic, artistic activity turns quite naturally to the making of playthings and toys.[18]

Considerations in relation to specific arts

Sculpture and music are the two art forms with special relevance for early childhood because they are directly related to the two major spiritual forces behind the growth and development of the child: the formative forces, active in the process of building up the physical body, and those soul-spiritual forces Steiner calls 'musical forces', which are related to the activity of the astral forces and the will within the child. Both of these art forms help older children in the kindergarten to balance their will forces with the emerging power of thinking.

Formative forces and the art of sculpture

Steiner describes the etheric body, the centre of formative activity, as an inward artist and the child as an inner sculptor:

> This etheric body is pre-eminently an inward artist in the child in the first seven years; it is a modeller, a sculptor ... If therefore you as teachers have a wide knowledge of the forms that occur in the human organism, and consequently know what kind of forms the child likes to mould out of plastic material ... then you will be able to give him the right guidance. But you yourselves must have a kind of artistic conception of the human organism. It is therefore of real importance for the teacher to try and do some modelling himself.[19]

Long before the child begins to mould or scribble, he experiences, albeit unconsciously, the processes of organ formation within his body. Sculptural activity involves working with polarities: expansion–contraction, angular–spherical, concave–convex, horizontal–vertical, as well as with processes of inversion and transformation. The child forms intuitively, while the teacher silences her thoughts in order to sense rather than think about the formative sculptural forces at work in nature and the human being. Thus the activity of moulding becomes a process driven by will and feeling rather than by the intellect.

As processes of fine-tuning of organs are still continuing in young children, Steiner perceives the child as a natural 'inner sculptor', rather than an 'outer sculptor'. Creating recognizable objects belongs to the later part of early childhood, and the sculpting of figurines and animals commences only around the sixth to seventh year and develops more fully in the ninth or tenth year.

The process of modelling starts in the horizontal plane and only gradually includes the vertical dimension. If provided with a wooden board and a soft piece of beeswax, the young child will begin by breaking off and scattering little lumps of beeswax all over the board. Gradually, after many 'chaotic' creations, patterns will appear: strings of lumps, piles, enclosures – all still mainly in the horizontal plane. A little later, cylindrical shapes may be created, first pressed flat on the board, then lifted up into the vertical. Several of these 'columns' may form a space reminiscent of ancient cultic sites, or be bent to create semicircular ornamental patterns. Eventually, forms resembling the human being will emerge, either by adding 'limbs' to flat-lying circles (heads), or created from cylindrical shapes.

We can observe how this development in children's sculpting coincides with a similar development in their drawing. It thus seems to make sense for Steiner to say that drawing emerges from the realm of activity of the sculptural forces.[20] 'It is the up-welling forces we employ then when we develop writing out of drawing, for what these forces really strive for, is to pass over into sculptural formation.'[21]

This purely intuitive modelling of the young child will gradually develop into a sculpting process that is based on observation. 'If the child is to learn to observe aright, it is a very good thing for him to begin, as early as possible, to occupy himself with modelling, to guide what he has seen from his head and eyes into the movements of fingers and hand.'[22]

Regarding the pedagogy of modelling with young children, Michael Howard has made some excellent suggestions,[23] including that modelling should arise more naturally as part of self-initiated play rather than as a structured group activity. Reviewing the ongoing professional debate on what medium to use, he suggests that besides the beautifully refined, warm and soft beeswax children should also model with materials they would find in their free outdoor play: mud, sand and clay. Also during outdoor play, modelling occurs best as an individual rather than a teacher-initiated activity. However, the time, place and materials for experimenting with the element of earth need careful consideration by the teacher. Modelling materials should be offered in their natural colours, as multiple colours will distract the child from the actual activity of moulding.

Musical forces and the 'Mood of the Fifth'

Throughout early childhood, soul-spiritual forces envelop the child, forming a sheath through which the child is united with the souls of the people closest to him. Part of these soul-spiritual forces have also been at work within the child in the process of learning to speak, and subsequently remain within the child, especially in the lower part of the body. Steiner calls these soul forces 'musical forces'. Musical forces are connected with the will nature of the human being. We can perceive their effects in the movements of the child, specifically in the young child's physical response to rhythm and beat.

According to Steiner there are powerful forces at work which should be left alone during early childhood.

> These other forces come from outside. Forcing their way through the sculptural forces and descending into the organism, they co-operate in what takes place, beginning with the seventh year, in the building up of the child's body. I can characterize these forces in no other way than as those active in speech and in music. They are forces of a musical nature, which we take up from the outer world.[24]

In perceiving tones and music the human being is able to form a connection not only to the natural and human environment but to the spiritual realm as well. When singing, for example, we may have the experience of the body acting as a musical instrument, the tones resounding through it as if the human being were an instrument for the music entering from somewhere else.

A single tone, melody and harmony are experienced within the whole human being: body, soul and spirit. The ear is the organ that receives the tone, but the actual experience of tone arises within the human soul. As Steiner puts it, the ear is a 'reflecting apparatus for the sensation of tone': the actual musical experience occurs within.

The experience of music within the body is closely linked to the system of movement in the lower body. Steiner points out that the musical element, being related to the human limb system, can pass over into dance. This holds especially true for the young child: 'The musical element that lives in the human being from birth and that ... finds particular expression during the third and fourth years as an inclination to dance, is inherently a will element carrying life within it.'[25]

These musical forces of the lower body exert such a strong influence on the child that he may be unable to control the resulting rhythmical movements of his limbs. Early childhood educators know from experience that music with a strong, pounding beat has such an effect on young children that they can move themselves into a frenzy and throw the entire group into chaos.

What kind of musical experiences should be brought to young children?

Some important principles of early music education in Steiner early childhood education:

- Music should be brought to the young child gradually, in accordance with the process of incarnation.
- Music should meet the child's natural liveliness but also bring order to the child's will forces.
- Music and the world of tone should be introduced to the child through singing and the element of melody, not through harmony or beat.
- Care should be taken to protect the child's natural fine perception of tone from exposure to harsh, loud sounds and to avoid strain on the vocal chords caused by loud and low singing.

Musical education has to take into account the nature of consciousness in the child's early years. Much of the Steiner curriculum is based on Rudolf Steiner's insight that the development of consciousness in each individual child mirrors the development of the consciousness of humanity. In different cultures and at different points in time the experience of musical intervals evoked different soul experiences in human beings. In his work on the evolution of music,[26] Steiner tells how in ancient times, music based on the interval of the seventh would have brought about a spiritual out-of-body experience. Later on, the interval of the fifth would have been experienced as surrounding the physical human being. As of the Renaissance, the interval of the third, which has since dominated Western music, would call up an inward experience in the human being.

The interval of the fifth has played a major part in the traditional music of parts of Asia, and in the form of pentatonic music it was the major musical experience in Greece and then in Europe all through the Middle Ages.

What Steiner calls the 'mood of the fifth' and recommends for the musical education of young children is based on elements of the early pentatonic music. It is characterized by the absence of harmony, musical scales and triads, which are so prevalent in post-medieval music. Melodic patterns move around a central tone rather than a base note or tonic, and songs are experienced as open, light, joyous and emotionally neutral: neither sad or melancholic nor exuberant.

As a result, songs in the mood of the fifth have qualities that match the developmental stage of the young child. Young children are still in the process of taking hold of their bodies, of incarnating. The inner life of the soul is still undeveloped. We could describe the situation of the child as being spiritually between heaven and earth. Music based on the interval of the fifth mirrors this in-between stage, whereas music based on scales with emphasis on the tonic conveys a more downward, earthly quality.

Steiner suggests that songs in the mood of the fifth should be part of musical education up to school age, or even up to age nine: 'Though it is not readily admitted, the child essentially dwells in moods of fifths. Naturally, one can resort in school to examples already containing thirds, but if one really wishes to reach the child, musical appreciation must be based on the appreciation of fifths; this is what is important.'[27] Steiner has only given brief indications on the importance of the mood of the fifth, but since his day, musicians have developed his ideas. Not only have they created songs for young children in the mood of the fifth, they have also developed and worked with instruments such as the children's lyre, which conveys the quality of free floating, objective tone. The tone of the lyre fills the surrounding space but does not put demands on inwardness of soul, a quality not yet developed in young children.[28]

Moreover, early childhood educators have understood that the mood of the fifth is not limited to musical experience as such but characterizes the entire atmosphere that should prevail around young children so that they are immersed in the qualities of this musical mood.[29]

As already mentioned, for the young child music and movement belong together. Beat and rhythm are the elements of music that the child experiences most strongly. The element of beat can have such an impact on the will of the child that it leads to an uncontrollable urge for frantic movement.

Lyre play. Samford Valley Steiner Pre-School, Brisbane. Author's collection

Rhythm is very different. Acccording to Steiner one has to use the musical element in teaching from an early age, but one should look more at the liveliness of rhythm rather than the content of music. With that one will establish a good foundation for the strength of the will.[30]

Melody, with its rhythmical flow, is the main means of musical education in early childhood, and the human voice is the main instrument. Thus singing and movement belong together: the rhythmical flow of song speaks directly to the child's will, and by focusing on the ever changing rhythm rather than the repetitive element of beat, the will can become harmoniously engaged without getting overexcited. In order to provide such experiences the adult needs to cultivate a singing voice as well as learn to work with the child's natural urge to move and dance.

> The musical element that lives in the human being from birth and that ... finds particular expression during the third and fourth years as an inclination to dance, is inherently a will element carrying life within it. Yet strange though this may sound, in the way it expresses itself in the child to start with it carries life too strongly, life that is too stunning and easily benumbs consciousness. This strong musical element very easily brings about a certain dazed state in the child's development. Therefore we have to say: The educational influence we exert by using the musical element must consist in a constant harmonizing ... something that is alive in the highest degree in the musical element has to be damped down so that in music it does not affect the human being too strongly. – This is the feeling with which we ought to bring music to the children.[31]

Since the early days of Steiner kindergartens these recommendations have been applied in the work with movement, song and speech in the daily morning circle, and also in the weekly eurythmy session provided by a trained eurythmist.

When singing with young children, the simplicity of song is important.[32] Simple melodies based on two, three or five tones are most appropriate and, provided they have a lively rhythm, the child will not get tired of them.

Steiner emphasizes that teachers must perform songs well. The quality of the teacher's singing voice is important because the child at this age is an imitator. It will make a difference whether the child hears a pleasant sound, a tone sung with ease and lightness or a tone forced out from stressed vocal cords. Not that teachers have to be singers, but they do need to be sensitive to using the appropriate pitch (higher than the average adult pitch) and to matching the lightness of children's voices. A teacher's voice needs to sound softly so that young children, who are imitators, do not strain their own voices and thus damage their vocal chords.

> To begin with, in the first seven years of life, the child learns everything by imitation, but then the child should learn to sing out of the inward joy experienced in building up melodies and rhythms ... You must have the feeling that, while singing ... every single child is a musical instrument and inwardly senses the pleasant feeling of sounds. [33]

The daily singing should be valued by the teacher as practising an art and should serve no other purpose than the experience and enjoyment of music.

Music is not a means for enticing children to do something they may not want to do, such as tidy up, come in from outside, or follow rules. In such cases the spoken word would be more appropriate. There is a difference between a song sung before story time in order to settle children and a song that captures the essence of a story just told and thus concludes story time. There is also a place for songs that prepare the child inwardly for the next step to come, or a song of grace at the beginning of a meal. There is a fine line between using music for purposes foreign to its nature and letting it take its rightful place as an art through which a mood appropriate for the education of the young child is established.[34]

Radiance of colour

The art of clothing

It might seem strange to mention clothing in the context of the arts. Yet colours in the environment, on fabrics and clothes, create deep impressions in young children long before they meet colour through painting or drawing.

Brightly coloured objects draw the attention of young children, and even babies, who regard them intensely. This attraction to colour should awaken in educators a sense of responsibility with respect to choosing which colours should surround the child.

In ancient cultures there was nothing arbitrary or meaningless about colour. In determining colours of clothing it was self-evident that people wore what corresponded to themselves, to their religion or place in society. According to Steiner, the joyous colourfulness of traditional clothing points to a special relationship to the gate of birth through which the human being enters this world. The love of colours still mirrors the spiritual world, and the way of dressing still expresses memories of a person's spiritual image.[35]

Later on in time, clothing and colour became a means of expressing the soul-spiritual qualities of a human being.

How does the enjoyment of colour manifest in young children? Children:

- show interest in and preferences for certain colours at kindergarten age;
- are attracted to radiant colours – in clothing as well as in drawing and painting;
- love to dress up. At times quite individual colour choices occur;
- comment on the clothes and colours a teacher is wearing;
- are attracted to sparkling jewellery, to gold, silver and the colours of precious stones;
- are fascinated by puppet shows. Next to the movement of the puppets, it is the colour symphony created by the teacher that speaks to the child.

Steiner describes colour as the bridge between spiritual light and earthly darkness.[36] The loss of the experience of the radiance of light and colour is part of the incarnating process. In the colour realm this is expressed in brown, which is not part of the radiant colours but has an earthly quality. Brown is used in the garments of monks, where it expresses human striving and virtue.

Steiner's comments should be of interest to kindergarten teachers. While there is no specific mention of appropriate colours for teachers to wear, we can work from the young children's affinity with the radiant colours, those colours which are closest to the light, to the colours of the rainbow.

Thinking about colour choices in this light may awaken consciousness regarding the colours not only of teachers' clothing but also of play equipment, materials and toys. The colours of the earth need to be present here, but also the colours of light. It is the task of the educator to find the right balance between both groups in the environment of the child.

In modern times, adults' clothing has become an expression of who a person is as an individual. Yet personal colour choices should be harmonized with the young child's affinity with the radiant colours, and also with the need of the young child to be protected from sensory overload by very bright, glaring colours so prevalent today in children's clothing and toys.

The enjoyment of colour also plays a role in handcraft in the kindergarten. Choosing materials or yarns from well-sorted baskets of multi-coloured cloth and thread can be a real feast for a young child. Coloured wisps of wool used for simple craft have the same effect. We could describe the early stages of handcraft as pure enjoyment of colour and texture, be it with respect to objects directly found in nature, or refined materials such as wool for felting, dyed fabric and silk.[37]

Steiner does not offer any advice about how to provide painting and drawing experiences for young children. He states, though, that painting and drawing *lessons* should begin at a very tender age.[38] No Waldorf kindergartens existed during Steiner's lifetime, and the situation did not arise for him to advise on specific areas of the kindergarten program. The content and form of early education has been a work in progress ever since the first Waldorf kindergarten started. It was Elisabeth Grunelius who described in detail the routines of a painting session. It is unclear whether these routines arose from her conversations with Rudolf Steiner in his last years of life, before she started the first Waldorf kindergarten in 1926. In any case, some of her suggestions as to how to conduct painting with young children are still used in Steiner kindergartens today.[39]

It is a natural consequence of imitation's importance in early childhood that painting should be based on imitation and the example of the adult. Here Steiner stresses the need to introduce real art – that is, the teacher must paint in earnest and not only for the purpose of demonstrating techniques.[40] Margrit Jünemann notes that painting is just as much a part of kindergarten life as domestic tasks such as baking, washing or cleaning.[41]

For adults, as well as for children, the main purpose of painting is to encounter and enjoy colour. Young children paint with great enthusiasm and give themselves wholly to the colour appearing on their paper. A brush of blue on the paper, and the child is the blue.[42] Thus colour evokes a strong experience within the child. The quality of the paint, the shades and hues of colours, need careful consideration and preparation by the adult.[43] In relation to children's experience of painting, Jünemann cautions against correcting anything that children do at kindergarten age, 'for they learn best if they do not have their conscious attention drawn to what they are doing'.[44]

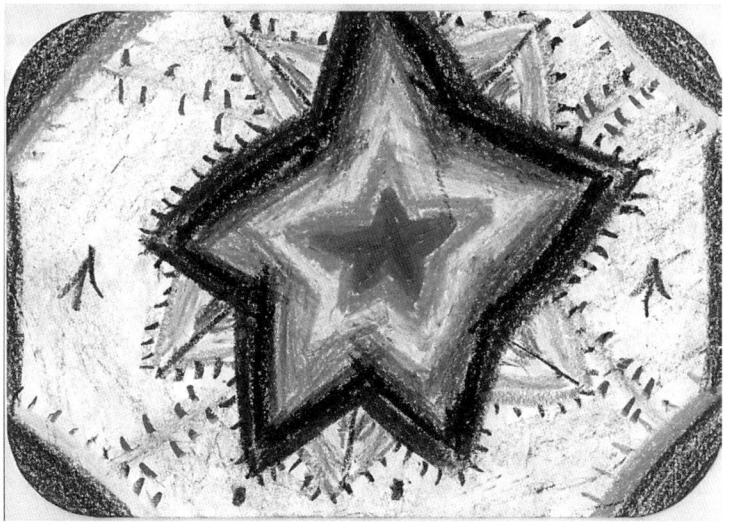

From Samford Valley Steiner Pre-School, Brisbane.
Author's collection

When we lead children to the experience of colour and set the mood for this activity, we should remember the importance of the preparation phase, as well as the tidy-up afterwards. Thus the colour experience forms the centre of a longer process in which the children are inwardly and outwardly prepared. There is much opportunity here for imitation and the children's active involvement.[45]

Enjoyment of colour also plays a major part in the activity of drawing. Presented with a beautiful selection of clean crayons from the spectrum of rainbow colours, the child's enjoyment begins even before reaching into the basket and taking hold of a crayon.[46] The enjoyment of colour is also recognizable in the richly coloured pictures that children are able to achieve with regular drawing experience.

Drawings by young children have become a diagnostic tool for developmental assessment rather than being valued as artistic experience. This is especially true for older children and the transition to school. In interpreting children's drawings the focus is on the details, the representation of objects and the overall composition. Within the assessment context, colour becomes a diagnostic indicator for temperament and psychological issues.[47]

This makes sense, given that Steiner describes the forces used in drawing – and later in writing – as will-forces seated in the lower body. We can expect drawings to tell us something about the soul-spiritual forces in relation to the physical body. Painting, especially with the wet-on-wet technique, is pure experience of colour. Drawing, on the other hand, has a component of formative activity, a kind of relationship to growth forces, so it is reasonable to look for clues about the developmental process in children's drawings. Michaela Strauss has pioneered research in this field,[48] which has led the kindergarten teacher Inger Brochmann to the discovery that children can even express in their drawings the state of specific organs in times of illness.[49]

Rudolf Steiner points to drawing as being a free activity, similar to play: 'The child's drawing is a kind of play, but while engaged in it, he is also communicating. We shall gain a real understanding of the child's drawing if we look upon it as a means of his communicating with the world. The child wants to tell us something about himself.'[50]

What is the child communicating? According to the general view in mainstream education, the child communicates ideas and feelings through art. Research in Steiner education has revealed that children's drawings communicate how the child lives and feels within his own body. Through his drawings the child communicates about bodily processes of which he is only dimly aware, and which he would never be able to describe in words. The child also expresses his relationship to other human beings, especially family, and to nature and the spiritual world.[51]

Steiner points to the benefits of drawing for the child's later years: 'What does a child really do when, up to the change of teeth, he draws pictures in a playful way? He is actually developing something which, later on in his twenties will mature into faculties of intelligence for using life experiences. These qualities are being developed through the ever-changing forms of his drawing activities.' In using and taking hold of the forces of will – and drawing is one way of doing this – the powers of comprehension will be enhanced, 'even if it be the still dormant and playful intellect of the young child which expresses itself in two-dimensional drawings as a means of communicating with the world'.[52]

In conclusion

Looking back to the questions posed at the beginning of this chapter about how artistic experiences can become part of early childhood education, we need to acknowledge that different approaches suit different art experiences.

Firstly, we should encourage teachers to become artists themselves: artists in how domestic work is done in the presence of children; musicians, painters, sculptors, craftspeople, pursuing their work under the watchful eyes of children.

With respect to children engaging in the arts themselves, no art experience should impinge on the time the child needs for play.

Modelling and drawing are experiences which we can expect to unfold best as part of self-initiated play.

Music based on the experience of the mood of the fifth, and connected with movement, needs to be brought to the child by the teacher and is an experience shared with the group.[53] However, the beginnings of experimenting with simple instruments and sounds of natural materials such as wooden sticks or copper rods can also become part of the child's self-initiated exploration in play.

Colour experiences through painting and simple handcraft need the example given by the teacher. They are not part of play but rather offered at a different time during the day or the week. Through the enjoyment of colour and form, these experiences will nurture the soul of the child and build a bridge from play through art experience to formal learning.

Endnotes

1. This chapter relates to a selection of art experiences only. Considerations are offered for modelling, music, drawing and painting. Considerations on eurythmy or storytelling, which are important in relation to early childhood practice as well, are made in: E. Bryer, *Eurythmy for the Young Child*, WECAN Publications, Spring Valley, NY, 2005; N. Mellon, *Storytelling with Children*, Hawthorn Press, Stroud, 2000.
2. E. Miller and J. Almon, *Crisis in the Kindergarten: Why Children Need to Play in School*, Alliance for Childhood, College Park, MD, 2009. Available online at: www.allianceforchildhood.org.
3. Miller and Almon, *Crisis in the Kindergarten*, p. 65.
4. *Belonging, Being and Becoming. The Early Years Learning Framework of Australia*, 2009. Available online at: http://www.earlychildhoodaustralia.org.au/resource_themes/eylf/eylf_early_years_learning_framework.html.
5. In: *Mentoring in Waldorf Early Childhood Education*, WECAN, Spring Valley, 2007, p. 15ff.
6. This is also the direction taken by M. Howard in the chapter on modelling in early childhood in his book. *Educating the Will*, Association of Waldorf Schools of North America, Fair Oaks, CA, 2004.
7. R. Steiner quoted from Susan Howard, 'Essentials of Waldorf Early Childhood Education', in *Mentoring in Waldorf Early Childhood Education*, p. 18.
8. Ibid.
9. 'How Do I Prepare Myself to be a Teacher of Young Children?' Photocopy of notes by H. v. Kügelgen.
10. R. Steiner, *Soul Economy and Waldorf Education*, Anthroposophic Press, Spring Valley, NY, 1986, p. 253.
11. Ibid., p. 254.

12 As a kindergarten teacher I have practised this many times following the suggestions by F. Jaffke, published in *Wir gestalten mit Holz für Kinder*, Verlag Freies Geistesleben, Stuttgart 1998.
13 R. Steiner in F. Jaffke, ed. *On the Play of the Child: Indications by Rudolf Steiner For Working with Young Children*, WECAN Publications, Spring Valley, New York, 2004, p. 28.
14 R. Steiner, *The Child's Changing Consciousness and Waldorf Education*, Anthroposophic Press, Hudson, NY, 1988, p. 82.
15 R. Steiner, *A Modern Art of Education*, Rudolf Steiner Press, London, 1972, Lecture 7, p. 127.
16 Steiner in *On the Play of the Child*, p. 40.
17 D. Dolder, 'Handwork in the Kindergarten', in J. Almon ed. *What is a Waldorf Kindergarten?* WECAN Publications, Spring Valley, NY, 2009, p. 20f.
18 Steiner in: *A Modern Art of Education*. p. 197. This refers to the older child. However, to some degree this is already the case in five- to six-year-old children in kindergarten.
19 R. Steiner, *The Kingdom of Childhood*, Rudolf Steiner Press, London, 1982, p. 110.
20 For the sequence of development which can be observed if children model freely without being given tasks of suggestions, see Hanne Huber, *Gestalten mit Bienenwachs im Vorschulalter* [Modelling with Beeswax in Early Childhood], Verlag Freies Geistesleben, Stuttgart, 2001.
21 R. Steiner, *Balance in Teaching*, Mercury Press, Spring Valley, NY, 1990, p. 17.
22 Steiner, *A Modern Art of Education*, p. 192.
23 Howard, *Educating the Will*, pp. 70–79.
24 Steiner, *Balance in Teaching*, p. 19. With respect to musical education in the time between 7 and 14 Steiner states: 'The astral body becomes emancipated between the change of teeth and puberty. And what emerges out of the essence of music forms humankind and makes them independent beings. No wonder, then, that the *music teacher who understands* these things, who *knows that human beings are permeated through and through with music*, will quite naturally allow this knowledge to enrich the singing lesson and the teaching of instrumental music. This is *why we try not only to introduce singing as early as possible into the education of children, but to allow those with sufficient aptitude to learn how to play a musical instrument* so that they have the opportunity really to grasp the musical element that lives in their form as it emancipates.' From *Human Values in Education*, lecture of 24 July 1924, quoted in M. Glöckler, *Education as Preventive Medicine*, Rudolf Steiner College Press, 2003, p. 203.

25 R. Steiner, *Practical Advice to Teachers,* Rudolf Steiner Press, London, 1976, p. 47.
26 R. Steiner, *The Inner Nature of Music and the Experience of Tone,* Anthroposophic Press, Hudson, NY, 1983, esp. chapters 5 and 6.
27 Ibid., p. 58.
28 Mention should be made of the book by R. Jacobs, *Music for Young Children,* Hawthorn Press, Stroud, 1991; and J. Knierim, *Quintenlieder: Music for Young Children in the Mood of the Fifth,* Rudolf Steiner College Press, 1994.
29 The magazine *Kindling* has devoted a recent issue (19/2011) to music for young children and how to work with the mood of the fifth in everyday kindergarten life. See especially articles by Jill Taplin and Sally Schweizer.
30 R. Steiner, *The Spiritual Ground of Education,* Anthroposophic Press, Great Barrington, MA, 2004, p. 62.
31 Steiner, *Practical Advice to Teachers,* pp. 47–48.
32 J. Knierim has created a wonderful resource of such songs (see above). Recently Karen Lonsky has published a collection of work songs which she has composed in the mood of the fifth: *A Day Full of Song,* WECAN Publications, Spring Valley, CA, 2010.
33 Quoted in M. Glöckler, *Education as Preventive Medicine,* p. 205.
34 Art itself must play its proper part in education and should be practised free of purposes which are not intrinsic to art itself. In: R. Steiner, *A Modern Art of Education,* p. 192f.
35 R. Steiner, *The Arts and Their Mission,* Anthroposophic Press, Spring Valley, NY 1964, pp. 29–30.
36 Ibid., p. 76f.
37 Handcraft as activity in the kindergarten is not discussed in this context. There is an excellent chapter on handcraft in early childhood by Dora Dolder in the booklet *What is a Waldorf Kindergarten?* In her publications on Handcrafts and Woodwork (available in German) F. Jaffke could demonstrate that embroidery or woodcarving done by adults in the presence of children are artistic practices which fill the kindergarten with a mood of creative activity and inspire the children to imitate or participate on their level.
38 Steiner, *A Modern Art of Education,* p. 192
39 E. Grunelius, *Early Childhood Education and the Waldorf School Plan,* Spring Valley, 1966. pp. 15–18.
40 Steiner, *A Modern Art of Education,* p. 203.
41 M. Jünemann and F. Weitmann, *Drawing and Painting in Rudolf Steiner Schools,* Hawthorn Press, Stroud, 1994. p. 37.
42 J. Almon (ed.) *What is a Waldorf Kindergarten?* WECAN Publications, Spring Valley, NY, 2009, p. 23.

43 Advice can be found in B. Müller, *Painting with Children*. Floris Books, Edinburgh, 2002; and Jüneman and Weitmann, *Drawing and Painting*.
44 Jünemann and Weitmann, *Drawing and Painting*, p. 38.
45 Recently S. Schweizer published a very informative essay on 'Art Around the Young Child in Painting and Drawing', *Kindling*, Issue 18, 2010. The entire Issue 18 of this magazine is about drawing and painting with young children.
46 Steiner gives no indication as to what kind of crayons to use in kindergarten. I do not wish to enter here into the issue whether children should be given the full range of the rainbow or just the primary red, yellow and blue. Nor do I want to enter into the debate on the use of stick crayons or block crayons in the kindergarten which has been going on for the last 10 years at least. Opinions range from open-mindedness to a very clear preference. The issue was raised by practitioners of The Extra Lesson, who observed a poor pencil grip in school children and concluded that this may be related to the use of block crayons in Steiner kindergartens. At this stage there is no clear evidence to substantiate this, nor is there evidence for the superiority of block crayons. The latest contributions to this debate among kindergarten teachers can be found in *Kindling* (18/2010), published in the UK.
47 See A. E. McAllen, *Reading Children's Drawings*, Rudolf Steiner College Press, 2004; Also E. Schoorel, 'The Child's Drawing as a Picture', in *The First Seven Years: Physiology of Childhood*, Rudolf Steiner College Press, Fair Oaks, CA, 2004.
48 M. Strauss, *Understanding Children's Drawings*, Rudolf Steiner Press, London, 1978.
49 Inger Brochmann, *Børnetegningerenes hemmeligheder*, Hernov, Denmark, 1995.
50 R. Steiner, *Renewal of Education*, Steiner School Fellowship, Forest Row, 1981, p. 176.
51 In my own collection of children's drawings there are a number of drawings which relate to birth, death and the life before birth.
52 Steiner, *Renewal of Education*, p. 176.
53 The same would be the case for speech and storytelling, which as art forms only live in the teacher and are brought to the kindergarten-age child by the teacher.

9

In Search for Reality: Self-development and Child Observation

Things are not what they seem: this is eminently true for child observation. Early childhood teachers are trained to observe children, their behaviour and abilities, using a range of observational methods developed to gain exact and reliable observational data. The data are then interpreted using concepts the teachers have acquired in their professional training. In connecting observations with concepts, mental images are formed within the observer, and a conclusion is drawn about the meaning of what was observed. The pedagogical judgement implicit in the conclusion will influence decisions on educational intervention.

This way of gathering and evaluating information is based on what is accessible to sense perception only. Teachers need to follow this process, however, as it will prevent them from making unfounded assumptions and generalizations about a child's behaviour.

The limitations of this way of observing become obvious the moment we feel that there is a deeper meaning to what we have seen, a meaning that cannot be brought to light using the methodology described above. We sense a discrepancy between what appears outwardly in the behaviour of a child and the hidden reality within the child.[1]

When Rudolf Steiner speaks about child observation as a task for the teacher, he emphasizes that it must lead to the reality of who the child really is. He called this 'reading the child'.[2] He also states that education would become ineffective if it derived its aims, content and methods from the observational data gained by using our sensory and intellectual faculties alone. Educational practice would be insufficiently informed and therefore unable to affect the inner life of the child.[3]

It is a shattering experience to recognize how little we know about the inner life of the children who are given into our care and whom we have to educate. However, if we allow this insight to enter our consciousness we have gained a starting point on the path towards knowing the child.

Self-development in meeting life's challenges

Rudolf Steiner has indicated that the gap between outward appearance and reality can only be bridged if the human being acquires more refined faculties of perception. The road to 'reading the child' will consist of developing such faculties.

Firstly, Steiner points to self-development through devoting ourselves to the tasks of everyday life, and thus developing the will. Intellectual faculties, which play such an important part in modern teacher training, are of little help for becoming a good observer and thus a good teacher.

To fulfil their everyday tasks early childhood teachers need to practise three virtues: gratitude, love and the will to do one's duty. 'Fundamentally, these are the three principal human virtues, to a certain extent encompassing all other virtues.'[4] What is developed in the practice of these three virtues will change the way in which we see and understand children, the world and ourselves.

Gratitude can be described as openness: as accepting what life holds in store according to individual destiny; as 'gratitude toward the world, towards the entire universe, thankfulness for being in this world'.[5] If gratitude becomes a daily exercise it will grow – not just in the teacher but in the child who, experiencing gratitude in the gestures and words of the adult, will absorb it.

Regarding love the situation is different, as the feeling of love cannot be willed. But we can practise taking an interest in the world, in children, in all living beings. Underlying the practice of being interested is a conscious effort to extend ourselves beyond our personal limitations, and this may become love of its own accord.[6]

Early childhood educators can practise doing their duty by attending to the practical aspects of kindergarten life, to domestic tasks and the children's well-being. Endeavouring to observe a child carefully, and taking the time to think about it, belongs to teacher's duties as well.[7]

Self-development of the inner life

Rudolf Steiner also mentions a second path of self-development, which runs side by side with the schooling of will through gratitude, love and doing our duty in the outer life. It is the schooling of thinking in our inner life.[8]

The schooling of our inner life will lead to drawing the right conclusions about life experiences. This is not to say that we become spiritual researchers ourselves.[9] Rather, it means that we become inwardly active in our life of thought. This includes acquiring the abilities to concentrate, to hold and move a particular thought at will, to remember and forget at will, to cultivate attentiveness and overcome inner nervousness such as flitting between thoughts.

What implications does this have for child observation? When observing children in the kindergarten the teacher should embrace what happens as open-mindedly as possible, holding back opinions and judgements while the situation unfolds. In the reflective process, however, the teacher must try to create an image of the child or situation in an effort to find what is essential and to separate out the non-essential. Through this inner focusing we will be able to find a direction of thought that brings order, depth and meaning to the multi-facetted phenomena we have observed.

In everyday life these processes are often reversed. During observation a teacher might already be focused on pre-existing ideas about a child. Or she might be concentrating on a practical task that diverts her full attention from the child. Thus the teacher may not be open enough to extend her consciousness to embrace the situation fully. When reflecting at the end of the day, a teacher may struggle to stay focused and produce only vague inner pictures of what has happened. In order to make sense of these vague recollections she may fall back on general behavioural labels. In doing so, the teacher will not be inwardly active enough for a new understanding to emerge.

In recognizing this we may become painfully aware of our own shortcomings. The realisation dawns that the ability to observe and understand is not a natural gift but needs to be developed through patient practice.[10]

Four steps for deepening understanding

1. The mood of wonder

> All human enquiry must proceed from wonder! ... In actual fact, in the soul that wants to penetrate to truth, this condition must first be present: the soul must stand before the universe in a mood of wonder and marvelling.

A little later Steiner states:

> Before we so much as begin to set our thinking in motion, we experience the condition of wonder. A thinking which is set in motion without the condition of wonder remains nothing but a mere play of thoughts.[11]

Cultivating a mood of wonder in child observation is the first step towards more understanding. We resist the temptation to accept the most obvious explanations for a child's difficult behaviour or the challenging social dynamics in a group. We will refrain from jumping too quickly to conclusions about 'what to do with this child' and the design of an action plan. Modern educational policy demands immediate action and pushes educators into programming for individual children too soon. It is difficult to resist this trend. Educators who realise that wonder is an essential step towards seeing more must withstand the push for action and allow time for looking, listening and finding the right question before considering answers.

2. Reverence

Whatever deep insights are gained in the process of observation, they are not to be understood as personal achievements but as belonging to the wisdom that pervades the world.

> After the mood of wonder must follow the mood of veneration, of reverence. Any thinking that is divorced from reverence, that does not behold in a reverent manner what is proffered to its view, will not be able to penetrate to reality. Thinking must never, so to say, go dancing through the world in a careless, light-footed way. It must, when it has passed the moment of wonder, take firm root in the feeling of reverence for the universe.[12]

The mood of wonder and reverence advocated here contradicts one of the major tenets of modern scientific observation: that of the impartial, uninvolved observer. According to this approach, the inner predisposition of an observer has no place in the research process and therefore should have no impact on the research results.

But not only should the scientifically informed process of observation be independent of the observer, it is only regarded as valid within a strictly defined setting. Steiner confirms that valid and correct discoveries can be made this way. However, he notes, with respect to the question of what is essential and what is not there will always be a feeling of uncertainty.

This holds true for child observation as well. Research on child development has produced an overwhelming abundance of very specific research results which provide pieces of a picture. But there is no meaningful framework for putting these pieces together. Questions about the essence of childhood or the individuality of a child are too broad and cannot therefore be researched using methods recognized as valid in the scientific community. Science, according to its own criteria, is unable to provide – it cannot even aim to provide – a full picture of the human being.[13]

Spiritual science asks observers to extend their observational abilities and use not only sense perception and thinking but also feeling as an organ of perception. The path begins with wonder and reverence.

3. Feeling the unity of I and world

In feeling, the human being is able to loosen the boundaries between self and world and to extend the inner being towards an experience of 'feeling oneself in wisdom-filled harmony with the laws of the world'.[14]

Steiner has given an exercise for this which is useful for the contemplative part of child observation. Firstly, visualize a circle with a point in the centre. Then let the centre become the periphery of the circle and the periphery become the centre. It is a meditative exercise of moving in thought between extending outwards and contracting inwards.[15]

This movement between centre and periphery is a helpful inner activity for educators because children are both at the centre and the periphery, depending on our angle of perception. They can be perceived as individual and unique (point), but also as living in and influenced by the people around them: their parents, teachers, other children (periphery). We need both perspectives if we are to understand the inner being of the child. In the deepest sense, this moving in thought between centre and periphery relates to the cosmic existence of the human being (periphery) and the incarnation of the human being on earth (point).

This exercise will enable the educator to remain in a state of observing for longer, to go out with our senses and receive impressions without judging what we observe. Any such judgement would pull us back into ourselves. Through abstaining from judgement and interpretation a chance is created that the observed phenomenon itself will reveal a truth which would not have been discovered otherwise.

Although we may:

> use all the efforts we may to judge correctly of something, error can always creep in. A true judgment can only result when we have attained a certain maturity, when we have

> waited for the judgement to 'jump' to us, not when we put ourselves about to find it, but when we take pains to make ourselves ripe for it to come to us. Then the judgement we form will belong to reality.[16]
>
> Our relation to thinking must not be that we make thinking sit in judgement upon objects but rather that we make it an instrument whereby the objects can express themselves. This is what placing oneself in harmony with objects means.[17]

In order to learn not to jump to conclusions but to let life speak for itself, we can make a habit of asking, upon observing certain behaviour in a child, whether there are instances of the opposite behaviour as well. Holding both ways of behaving in our thoughts, we can then avoid falling into the trap of being drawn to what stands out most and becoming blind to other possibilities.

Life is beyond logic, and opposites may well stand side by side. Learning to work with polarities in observation and subsequent contemplation may bring the truth closer. The spiritual reality of the human being is characterized by many such polarities: thinking and will, the upper and the lower pole in the human organism, opposites in the temperaments, to name but a few. Working with polarities requires the observer to be open and flexible, to resist the temptation to label behaviour. Polarities indicate a field of possibilities rather than one single point. Working with these in observation and interpretation will prevent the observer from drawing conclusions too quickly and will prepare the observer for letting the phenomena themselves speak their meaning.

4. Surrender

When we have learned to let the child reveal her own secrets, and when reverence and wonder have become soul habits, then our personal likes and dislikes will gradually move into the background and cease to interfere with the process of observation and understanding. We become able to silence hidden intentions – and even ambitions – and wait with inner openness and patience.

> Surrender does not set out to force an entrance, as it were, into this or that truth, rather do we seek to educate ourselves and then quietly wait until we attain to that stage of maturity where the truth flows to us from the things of the world ... To work with patience, knowing that patience will bring us further and further in wise self-education – that is the mood of surrender.[18]

Through the mood of surrender in observation we experience ourselves as if standing beside the child, and walking with the child. We adapt to how a particular child steps into and communicates with the world.

We can practise this stepping out of ourselves into 'somebody else's shoes' by emulating a child's particular way of walking or moving when we reflect on the child. This helps us to become more sensitive to how it might feel for the child to move that way, and to understand some of her struggles and behaviour. Another option, suggested by Heiner Priess, is to form inner images by finding a plant, animal, landscape, or garden that expresses something of the inner being of the child.[19] Henning Köhler, a child therapist, wrote poetry and thus created images around children he had worked and formed a therapeutic relationship with.[20] He is working with his observations and questions rather than with immediate answers. Such an activity of inner visualization will strengthen the teacher's perceptive abilities and contribute to an in-depth understanding of children that uses the trained capacity of feeling as much as of thinking.

Things are not what they seem – an example to demonstrate the challenges of observing and understanding

In place of a conclusion I would like to present an observation record here which highlights the complexity of child observation. Of course, in real life situations not just one but a whole range of observations would be necessary. The example presented here was chosen because the child in question does not live up to conventional expectations of behaviour. The situation reveals contradictions in the behaviour of the child and therefore this child presents a riddle to the observer.

For reasons of space, what follows is a shortened version of several more detailed observations that were written down shortly after the events occurred. This kind of observational summary is particularly common among educators, and considerations of what to do with a child are frequently derived from such work.

Boy 'Tim', six years:

> The morning circle was based on the story of the three little pigs. As the morning circle started, Tim seemed to be immersed in the activity, however he did not sing unless the teacher made eye contact with him and then he merely mouthed the words. Tim appeared to imitate some gestures, mainly he gesticulated actions that expressed animal gestures or animal behaviours. When the teacher recited a particular verse of the circle, Tim became especially animated when the wolf was described as trotting after the pigs. Otherwise Tim did not respond very much to the rest of the verse. He intently observed the gestures of the teacher but did not make any physical movement except to move his head from side to side. When the verse repeated the trotting of the wolf, Tim immediately exaggerated the movements. This situation is found to occur on a daily basis with regards to the morning circle of the three pigs.

Additional observations were made and information collected in order to establish whether the child reacted differently in other situations. The following is a summary of those observations:

> Tim is usually very measured and controlled with his outer expressions and gestures. According to his mother he has a deep sensitivity for animals and has shown compassion for animals from a very early age.

When Tim is at home, he expresses himself musically through what can only be termed as a great musical sensitivity. According to his mother, Tim loves to sing at home and from all accounts seems to have a beautiful singing voice. When in the kindergarten, Tim never sings and at times mouths the words in a bid to appear to be singing.[21]

The observations of this child reveal polarities in his behaviour: Tim is singing at home but not in the kindergarten. He shows a love for animals, yet he is acting the wolf, the aggressive animal in the fairytale. He is usually controlled in his movements, but in the circle he performs exaggerated movements. Either he does it because the teacher has requested his participation and he is obliging reluctantly, or he temporarily identifies with the wolf quality.

Observing behavioural polarities helps in perceiving the complexity of behaviour. We catch a glimpse of the depth of the child's soul, we intuit the simultaneous presence of aggression and fear, love and hate, high sensitivity, being open and closed, even rejection. Without reflecting on such polarities in behaviour and the riddle they pose, we might conclude that this child displays typical behaviour for a six-year-old child who likes doing his own thing and testing the teacher's strength. We could also assume that the child is not interested in the circle and therefore causes disruption.

However, these interpretations do not quite fit. The child makes no attempt to entice other children into disruptive behaviour, which is usually the case when older children test a teacher's resolve. Also, a child who sings beautifully at home will do so out of a love for and enjoyment of singing. So why does the child not sing in the morning circle? What is preventing him from doing so?

We need to consider that this child is gifted with exceptionally fine hearing, maybe even with perfect pitch, and that the less than perfect singing in the kindergarten group might be an unpleasant experience for him. Which goes to show that things may not be as they outwardly present themselves.

Patience and further observation would be required, embracing this and other aspects of the child's being, to find out what is troubling him. If these investigations are pursued in an attitude of wonder and reverence, looking, listening and feeling into the child and his life situation, then there is a chance we can come closer to what is essential to him.

These are only limited indications about a very complex process of searching for reality behind outer phenomena. However, the example given here may demonstrate the intimate connection between the teacher's path of self-development and the ability to observe and understand. As Steiner suggests,

> if as a teacher and educator, you represent the knowledge of the human being with the necessary love, devotion and selflessness, something quite remarkable ensues. In associating with the children you become – do not misunderstand the word, it is not meant in a bragging sense – you become wiser and wiser. As it were, you yourself discover how to evaluate a given faculty or achievement of the child. You learn fully to enter in a living way into the child's nature and to do so comparatively quickly.[22]

Endnotes

1 Steiner speaks about the phenomenon and the reality behind in: *The World of the Senses and the World of the Spirit*, Steiner Book Centre Inc., Vancouver, 1979, Lecture 1.
2 R. Steiner, *A Modern Art of Education*, Rudolf Steiner Press, London, 1972, Lecture 4.
3 R. Steiner, *The Fall of the Spirits of Darkness,* Rudolf Steiner Press, Bristol, 1993, Lecture 11, p. 166.
'Children and young people we see do not show their true nature in what we see on the outside, beside it runs ... a hidden inner life to which we must pay real attention.'
4 R. Steiner, *The Child's Changing Consciousness,* Anthroposophic Press, Hudson, NY, 1988, Lecture 6, p. 127.

5 Ibid., p. 131.
6 Ibid., p. 133. Steiner: Gratitude grows, love awakens.
7 Steiner points to the lack of this inner work of pondering in observing in experimental settings: 'How is man's mental life nowadays affected by experiments? There is not active participation, for he simply looks on and tries to eliminate activity as much as possible; he wants to let the experiment tell him everything and regards as fanciful anything that is the outcome of his own inner activity.' In: *Man and the World of Stars: The Spiritual Communion of Mankind*, Anthroposophic Press, New York, 1963, p. 91.
8 R. Steiner, *Self-Education in the Light of Spiritual Science*, Mercury Press, Spring Valley, NY, 1995.
9 The path leading to direct perception of spiritual reality is described by Steiner in *Knowledge of Higher Worlds* and other publications. What is meant here with 'schooling of one's inner life' relates only to the initial stages of self-development as described in these publications.
10 This Steiner calls the 'culture of inner life' through which the human being can come to an experience of what is essential and to be able to view life experiences in the light of these essentials. In: *Self Education in the Light of Spiritual Science*, pp. 18–21.
11 Ibid., pp. 13–14.
12 Steiner, *World of the Senses*, p. 14.
13 'It is really essential to be inwardly sustained and upheld all the time by the consciousness that with all one's strict and precise thinking one can, as a matter of fact, get nowhere at all in the domain of reality.' Steiner, *World of the Senses*, p. 17.
14 Ibid., p. 15.
15 R. Steiner, *Curative Education: Twelve Lectures for Doctors and Curative Teachers*, Rudolf Steiner Press London, 1972, p. 178.
16 Steiner, *World of the Senses*, p. 17.
17 Ibid., p. 18.
18 Ibid., p. 24.
19 H. Priess, *The Practice of Child Observation*, reprinted from *Kindling* in *Star Weavings*, No. 21.
20 H. Köhler, *Difficult Children: There Is No Such Thing*, AWSNA Publications, Fair Oaks, CA, 2003.
21 This observation was made by Carol, a former early childhood student at Sydney Rudolf Steiner College.
22 R. Steiner, *Human Values in Education*, quoted in M. Glöckler, *Education as Preventive Medicine*, p. 60.

10

'Under the Stars'

Self-development is an ongoing task for anyone who works with young children. There are many different pathways of self-development. In the first part of this chapter I suggest that the particular path for Steiner early childhood educators begins with the deepening of their understanding of the incarnation process. In the second part I look at how this path continues with insight into our earthly endeavours, the life of the will.

Part 1: The incarnation process as a guide for the self-development of the early childhood teacher

Rudolf Steiner has encouraged educators to look at the big cosmic picture of incarnation and to include the cosmic dimension in their understanding and education of children:

> The time is now that the human being must extract the essentials of education from the knowledge of the connection of the human being with the cosmos. The growing child experiences the continuation of happenings which have occurred in the supersensible world before birth.[1]

What characterizes this connection between the incarnation process and the cosmos?

On the one hand, from the cosmos, the zodiac and the planets, originate those etheric and astral forces which form the child's body in the womb and continue their formative activity all through the first seven years. On the other hand, once the child is born, there is a continuation of experiences in the inner being of the child which relate to the state of 'unbornness'. These are 'archetypal experiences', which are shared by all children around the world.

According to Steiner these archetypal experiences are connected with specific spiritual qualities behind each sign of the Zodiac. For the incarnation process in particular, Steiner speaks about the signs of Aries, Taurus, Gemini and Cancer as significant powers: 'When we arrive in the world, the first four powers or impulses [meaning the first four signs of the Zodiac. – RLB] are already in us, though we only develop them afterwards.'[2] The younger the child, the closer he still is to these four powers of incarnation.

Once, on a trip to Thailand, I discovered a woodcarving in the entrance area of an old house. It showed two figures sitting in a gateway. One of them, who could be male, is lifting up a baby and handing it to the female figure, who could be the mother. Encircling the scene are the twelve signs of the zodiac. These in turn are encircled by the animals representing each year in a 12-year cycle as known in the Chinese tradition.

Woodcarving, Thailand. Photo by author

What made the composition so special were the beings mounted on each of the outer animal signs and, in the case of the dragon and the snake, keeping them under control.

In Thai culture these beings would be regarded as 'Devas', lower divine beings. But we could also see in them images of the higher self of the human being overcoming, or 'taming', the animal forces present within the human being. Thus the outer circle could be pointing to moral forces in the cosmos, beyond the zodiac.[3] The family group in the centre is surrounded by and part of the world of cosmic forces and the spiritual world of morality.

A second experience occurred at a kindergarten in New Zealand. The kindergarten room had a most unusual play house. Instead of the usual roof-like draping it had a specially decorated back wall. In accord with the Maori creation myth the wall was hung with a woven arch, above which stars representing the Zodiac could be seen. In front of them stars were hanging, representing the planets. Below this was a pedestal on which wooden figures were standing, depicting the ancestors. Then on the floor were the dolls, lying asleep with a special woven fabric behind their beds. What a wonderful picture of children's connection to the cosmos!

Play house. Taikuna Steiner School Kindergarten, Hastings, New Zealand. Photo by Heather van Zyl

While the child's connection to the cosmos is natural, a 'gift of heaven',[4] as it were, adults have emancipated themselves from it. Building a relationship to the world of stars does not come naturally anymore. The formation of the body has long been completed; the ties to the past are cut. In the act of thinking and in the performing of deeds, the human being experiences, to a certain degree, a sense of freedom and independence. Only within the life of feeling have certain memories remained.

> Man has renounced the universe at the head end and at the limb end so that we are only wholly given up to the rhythm of the universe in so far as we are rhythmical human beings.[5]

We experience this connection to the universe when working with the rhythms of life in the kindergarten: the connection between the planets and the days of the week, the monthly rhythm of the moon and the rhythm of the year as the passage of the sun through the signs of the Zodiac, as observed from the earth, or as the passage of the earth around the sun, which causes the seasonal changes. These rhythms are part of the sun's relationship to the earth, affecting not only nature but the human body and soul as well.

We take a step further into the contemplation of the cosmos when we embrace the regions of the zodiac. Rudolf Steiner indicates that this means the beginning of a spiritual practice of the different moral qualities, the 'twelve virtues'.[6]

Of especial interest for educators wishing to gain a deeper understanding of the incarnation process of the child are the virtues that correspond to the first four signs: Aries, Taurus, Gemini and Cancer.

Images of Incarnation

Aries in relation to the child: the ram looking back

The image Steiner describes is of the ram with his head turned back, a frequent representation of this zodiacal sign.[7] 'Looking back' is also one of the gestures of the young child – not as a conscious act but as a kind of 'spiritual habit'. The young child still holds a connection to the spiritual world, which becomes visible in his way of relating to human beings. It is from the spiritual existence that the child's ability to imitate and live in total trust originates. After birth this becomes trust in the goodness of the world and the human beings surrounding the child.

Young children are still travellers between two worlds, the spiritual and the earthly. Therefore the spiritual continuity of existence beyond birth and death is a reality for them, unless they are told otherwise. We can observe the ease with which children connect to other realms than the physical life on earth, and how they slip into images depicting other worlds, such as from fairy tales, or archetypal images from long-gone cultures which now appear in their play.

How can educators embrace this? What is the adult's gesture of 'looking back'?

Aries in relation to the adult: the virtue of devotion

As educators we should meet with respect this connection between child and spiritual world, as symbolized by the ram looking backwards. We might follow the child's impulse to consciously build an individual relationship with the spiritual cosmos by cultivating our awareness that there is a spiritual dimension in and beyond the things we see and do. In the presence of people who are open to the spiritual realm the child will feel at home and accepted.

To warmly embrace children who are still easily traversing the border between worlds, we also need to offer them an environment that suits their in-between stage of existence. The child's entry into the earthly world can be helped if the environment contains elements that remind him of his heavenly home. This does not mean prescribing what kind of cubby house, dolls or soft toys to use, as these are only the outer expressions of something less tangible. The heavenly quality lives first and foremost in the inner mood of the teacher, from where it radiates out into the environment and shapes it.

When the educator works with devotion on her daily tasks, a sacred space is created. This is the adult's way of looking back, of relating to the spiritual world. Devotion is more than performing one's duty. It requires that we feel we are working in the presence of spiritual powers and toward the highest possibilities of the human being. This the educator can bring to the children as a mood.

Creating a mood of devotion demands, at times, that we let go of tight schedules and a continuous succession of planned activities.

When the educator becomes less driven by schedules and more able to live the sacred quality of work with the young child, then the children will sense that their teacher is also 'looking back' and sharing the connection to the other world.

Taurus in relation to the child: movement and balance

The archetypal image Steiner refers to is the jumping bull. This expresses movement and balance at the same time, and what better picture could be given for the young child! Through movement the child adjusts himself to the new world, to space. In moving he learns about his body and what this body can do: the twists, the turns, the bends, the walking and running. In the practice of movement and balance the child has his first experience of what it means to be on earth, to live within the laws of gravity and spatial dynamics.

There is a second aspect as well: inherent in movement is the gesture of going towards the future, the new. Young children are immensely curious about the world and eager to learn. They learn from the moment they wake up to the moment they go to sleep, and, if healthy, they are in movement for most of this time. What a tremendous will activity!

When working with young children, rhythm in speech and movement is used to help the child enter into new movement patterns. Rhythmical movement in the morning circle, in hand gesture games or in nursery rhymes can help children to incarnate into their bodies.

Here is a wonderful instance of this, related by M. L. Nüesch:[8]

> He got to know the kindergarten and the teacher only recently, but he quickly learned that the teacher understood his language. He did not take any initiative in play himself. If he played with others, he could do so only in the role of a wild animal or a monster. One morning he says: 'You are my mummy now and you must go and get me from the back there, because I am frozen into an ice block.' He really stands there like an ice block, without any movement.

Some children help me to carry him away. 'You have to bring me into a warm country,' he says. But this does not help. He hides in a cave (under a table). He obviously needs protection and quiet. 'Now something will come out,' he announces. But it is not a 'thawed' child who appears, but another horrible monster ...

Many weeks later he comes back to the theme.
'Look, I am all frozen,' he says. He stands there in a twisted position, even his eyes and hair look as if affected by stiffness. This time the teacher takes him on her lap and starts to massage his arms and legs firmly while talking to him with humour.

'The ears as well', he says. (He has had surgery because he did not hear well.)

The teacher shakes him a little, and he is satisfied when she tells him that the 'frozenness' is now flowing out. He says it has to flow out from both his ears. Then the teacher takes him on the lap like a little parcel, kneels down herself and rocks him backward and forward.

'I am not a baby,' he cries, but he sounds content. The teacher says that this is what you do if somebody is 'frozen'. After a while the teacher lets him go with a little friendly smack. His face is now relaxed.

This is an example of working with the Taurus quality. It takes courage to try new ways, and acceptance that not every goal can be achieved.

Taurus in relation to the adult: balance becomes progress

There is no easy recipe for living the virtue of balance. Finding balance in working with children is an act of attuning our inner perception to the child's needs as well as considering our own strengths and limitations. We may have to leave behind familiar ideas, habits and conventions in order to experience that there is a rhythm between the 'old' and the 'new', between how we have worked so far and what the next step demands. The past and the future belong together and the gesture of moving forward needs to relate to both.

Steiner describes this in his youth lectures with respect to the relationship between the younger generation and the older generation.

He speaks of three enemies for Waldorf education: set phrases, conventions and set routines.

To use an example from kindergarten practice, 'gentle hands' or 'inside voices', used over and over again, can become a set phrase. While there is a place for repetition in early childhood, there are many situations where a new way of saying things is preferable, where the right thing to say can be found through tuning into the actual situation rather than quoting from a different context.

Convention has taken over when an educator continues to do something that has lost its meaning, without being aware of the fact. Take lighting a candle, for example. Unless the educator has reflected on why she is doing it, unless she is convinced of its relevance for a particular situation, it is better to not light a candle. The children will sense if it has become a convention, an empty ritual, and they may react by misbehaving.

When considering set routines in an early childhood context we have to acknowledge, of course, that young children need them. But routines require a rhythmical quality, a moving quality as well, which allows for small variations. While not wanting to break the rhythm of the day we could allow some flexibility within the daily schedule, thus giving it a living 'Taurus' quality.

The child is so eager to do both: to move forward as well as look back. How well can the educator tolerate the new? How does she work with staying in movement within herself so that rigidity is avoided? If we become aware of the risks of stagnation in the set phrase, convention and routine, we can at one and the same time retain the need for stability and combine it with openness for change. Then there is not only balance but progress as well.

Gemini in relation to the child: the I meets the self

The image of Gemini is 'twoness in oneness', the twins holding hands. Consciousness of self is possible only in the realm of matter where there are borders around things and where beings are physically separated from one another. It is a big transition from the spiritual world to the physical world, from being able to merge with and live within other beings in the spiritual world, to separation and individualization. It takes years for the child to go through this process.

The innate ability of the child to imitate is a great helper in this transition, and parents and educators play a crucial role in the process. From birth onwards there is 'twoness in oneness' – the adult and child 'holding hands', literally and metaphorically. The self of the child rests within the selves of the mother and carers, the earthly helpers of spiritual powers. From around age three to the end of early childhood, the time of holding hands continues, but now the child also becomes aware of himself as a separate being. When he says 'I am Thomas,' or 'I don't want to,' or 'I don't like my drawing,' then the child has learned to look at himself in the gesture of I, who has done the drawing, and self, who is judging it, facing each other. In some children this individualization does not come about easily.

There is a wonderful account of this process of discovering oneself as an I in Virginia Axline's book *Dibs: In Search of Self*.[9] Axline writes about the first session of play therapy with a five-year-old boy:

> When we got into the playroom, Dibs walked slowly around, touching the materials, naming the items with the same questioning inflection he had used on the first visit to the other playroom. Sandbox? Easel? Chair? Paint? Car? Doll? Every item he touched, he named in that manner. Then he varies it a little. 'Is this a car? This is a car. Is this sand? This is sand ... After he had completed the first circuit of the room, I said, 'Yes. There are many different things in this room, aren't there? And you have touched and named most of them.' 'That's right,' he said, softly. I did not want to rush him. Give him time to look around ... He stopped in the middle of the room.
> After a while I ask him, 'I say, Dibs! Would you like to take off your hat and coat?' 'That's right,' he said. 'You take off your hat and coat, Dibs. You take off your hat. You take off your coat, Dibs.' He made no motion to do anything about it. All right, I replied, Take off your

mittens and your boots too, if you want to. 'That's right,' he said almost in a whisper. He stood there, plucking idly and restlessly at his coat sleeves. He began to whimper. He stood in front of me, hanging his head, whimpering. 'You would like to take them off, but you want me to help you? Is that it?' I asked. 'That's right,' he said. There was a sob in his voice as he replied.' [Then she helps him on his request.]

It is obvious that this child has not been able to find his own identity, that he speaks about himself in the third person as if he were an onlooker with no relationship to himself. In the therapeutic process he comes to the discovery of himself as a human being who relates to himself as an I, as well as to the expression of feelings he can identify as his own:

12th session.

> He ran over to the table, got the nursing bottle, and went back to the sandbox. He lay down and sucked on the bottle like a small baby. He closed his eyes. 'When I was a baby,' he said ... Then he suddenly sat up. 'No, no, no.' He said and got quickly out of the sandbox. 'I am not a baby. I was never a baby ...' (He changes subject). Later: He got the nursing bottle, took it to the sink, refilled it, tried to put the nipple on, but it was too slippery. 'Miss A will do it for you, Dibs,' he said. 'Miss A will not turn you down.'
>
> [She:] 'You think I'll fix it for you?' 'That's right,' said Dibs. 'I know you will.' He handed me the bottle ... [She does it and returns the bottle to him]. He stood in front of me sucking on the bottle looking steadily at me. 'You do not call me stupid,' he said. 'I say help, you help. I say I don't know, you know. I say I can't, you can.' 'And how does that make you feel?' I asked.

'Like that,' he said. 'I feel.' He looked at me steadily, seriously. (Then he goes to the sink and starts splashing water).[10]

Gemini in relation to the adult: perseverance becomes faithfulness

There is a lesson about the virtue of perseverance in the above story of a therapist who walks alongside the child, 'holding hands'. She loves him in a form of objective devotion. She serves him (taking off his mittens, helping with the bottle) even though she knows he can do it himself. She does not ask for acts of independence he may be able to perform but does not want to just yet. She follows his steps. She mirrors his actions and intentions out of the deep conviction that what the child harbours in the depth of his soul is valuable and that in due course he will bring forth his inner treasures. This is the virtue of perseverance and faithfulness: to take the place of self of the child at a time when he cannot do it for himself. Temporarily she becomes one of the twins.

In the education of healthy children we work with mirroring as well, but here the child is capable of doing the mirroring or imitating himself. He is able to actively accept the adult as his 'twin'. Rudolf Steiner points out that the benefit for a child is greater the more he is able to live not in his own soul but in those within his environment.[11] This ability to live in the soul of the people around him forms the basis for the child's experience of trust and belonging.

The adult's contribution to forming relationships of trust and belonging is the virtue of faithfulness: faithfulness to what the child is not yet, but wants to become. We can do this by holding within ourselves the picture of the child's higher being, who will lead him to his destiny. To take the other into oneself is the gesture of love.

By persevering to be a model for the children for as long as they need it, the teacher helps them to become individualized and independent when they are ready. That imitating should lead to freedom might seem contradictory, but such is the way of finding the self: the way of the twins.

Cancer in relation to the child: enclosing, embodiment

> All the way to where we enclose ourselves, using the crab principle, we are head. This is the gift of heaven and we do not have to contribute.[12]

The essentials of incarnation contained in the first four signs of the Zodiac are all linked to the process of the embodiment of the I. They relate to what works in the child from the head down as well as from the limbs upward when the I takes hold of the body and uprightness is acquired. With respect to the sign of Cancer, the head pole is of special importance. The skull itself can be understood as an image of the hard shell of the crab, protecting the brain, the delicate organ of human thinking, which is an image of the cosmos. The crab principle is the building of a bodily house around the soul and spirit of the child. As of age three, the child will act out this fundamental need for enclosing and protecting in his play. The child will build or seek out cubby houses and hiding places. The cubby is a wonderful image for the body house of the human being.

A most beautiful depiction of incarnation is Raphael's painting of the Sistine Madonna, depicting the Madonna as she carries the child from the realm of the heavens towards earthly life, holding the child close to her heart and surrounding it with her veil.

Infancy and childhood are times of being protected, nurtured, carried, embraced, surrounded by human warmth. Being served, being nurtured and loved is the necessary foundation for developing selflessness later in life. The child experiences the mother or primary caregiver as the one who fulfils his needs and who can be trusted. His trust in the world grows through this experience.

Cancer in relation to the adult: selflessness becomes catharsis.

So essential when looking after young children, selflessness is a virtue which cannot be demanded of a person. Either one is selfless or one is not. Otherwise, selfless behaviour becomes pretence. There are reasons why a person may be unable to be selfless. In striving for self-knowledge the educator may discover these reasons better and ultimately, perhaps, be able to overcome them.

Children are outwardly and inwardly dependent on the selflessness of adults in their environment. They rely on our ability to give freely rather than pursue our own needs and wishes when these collide with the needs of the child. It is one of the great illnesses of our time that more and more parents and teachers experience the forgoing of their own needs and wishes emotionally and physically as very difficult or even impossible. In wrestling with such inner resistance, mothering, teaching and caring can become a path of initiation. It opens up the potential of becoming a different, spiritually more aware person. It encourages a process of transformation from the closing-off, 'egotistical' gesture of the crab to inner openness and empathy for the needs of others.

Thus four essentials of incarnation are written in the signs of the Zodiac as archetypal processes in becoming a human being:

- *in Aries*: the preserving of the connection to the spirit world from whence the child comes;
- *in Taurus*: the child's desire to move forward and orientate himself towards the future;
- *in Gemini*: the process of developing a consciousness of self;
- *in Cancer*: the child's need for embodiment, enclosing and nurturing.

The question is how to respond to these essentials. The way suggested here is to make the four virtues of devotion, balance, faithfulness and selflessness part of our inner work in order to deepen the pedagogical work and to meet the spiritual needs of the incarnating child.

Part 2: The Zodiac, the Adult's Work and the Child's Play

The self-education of the will relies on placing ourselves in the middle of life with openness to what life brings in an attitude of gratitude and acceptance of our destiny. If the educator takes children into this stream of will activity and is fully present in her work, then the children are able to experience the adult as an example of a fully and harmoniously developed human being.

Through her activity the educator also builds up a field of warmth around the child in which he can experience closeness to another human soul. The working context allows for a warm, activity-centred and emotionally objective closeness which will not burden the child with emotional sentiment.

Steiner speaks about what will happen if we take the children into our sphere of will activity and thus provide the opportunity for imitation: 'This living interest, devotion and sympathy will be there if at the right age we permeate all branches of our teaching and education with the principle of imitation.'[13]

Regarding the self-development of the teacher the focus will now be on will activity, on human work, which Steiner relates to the zodiacal signs of Sagittarius, Capricorn, Aquarius, and Pisces.[14]

Steiner calls these four signs 'will signs', adding that they do not influence human deeds directly. The picture he gives us is of the human being standing on earth with the zodiacal signs from Aries to Scorpio in a semicircular arc overhead. In contrast, the signs from Sagittarius to Pisces have to be envisaged as below the feet, coming from the opposite side of the earth. Because the sphere of the earth separates the human being from these zodiacal signs, their influence is only indirect and weak and leaves us free in our activity of will. Through will activity, therefore, something new can be created which is independent of the cosmos and more influenced by the earth.[15]

Steiner describes the qualities of Sagittarius, Capricorn, Aquarius and Pisces as related to archetypal forms of human work. However, these archetypal activities have changed in recent times and are no longer to be found in their original form. We have to go back to older civilizations to discover the archetypal forms of work, which Steiner names as hunting (Sagittarius), animal breeding (Capricorn), tilling the soil (Water carrier) and trading/travelling (Pisces):

> To the stars down there on the opposite side, which are covered by the earth, human beings owe their existence as hunters, animal breeders, tillers of the soil walking across the field carrying urns to water the fields and we are traders thanks to the part of the starry heavens that takes us across the seas – in far distant times boats were built to look similar to fish, and two ships side by side that have sailed the seas in pursuit of trade are the symbol for trade … In the past, people really had a feeling for the way the human being is connected with the universe and the earth.[16]

Over time, many more occupations were added to these original four, and no attempt should be made to try to relate them all to these four archetypal activities. Steiner says that in moving into the age of Pisces, the age in which modern industrialized civilisation has developed, the 'four honest occupations' have been somewhat modified.

However, for the time of childhood in which the consciousness of the child does not yet correspond to our modern consciousness it seems relevant to turn to these archetypal activities. The young child's consciousness has an affinity with them, which we can observe and study in the child's play.

Sagittarius: the hunter

The image:

Is the archer, human in his upper body and animal in his lower body. Such a figure is known in Greek mythology as the centaur, a being half animal, half man. The centaur represents the lower nature of the human being, as yet untransformed. The upper part of the human being, thinking, has to master the animal nature eventually.

The activity:

Depicted in this sign is hunting. The archer holds a bow and arrow. Gathering can be regarded as a gentler version of hunting: it is a kind of 'hunting' in the plant realm.

Hunting and gathering, the ancient ways of securing food, live on to this day, albeit in different forms. Take the medieval merchant or the modern businessman, for example: searching out and hunting for good markets, and gathering goods. For young children, gathering the gifts of the earth and hunting for treasures are important activities.

With the teacher's help children can find good hunting grounds outdoors. But even during inside time we can observe such play: gathering toys, piling them up. Hunting and gathering are part of children's archetypal play. Some hunt for treasures, some for specific toys, and children may even snatch them from others. These are unrefined hunting gestures. There is still much learning ahead for the child in order to be fully human.

Educators can model the treasure hunting and gathering on the many walks and outings on which the children are taken. They can express interest in the natural surroundings, gratitude for what can be found there and joy at the beauty and richness of the world. Gathering can also be cultivated by harvesting fruits and vegetables to prepare meals and preserve food.

There is a great temptation in the hunter and gatherer to live out his lower instincts, to do business according to his own advantage. But hunting and gathering can also become honest and noble.

The virtue:

Related to this sign is truthfulness: truthfulness – that is, honesty – in conducting business, truthfulness in words, thoughts and deeds.

In kindergarten there are children who are cunning, who cheat and sometimes lie. What is this? Deep down a child may not really want to cheat, but something is taking over which, once the situation has passed, leaves the child unsatisfied. Deep within each child is a longing to experience truth, but the child's learning relies on the deeds and words of the people around him.

Educators are asked to look at their unrefined soul aspects and come to know them. Truthfulness in this respect means that we do not delude ourselves as to the motives behind our actions, or as to who we truly are.[17]

Capricorn

The image:

Is the goat-fish. Steiner says that the symbol of the goat-fish has no a counterpart in the natural world. It may be understood as a representation of the activity of animal breeding, an activity that followed, culturally, the stage of hunting and gathering.[18]

The activity:

Is animal breeding. As archetypal activity, animal breeding implies looking after animals, caring, providing nourishment, comforting and nursing the sick. It embraces the entire range of what is called the caring/social professions today. We could say that the caring professions are derived from the work of animal breeders. Education belongs to a certain extent to the realm of caring as well. Here, as with animal breeding, human intervention can be for the good or ill.

Already at a young age there are children who are concerned about caring for others and who also act out care situations in their play. There is an archetypal quality to role play such as mother and baby or nursing the sick. I would like to summarize a description by M.L. Nüesch of such a play situation in which she modelled caring for others:

> Nine children are playing together, the teacher is sitting close by, sewing.
>
> Three girls live in a house made from cloths. One is cooking and distributes 'coffee and soup'. One is shopping. This girl buys so many things that the house becomes very full and at last there is no room left 'to be' in the house. This girl is ceaselessly busy. She has two hunting dogs, two boys who wanted to play as well, but did not dare to offer themselves as father or children. These dogs soon became ill, one of them seriously. One dog's paws are limp; the other dog has a broken leg. The owner remains detached

in the face of this suffering, still shopping busily. 'You can look after them,' she says to the teacher.

Then the teacher starts to nurse the sick animals, put cream on their limbs, and bandages. More and more animals come, all very ill. Some die and the teacher covers them with a cloth. But luckily new puppies come forth from under the cloths. Now the dog owner quickly becomes a little kitten herself, newly born. The kitten is blind and roams about for a long time. Then the blind kitten comes very close to the teacher who had resumed the sewing. The kitten wants to sleep very close by. The kitten sleeps very restlessly and needs to be caressed and calmed down again and again.[19]

We may ask whether it is appropriate for a teacher to become so involved in the children's play. If the teacher decides to do so, it must be for a good reason. In this example the children expressed their need for special loving attention and care through becoming sick animals. Nüesch had sensed that behind the rough outer façade of the dog owner was a needy child. It is pedagogical intuition which informs such actions for the sake of a child or group of children.

The virtue:

Related to the sign of Capricorn is courage. Not courage in the sense of bravery or heroism, but in the sense of accepting mistakes, accepting the truth even if it hurts, and never giving up. Courage is the determination not to go backwards or 'drop out', but rather to stay engaged even if the situation is difficult. This courage to go forward despite mistakes is important for the teacher.

Kindergarten work offers many opportunites for practising courage. Often the amount of selflessness required for educating and caring for young children makes it hard to keep going. This feeling of near-exhaustion is common to all caring professions. The inner strength to carry on is the practice of the virtue of courage.

Aquarius

The image and the activity:

Is the water carrier. Agriculture is represented by the water carrier. There is a certain spiritual justification for thinking in terms of water, but what matters is the way he walks across the field. He holds an urn in each hand and pours water from these. This is the gardener and the tiller of the soil.[20] The image of the water carrier and the activity of caring for the land lead our thoughts to the nurturing of the etheric forces in human beings and in nature. In early childhood education it is essential for the teacher to be visibly active during outside time by gardening, watering the plants, digging the soil, weeding and planting, often with the help of some children.

I remember a strongly-built boy in my kindergarten group whose grandfather ran a bulb nursery. During a home visit, this child took me into the nursery gardens and proudly and precisely explained the workings of the watering system. He spoke as if it was his own invention, so deeply had he taken in his grandfather's caring for the plants. When plants needed watering in the kindergarten, he was there immediately. Watering was not a chore for him, it was a natural, joyous activity. Where other activities were concerned this boy was phlegmatic and it was difficult to motivate him to do anything that demanded effort.

This was a lesson for me in how deeply the work of the adult sinks into the unconscious, bodily responses of the child, and how this 'slipping into' the adult through imitation brings about an intensity of will activity which we may not reach in any other way.

The virtue:

The human response to the quality of this star sign is discretion: the act of creating inner stillness, of pausing, observing, waiting before one speaks, acts and makes judgements. Out of the space of silence, out of the space of discernment, the right decision can be found.[21] A gardener knows the value of waiting, of not uprooting a plant too soon. He understands that to wait is to improve his perception of every facet of his plants' needs.

Kindergarten teachers and caregivers are well advised to do the same, to avoid stepping in too quickly in a conflict situation, to act out of their realm of inner stillness instead of getting agitated when a child has done something wrong. Then we can achieve an attitude of soul where our own emotional reaction does not blur the recognition of what has happened. Educators need this inner stillness so that they do not fall into a superficial educational activism.

Familiarity with our own space of inner silence and discernment equips us better to calm a noisy, restless group of children. To become still in the middle of chaos is a challenge for the adult. When we can do this we give our strength to the children and they in turn can find their way out of the turmoil more easily.

Pisces

The image:

Is the fishes. Steiner says that the sign of the fishes actually depicts two boats sailing together across the sea. This is a big picture. It conveys a mood of opening the soul wide to the world, embracing not only what is nearby but also what is out far away.

> 'We are traders thanks to the part of the starry heavens that takes us across the seas.'[22]

Traders are travellers. They roam the world. They are also adventurers and risk takers. Risks are always present when the field of activity widens. To travel and seek adventures is a major part of life for many young and older people today. We are living, after all, in the age of Pisces.

In their play, young children are strongly drawn to the activity of travelling. It is actually a favourite play activity for many children and appears in many variations: creating means of transportation and travelling in various kinds of vehicles, including boats, trains, aeroplanes and rockets, trucks, cranes and bob cats. Here is an example from a Steiner early childhood centre in Bangkok:

A group of six boys turn a table upside down, attach cords to it and pull it across the floor as a carriage. They experience difficulties as the table top drags on the floor, and the carriage with at least one child sitting in it is hard to pull along. They manage to get a blanket underneath, making the carriage easier to push. After many rides, the carriage becomes a car, pushed along by one child. The car is stopped by a child in the role of parking lot guard with a whistle, waving the car with professional gestures into a parking slot. The child plays the guard perfectly. In another part of the room, an upside down table became a removal truck and is loaded with big furniture: three freestanding shelves used to hold toys are loaded, and other smaller things. The load is secured with lots of ropes. Next to the truck, three girls have set up a food shop. As the truck starts moving, the shop is in danger, so the shopkeepers pack up very quickly and move to a big table further away. The shop is re-established on top of the table, but then moved again under the table, where it stays until the end of playtime. These children make no complaint about the removal truck disturbing their play. Travelling and moving are just part of life.

The virtue:

Related to Pisces is magnanimity, as displayed by the children who moved their shop in order to accommodate the truck. Magnanimity means going beyond our personal wishes, feelings, and attachments. The child needs to experience that adults can open their souls wide and embrace them, their parents and the school community. Steiner suggests that we read the news and hold world events inwardly, even if this is painful. The practice of magnanimity, of the wide-open heart, will increase our ability to love. It will counteract the common practice of passing by our fellow human beings without bothering to know them.

Love cannot be demanded or forced, it has to grow and be given freely. But magnanimity and developing an interest in other human beings can be practised and become an exercise of everyday life.

With this, the picture of the four spiritual virtues of the will is complete: truthfulness, courage, discretion and magnanimity. They have in common the gesture of inner openness. Openness to the spiritual world is part of the gesture of Aries, of the practice of devotion to the spiritual world. Openness and magnanimity are the beginning of the practice of love for the needs of the earth. Aries and Pisces – these two belong together as the beginning and ending of the journey of the soul through the moral landscape of the signs of the zodiac and the working fields of the will.

Endnotes

1 R. Steiner, *Practical Advice to Teachers*, Rudolf Steiner Press, London, 1976, Lecture 2, p. 37.
2 R. Steiner, *Cosmosophy Volume 2*, (GA 208) Completion Press, Moorooka, Australia, 1997, p. 78.
3 In Chinese tradition morality is seen as the highest principle, ruling not only the cosmos beyond the zodiac but also demanding the highest moral qualities from each human being.
4 Steiner, *Cosmosophy 2*, p. 80.
5 Ibid., p. 118.
6 The descriptions of these spiritual virtues first became known through the work of Madame Blavatsky. Her findings were confirmed as spiritually correct by Steiner. A more recent work is Robert Sardello's comprehensive publication on working with the spiritual virtues related to the zodiac: *The Power of Soul: Living the Twelve Virtues*, Hampton Roads Publishing, Charlottesville, VA, 2002.
7 Steiner, *Cosmosophy 2*, p. 73.
8 In: M. L. Nüesch, *Spiel aus der Tiefe: Von der Fähigkeit der Kinder sich gesund zu spielen*, K2 Verlag, Schaffhausen, 2004, p. 87.
9 V. Axline, *Dibs: In Search of Self*, Penguin Books, New York, 1986, pp. 33–34.
10 Axline, *Dibs*, p. 126f.
11 R. Steiner, *Education as a Social Problem*, Anthroposophic Press, Hudson, NY, 1984, p. 13.
12 Steiner, *Cosmosophy 2*, p. 80.

13 R. Steiner, *The Roots of Education*, Anthroposophic Press, New York, 1997, p. 93.
14 Leo, Virgo, Libra, and Scorpio, which Steiner relates to the life of feeling, will not be addressed here. They have more to do with relationships to other adults. The virtues related to these signs would be important for working with parents and in communities.
15 Steiner, *Cosmosophy 2*, p. 70f.
16 Ibid., p. 72f.
17 I would like to express gratitude to the work by R. Sardello on the practice of the virtues in the self-development of adults. Sardello provides a wealth of wisdom related to the deeper understanding of the human soul. See Sardello, *The Power of Soul*.
18 Steiner, *Cosmosophy 2*, pp. 72, 74.
19 Nüesch, *Spiel aus der Tiefe*, p. 73.
20 Steiner, *Cosmosophy 2*, p. 74.
21 Sardello has pointed to the special connection between silence and discernment. See *The Power of Soul*, p. 181.
22 Steiner, *Cosmosophy 2*, p. 72.

Bibliography

Books

Drummond, M.J. and Jenkinson, S. (2009) *Meeting the Child: Approaches to Observation and Assessment in Steiner Kindergartens*, University of Plymouth, UK
Ellersiek, W. (2003) *Giving Love – Bringing Joy: Hand Gesture Games and Lullabies in the Mood of the Fifth*, WECAN, Spring Valley, NY
Goddard, S. (2002) *Reflexes, Learning and Behaviour*, Fern Ridge Press, Oregon
Goddard Blythe, S. (2003) *The Well Balanced Child: Movement and Early Learning*, Hawthorn Press, Stroud
Glöckler, M. (2000) *A Healing Education: How Can Waldorf Education Meet the Needs of Children?* Rudolf Steiner College Press, Fair Oaks, CA
Howard, M. (2004) *Educating the Will*, AWSNA, Fair Oaks, CA
Jacobs, R. (1991) *Music for Young Children*, Hawthorn Press, Stroud
Jaffke, F. (1996) *Work and Play in Early Childhood*, Floris Books, Edinburgh
Jaffke, F. (ed.) (2004) *On the Play of the Child: Indications by Rudolf Steiner For Working with Young Children*, WECAN Publications, Spring Valley, NY
Jenkinson, S. (2001) *The Genius of Play: Celebrating the Spirit of Childhood*, Hawthorn Press, Stroud
Jünemann, M. and Weitmann, F. (1994) *Drawing and Painting in Rudolf Steiner Schools*, Hawthorn Press, Stroud
Knierim, J. (1994) *Quintenlieder: Music for Young Children in the Mood of the Fifth*, trans. P. and K. Klaveness, Rudolf Steiner College Press, Fair Oaks, CA
Köhler, H. (2002) *War Michel aus Lönneberga aufmerksamkeitsgestört?* Verlag Freies Geistesleben, Stuttgart
Köhler, H. (2003) *Difficult Children: There Is No Such Thing*, AWSNA Publications, Fair Oaks, CA
König, K. (1984) *The First Three Years of the Child*, Floris Books, Edinburgh
König, K. (1989) *Being Human: Diagnosis in Curative Education*, Anthroposophic Press, New York

Kühlewind, G. (2004) *Star Children: Understanding Children Who Set Us Special Tasks and Challenges*, Temple Lodge Publishing, Forest Row

Long-Breipohl, R. (2010) *Supporting Self-directed Play in Steiner/Waldorf Early Childhood Education*, WECAN Publications, Spring Valley, NY

Marti, E. (2011) *The Four Ethers*, Schaumburg Publications, Illinois

McAllen, A. (2004) *Reading Children's Drawings*, Rudolf Steiner College Press, Fair Oaks, CA

Miller, E. and Almon, J. (2009) *Crisis in the Kindergarten: Why Children Need to Play in School*, Alliance for Childhood, College Park, MD

Müller, B. (2002) *Painting with Children*, trans. D. Maclean, Floris Books, Edinburgh

Nüesch, M. L. (2004) S*piel aus der Tiefe: Von der Fähigkeit der Kinder sich gesund zu spielen*, K2 Verlag, Schaffhausen

Oppenheimer, S and Almon, J. (ed.) (2008) *What is a Waldorf Kindergarten?* SteinerBooks, Great Barrington, MA

Poppelbaum, H. (1955) *The Etheric Body in Idea and Action*, Anthroposophical Publishing Co., London

Sardello, R. (2002) *The Power of Soul: Living the Twelve Virtues*, Hampton Roads Publishing, Charlottesville, VA

Schoorel, E. (2004) *The First Seven Years: Physiology of Childhood*, Rudolf Steiner College Press, Fair Oaks, CA

Schwartz, E. (1999) *Millennial Child: Transforming Education in the Twenty-first Century*, Anthroposophic Press, Great Barrington, MA

Steiner, R. (1972) *A Modern Art of Education*, Rudolf Steiner Press, London

Steiner, R. (1976) *Practical Advice to Teachers*, Rudolf Steiner Press, London

Steiner, R. (1979) *The World of the Senses and the World of the Spirit*, Steiner Book Centre, Vancouver

Steiner, R. (1981) *The Renewal of Education*, Steiner School Fellowship Publications, Forest Row

Steiner, R. (1982) *The Essentials of Education*, Rudolf Steiner Press, London

Steiner, R. (1982) *The Kingdom of Childhood*, trans. H. Fox, Rudolf Steiner Press, London

Steiner, R. (1983) *Deeper Insights into Education: The Waldorf Approach*, Anthroposophic Press, Spring Valley, NY

Steiner, R. (1983) *The Inner Nature of Music and the Experience of Tone*, Anthroposophic Press, Hudson, NY

Steiner, R. (1984) *Education as a Social Problem*, Anthroposophic Press, Hudson, NY

Steiner, R. (1984) *The Human Soul in Relation to World Evolution*. Anthroposophic Press, New York

Steiner, R. (1986) *Soul Economy and Waldorf Education*, Anthroposphic Press, Spring Valley, NY

Steiner, R. (1988) *The Child's Changing Consciousness and Waldorf Education*, Anthroposophic Press, Hudson, NY
Steiner, R. (1990) *Balance in Teaching*, Mercury Press, Spring Valley, NY
Steiner, R. (1992) *The Spiritual Guidance of the Individual and Humanity*, Anthroposophic Press, Hudson, NY
Steiner, R. (1994) *Understanding Young Children: Excerpts from Lectures by Rudolf Steiner Compiled for the Use of Kindergarten Teachers*, Waldorf Kindergarten Association (distributed by WECAN) Silver Spring, MD
Steiner, R. (1995) *Self-Education in the Light of Spiritual Science*, Mercury Press, Spring Valley, NY
Steiner, R. (1996) *The Education of the Child and Early Lectures on Education*, Anthroposophic Press, Hudson, New York
Steiner, R. (1996) *The Foundations of Human Experience*, Anthroposphic Press, New York
Steiner, R. (1997) *Cosmosophy Volume 2: Cosmic Influences on the Human Being*, (GA 208), Completion Press, Moorooka, Australia
Steiner, R. (1997) *The Roots of Education*, Anthroposophic Press, Hudson, NY
Strauss, M. (1978) *Understanding Children's Drawings*, trans. P. Wehrle, Rudolf Steiner Press, London
Wachsmuth, G. (1965) *Erde und Mensch. Ihre Bildekräfte, Rhythmen und Lebensprozesse, Vol. 1 (Third edition) Verlag am Goetheanum, Dornach
Woitinas, S. (2002) Wer sind die Indigo-Kinder? Herausforderungen einer neuen Zeit*, Verlag Urachhaus, Stuttgart

Websites

Rota Therapy: www.rota-therapie.de

Index

activities, structured learning	34
activity, etheric	xx-xxi
ADD	91
ADHD	xxvii, 87–8, 91
adolescence	65
adult role models	34
adult:	
importance of inner life	77
relationships with	79
self-development	35
self-education of	63, 79
'Adult Attachment Interviews'	75
Alliance for the Childhood in the USA	140
anthroposophical therapies	108
anthroposophy	xv
Aquarius	187, 192–3
archetypal:	
activities	188–90
images	178
play	189
Aries	177–9, 186–7
'Art Experiences in Early Childhood Education'	xxx-xxxi
Asperger syndrome	88
astral body	6, 46, 47, 48, 118
activity of	118
astral forces	145, 175
attachment	81
avoidant	75
bonding, imitation and secondary	73–4
disoriented	76
four stages in the development of secure	xxv-xxvi
indiscriminate	70

insecure	75–6
resistant	76
secondary	73
secure	74–5, 81–2
secure and insecure	74
specific	71
'attention span, short'	91
auditory capacities	110
Australian Early Years Framework	141
autism	88
Axline, Virginia	182
balance	14, 15, 103, 181, 186
sense of	105
virtue of	180
balance and hearing, sense of	117
Bartel, Doris	107–8
behaviour, changes in children's	87
behaviour, difficult	165
behaviour, hyperactive	91
behavioural disturbance	91
Bein-Wierzbinski, Wibke	105–7
Berk, Laura	33
'bodily geometry'	28
'bodily religion'	104
body stretch	106-7
'bond'	71
bonding	779-
act of	69
primary	79
Bowlby, John	xxv
brain	25–6, 28, 30, 93
brain structure, changes in	92
breathing	118
Brochman, Inger	156
Camphill Movement	102
Cancer	177, 185–6
Capricorn	187 190–1
Carroll, Lee	87, 89
centre and periphery, movement between	167

chid:
- and teacher, relationship — 74
- as a spiritual being, the — xxi-xxii
- behaviour in — 168
- –child relationship — 79–80
- cognitive and social development of — 74
- consciousness of — 115
- contradictions in the behaviour of — 169
- creativity of the — 126
- development and thinking — 24–25
- development of movement in the young — 103
- essential nature of the — xi
- growth and transformation in the young — 6
- individuality of — 127, 166
- inner being of the — 169
- inner life of — 163
- inner mobility of — 125
- intellectual faculties — 18
- observation and self-development — 162–72
- observation, contemplative part of — 167
- soul-spiritual — xii
- the anxious — 78
- the 'defiant' — 82–3
- the dependent — 80–1
- who does what he wants — 83–5
- will of the — xxii-xxv

childhood:
- attachment and separation in early — 68–73
- essence of — 166
- moral education in early — 60–6
- relationships in early — 68–85
- working with movement in early — 113–19

children:
- change in modern — 87
- changes in developmental patterns — 92
- development patterns in — 94
- difficult — 93
- in the modern world — 87–100
- new generation — xxvi-xxvii

'Children in the Modern World' — xxvi-xxvii
cognition, intuitional — xviii

cognitive disabilities	102
colour, radiance of	152–7
connecting, imitating	17
consciousness	135, 140, 164, 188
dreamlike state of	123
extended	95
higher	95
nature of	148
shift in human	93
soul	xxiv, 61, 66
state of	36, 132–4
correlation, law of	6
'cosmic movement'	119
cosmos	174–5
spiritual	178
cosmos and earth, relationship between	xxxiii
courage	195
virtue of	191
dentition, first	38
dentition, second	13, 38, 42, 142
destiny	184, 187
individual	51, 163
development:	
hindrances to normal	108
learning disturbances	108
natural sequence of	33
devotion	178
four virtues of	186
Dibs: In Search of Self	182
discretion	192, 195
Early Childhood Education and the Waldorf School Plan	xii
early childhood education, art experiences	140–58
early childhood, self-directed play	122–37
early years, supporting movement development	102–19
earth realm, uprightness and incarnation	103–9
'earth stage'	72
earthly faculty	26
education	
three seven-year phases of	xxiv
values in	60

educational policy, modern	165
'elements'	2
Ellersiek, Wilma	xxviii, 111, 116
embryonic development	7
environment	37, 49, 131, 137, 141, 147, 152–3, 184
self-directed	126
environmental influences	20
'Essentials of Waldorf Early Childhood Education'	141
ether body, forces of	31
ether	3
activity of light	11
etheric body	42, 47, 48, 118, 145
activity of	118
loosening of	95
etheric forces	1–15, 26, 38, 40, 48, 50, 105, 108, 175, 192
battle and balance	13–15
battle of	51
cosmic	7
forms of archetypal activity	8
growth	41
juxtaposition, polarity	11–13
role in child development	2–15
variation, refinement and enhancement	9–11
etheric qualities	15
ethers, functions of the four	15
eurythmy	112–13, 115–16
evolutionary:	
conditions, four	xxv
shift	xxvii
existence, transitional stage of	xviii
expansion and contraction	116–17
polarity	107
faculties:	
higher human	37
three fundamental human	33
faithfulness	184, 186
feeling	46, 89
shift in	94
feelings, expression of	183
feeling-will	50
forces	xix-xx

astral	13
formation and growth	26
formative	6, 10
formative and musical	42
growth	11
life	13
life ether	19
other or *musical*	38
sculptural	42
sculptural or *growth*	38
'Forming Relationships in Early Childhood'	xxv–xxvi
free play, disappearance of	xxix
frontal plane	103, 111–12
Gemini	177, 181–4, 186
'Gestalt'	5
Goddard Blythe, Sally	xxi, 102, 104–5, 113
goodness, quality of	64
growing up, three seven-year phases of	xxiv
growth forces	28, 156
Grunelius, Elizabeth	xi–xiii, 142, 165
habits, establishing	55
hand gesture games	111, 116
Hanna, Paulene	15, 114, 129–32, 134
Hattermann, Klara	xii
head rotation, free	108
head spirit	57
health, physical, soul and spiritual	140
Heiner Priess	169
'hermit'	49
horizontal plane	103, 146
Howard, Michael	xxx
Howard, Susan	141
Huber, Hanne	xxx
human being	
faculty of thinking	24
four bodies of the	xix, 4
how does the will work	47–8
individuality of	126
spiritual biography of	xxiii
spiritual 'bodies' of	118–19

spiritual reality of 168
human relationships, establishing positive 17
human soul-spirit 28
hyperactive 84

I 28, 46, 48, 49, 89, 92, 118
   and the astral body 49
   and world, feeling the unity of 167
   consciousness of 34, 37, 43, 81
   gesture of 182
   incarnation of 58
I-activity 43
I-being 36, 54
I-consciousness 33, 103, 113
imagery 42
imagination 126
   free 140
imitate 27, 74, 135, 170, 177, 182
   desire to 124
imitated 131
imitates 92
imitating 57, 119, 142, 184
imitation 29 35, 36, 42, 49, 52, 53, 62, 80, 116, 140–2, 156, 187, 192
   learning by 34
imitation and example 73, 98
imitator 151–2
incarnate 179
incarnating 149
   process 152
incarnation xviii-xix, xxxiii, 48, 103, 167, 185–6
   process 174
   images of 177–94
   powers of 175
incarnation, process of 70, 104, 148
independence 72–3, 81, 184
Indigo Children xxvi, 94
individual, conscious of being 81
inner development, aspects of xxxi-xxxii
inner stillness 192–3
integration, sensory-motor 102
intellect 57, 157
intellectual

development	20
faculties	163
understanding	52, 64
International Association of Waldorf Kindergartens (IAWK)	xii–xiv
I-organization	47
'In Search for Reality'	xxxi-xxxii
Jaffke, Freya	40
Jünemann, Margrit	155
kindergarten, rhythms of life	177
Köhler, Henning	84, 88, 91–2, 93, 97, 169
König, Karl	xxviii, 29, 102–3, 109, 111, 116, 118–19
Kühlewind, Georg	27, 93
language development	134
learning	
cognitive	35
early adult-directed	32
early intellectual	34
structured	31
'to see'	98–9
life challenges	163–4
Life Forces of the Young Child, Recognising and Nurturing	1–20
life forces	2
depletion of	19
final liberation of	39
life processes	19
rhythms of	20
life	
conditions of modern	88
first and second year in relation to thinking	25–30
first year of	28
inner	84
mission in	65
modern	xiii, 90
rhythms and habits of	87
self-development of the inner	164–72
seven years	32
thinking in third year	30–4
life, third year	9, 30, 34–6
'light'	73

limbs, movement of	129
love	163–4, 184, 194–5
Mackenzie, Dr Millicent	xv-xvi
magnanimity	195
Marti, Ernst	xx, 2
matter, different states of	2
McAllen, Audrey	102, 105
meditation	97
memory	50
metabolic system	77
'metacognition'	33
Michaela Glöcker	41
milestones	108
modern culture	19
modern life	100, 117
'Mood of the Fifth'	xxxi, 147–50, 157
mood of wonder, the	165–6
moral education	xxiv, 63
morality	60–1, 64
internalising	62
morning circle	56, 112, 115, 151, 170–1, 179
Moro reflex	104
'mother's internal working model'	76
movement and play	99
movement	10, 109, 157
development of	131
disturbances	105
imitating	115
lack of control of	91
quality of	119
self-directed	114
'Moving with Soul'	xxvii-xxix, 116
music education, recommendations for	xxxi
musical experiences	148–52
musical forces	147–8
nerve-sense system	77
'new will'	48–9
Nüesch, M. L.	179, 190–1
observation	97, 169

process of	166
observe and understand	172
observing	54
oneness	62, 70, 73
consciousness of	xi
openness	195
organization:	
physical-etheric	5
soul-spiritual	5
outer word, experience of	xviii
path, individual	65
perseverance, virtue of	184
physical body	48, 118
developing	20
three systems	25, 30
physical earth environment	xvii-xviii
physical growth, connecting and repeating	8
physical world, transition	181
physical-etheric forces	46
duality of	
Piaget	xii
Pisces	187, 193–4
Plan und Praxis des Waldorfkindergartens (Plan and	xiv
planets	7
play	10, 43, 90, 122–37
-based activities	122
developmental aspects of	126
facilitating	135–7
imaginative	38
initiative in	179
model for understanding	128
nature of	124–5
self-directed	126–7, 135–7, 140–1
self-initiated	11, 124, 136, 141, 146, 157–8
solitary	29
solitary, outwardly non-verbal	30
solitary, self-initiated	35
therapy	182
value of	126
polarities, observing behavioural	170
Poppelbaum, Hermann	xx, 8

posture:	
maintaining	109
upright	108
pretend	33
psychological issues	156
punishment	90
Raphael	185
refinement and enhancement	18–19
reflex patterns	108
reflexes	104–8
relationships	97
attachment	84
child–teacher	77
lack of warmth in human	90
teacher–child	85
remember	33
remembering and *forgetting*	50
repetition and rhythm	17–18
reverence	166, 171
rhythm	147, 150–1
rhythm and form	85
rhythmical:	
speech	58
system	38, 110
right–left discrimination	111–12
role play	190
'Rota-Therapy'	107–8
'rough and tumble'	130
Ruhrmann, Ingrid	108
sagittal plane	103, 111–12
Sagittarius	187, 188–9
Schwartz, Eugene	xxvii, 94
Science:	
natural	xvi
relationship to spiritual	xvi-xvii
Scorpio	187
sculptural forces	146–7
sculpture, art of	145–6
'secure attachment'	73
self and others, awareness of	88

self and world, perception of	72
self, consciousness of	10, 33–7, 42, 81, 89, 95
self development	174
self, psychological, emergence of	33
self, sense of	114
self-conscious	115
self-development	98
and child observation	162–72
self-education	169
self-expression	115
selflessness	185–6
self-reflection	98
sensory exploration	52
separation	72, 81
separation anxiety	69, 74–5, 77–9
Sistine Madonna	185
social dynamics in a group	165
soul	104, 119, 149–50, 165
attitude of	192
'habit'	9
human	187
knowing	96
'moving with'	102–19
three powers of the human	89
soul activity, inner	43
soul development	134
soul faculty, independent	43
soul forces	38, 43, 58, 62, 147
three	46
soul level	41
reaction on	56
soul life	31, 55
transformation of the human	94
soul moods	65
soul qualities	55
soul-spiritual forces	30, 36, 46, xix-xx, 145, 147, 156
spatial dimensions	117
spatial dynamics	179
spatial existence	128
speaking	25
speech	10, 30

and movement, rhythm in	179
and play, development of	110
spirit, longing for	94
spiritual:	
dual	48
force	57
science	96–7, 166
sheath	54
transition	181
world	xxxiii, 7, 152
'Spiritual Values in Education and Social Life'	xv
Spitalny, Stephen	116
Steiner	
Steiner, Rudolf xi–xiii, xviii–xxv, xxvii–xxviii, xxx–xxxiii, 1, 4, 6, 8, 23, 25, 27, 50, 73, 103	
stimulation	30
early intellectual	33
of the vestibular system	105
Strauss, Michaela	156
surrender	169–70
swoul, interests in	118
Taurus	177, 179–81, 186
teacher:	
attachment to	78
relationship with	79, 81
–child relationship	136
teeth:	
birth of second	41
change of	38–42, 57, 124, 137, 157
temperament	156
'The Development and Education of the Will'	xxii–xxv
The Education of the Child in the Light of Spiritual Science	xi, xv
The Indigo Children	87–8
The Millennial Child	xxvii, 87
the spiritual cosmos	xvii–xviii
The Spiritual Guidance of the Individual and Humanity	24
think	33
thinking	10, 23–25, 28, 36, 89, 165
abstract	140
foundations of	114
intellectual	42

relation to	168
shift in	94
three moral predispositions	xxiv-xxv
time, sense of	72
Tober, Jan	87, 89
trust and belonging	184
truthfulness	189, 195
'twelve virtues'	177
'twoness in oneness'	181–2
'Under the Stars'	174–95
understanding, four steps for deepening	165–9
uprightness	106, 109, 185
complex posture of	104
veneration, mood of	166
vertical dimension	146
vertical plane	103
vestibular stimulation	113–14
virtues	163
vitality, natural	115
Vom Wesen des kleinen Kindes/Understanding Young Children	xiii
von Goeethe, Johann Wolfgang	6
Von Kügelgen, Dr Helmut	xii, xiv
Vygotsky, Lev	30
'waking-up'	51
Waldorf education, three enemies of	181
walking	25
Wiechert, Christoph	52
will	49, 150, 168
activity	187, 192
and feeling	145
and imagination, lack of	20
and thinking	58
at the time of the awakening of thinking	57–9
consciousness and a new strength of	97
design nature of	49
developing the	163
development and education of	46–66
development of, between 5 and 7	50–1
development of, birth and age 2½	48

development of, first seven years	48
development, 2½ and 5	49–50
educating feeling in	55–7
educating three- to five-year-old	56
education of the	51–4
engaging the	59, 143
'feeling in'	49
forces	51, 57, 115, 94–5, 148, 157
four spiritual virtues of	195
further developments of	58
grown old	
higher forms of	54
instinctual	49
lack of	52
life of the	174
lower forms of	54
new impulse in	94
operation of the	125
self-education of	186
'signs'	187
strength of	58
weakness of	52
working fields of the	195
willing	46, 89
wills, power struggle between two	53
wonder	168, 171
mood of	166
word, spoken	152
Work and Play in Early Childhood	40
year:	
fifth	11
first	25
first and second	91
fourth	36–7
fourth to seventh	38
ninth	112
ninth to tenth	145
second	25, 29
seventh	7, 12, 14, 25, 35, 39, 43, 51, 105, 140, 147
sixth	12
sixth and seventh	40

sixth to seventh	145
third	31, 34–5
third and fourth	148, 151
three to five	43
young child, thinking and consciousness of	23–43
young children, death forces and their impact	19–20
'youth movement'	94
zodiac, signs of	175
Zodiac, spiritual significance	xxxii
zodiac, the	7

Other books from Hawthorn Press

Storytelling with Children

Nancy Mellon

Telling stories is a peaceful, magical way of creating special occasions with children, whether it is at bedtime, around the fire or on rainy days. Nancy Mellon believes every parent can, and should, become a confident, creative storyteller. A story told by you is a gift to your child; a wonderful act of sharing and communication which enriches family life. Nancy's gentle, practical advice is illustrated with many beautiful, funny and wise stories created by families who have discovered how the power of story transforms lives and relationships.

'Nancy Mellon's experience, advice and suggestions work wonders. They are potent seeds that give you the creative confidence to find your own style of storytelling.'

Ashley Ramsden, Director of the School of Storytelling, Emerson College

'Here is a treasure-trove for professionals and beginners – a book borne of years of experience, written from the heart and stirring to the soul. Reading it, I feel the urge to pull my own children close, to light a candle, to begin ... Nancy Mellon inspires us all to be storytellers ...'

Katrina Kenison, editor, *Best American Short Stories*

192pp; 216 x 138mm; 978-1-907359-26-2; pb

What Babies and Children Really Need

How mothers and fathers can nurture children's growth for health and well being

Sally Goddard Blythe

This book draws on the latest scientific research to show how a baby's relationship with its mother has a lasting and fundamental impact. Sally Goddard Blythe calls for a new Charter for Childhood in which nutrition, play, affection and discipline are valued as the basic building blocks for meeting children's needs.

224pp; 234 x 156mm; 978-1-903458-76-1; pb

You Are Your Child's First Teacher

What parents can do with and for their children from birth to age six

Rahima Baldwin Dancy

This lucid, practical and common-sense guide will help you navigate safely through the early years of childhood and find solutions that work for your own family situation. Create your own family rituals to ease the daily routine, nourish your child's imagination with simple, home-made toys and materials from the garden and kitchen cupboard, and use imitation, repetition and setting limits to promote a harmonious family life.

400pp; 234 x 156mm; 978-1-903458-65-5; pb

Pancakes *for* Findus
Sven Nordqvist

It is Findus' birthday, so Farmer Pettson wants to bake a big stack of pancakes for him. But before he can start, Pettson has to fix a puncture in his bike, find the keys to the shed and distract Anderson's bull. Only then can he bike to the shop to buy flour for the pancakes.

28pp; 297 × 210mm; 978-1-903458-79-2; hb

When Findus Was Little and Disappeared
Sven Nordqvist

Farmer Pettson lives with his hens in an old red farmhouse. He sometimes feels lonely. One day his neighbour Mrs Anderson visits with the present of a tiny kitten in a cardboard box labelled *Findus Green Peas* …

28pp; 297 × 210mm; 978-1-903458-83-9; hb

Findus Plants Meatballs
Sven Nordqvist

Farmer Pettson begins to sow his vegetables and because Findus doesn't like vegetables he decides to plant one of his meatballs instead. However keeping the vegetable garden safe from the farm animals proves a hard task for Findus and Pettson.

28 pp; 297 by 210 mm; 978-1-907359-29-3; hb

ORDERING BOOKS

If you have difficulties ordering Hawthorn Press books from a bookshop, you can order online at **www.hawthornpress.com** or you can order direct from:

United Kingdom
Booksource
50 Cambuslang Road, Glasgow
G32 8NB
Tel: (0845) 370 0063
Fax: (0845) 370 0064
E-mail: orders@booksource.net

USA/North America
Steiner Books
PO Box 960, Herndon
VA 20172-0960
Tel: (800) 856 8664
Fax: (703) 661 1501
E-mail: service@steinerbooks.org

Australia
Footprint Books
1/6a Prosperity Parade
Warriewood
NSW 2102
Tel: (02) 9997 3973
Fax: (02) 9997 3185
info@footprint.com.uk
www.footprint.com.au

New Zealand
Ceres Books
Ceres Enterprises Ltd
121 Carbine Road
Mt Wellington, Auckland
Tel: 9574 3356
Fax: 9527 4513
info@ceresbooks.co.nz
www.ceresbooks.co.nz

South Africa
Rudolf Steiner Publications
PO Box 71925
235 Bryanston Drive
Bryanston 2021
Tel: (11) 706 8544
Fax: (11) 462 5180
Steinerp@netactive.co.za

Canada
Tri-Fold Books
PO Box 32, Guelph
Ontario, NIH 6J6
Tel: (519) 821 9901
Fax: (519) 821 5333
info@trifoldbooks.com